Changing the Playbook

SPORT AND SOCIETY

Series Editors
Randy Roberts
Aram Goudsouzian

Founding Editors
Benjamin G. Rader
Randy Roberts

*A list of books in the series appears at
the end of this book.*

a grant for sanity
Figure Foundation
editing the future

Changing the Playbook

How Power, Profit, and Politics Transformed College Sports

HOWARD P. CHUDACOFF

University of Illinois Press

URBANA, CHICAGO, AND SPRINGFIELD

Library of Congress Cataloging-in-Publication Data
Chudacoff, Howard P.
Changing the playbook : how power, profit, and politics transformed
college sports / Howard P Chudacoff.
   pages cm. — (Sport and society)
Includes bibliographical references and index.
ISBN 978-0-252-03978-2 (hardback) — ISBN 978-0-252-08132-3
(paperback) — ISBN ISBN-0-252-09788-1 (e-book)
1. College sports—United States. 2. College sports—Social aspects.
3. College sports—Moral and ethical aspects. 4. College sports—
Economic aspects. 5. College athletes—United States. 6. National
Collegiate Athletic Association. 7. Education, Higher—Aims and
objectives—United States. I. Title.
GV351.C487   2015
796.04'3—dc23   2015022456

To Nancy: the best teammate one could ever want.

Contents

Acknowledgments

My point of view derives from more than thirty years of teaching about sports in America and more than fifteen years as Brown University's faculty athletic representative to the National Collegiate Athletic Association (NCAA). The inspiration and provocation for this book that I have received from countless contacts with students, colleagues, and sports enthusiasts and critics are too numerous to acknowledge individually. A few individuals stand out, however. In 2007, as I was contemplating a new book project, I attended the annual Fall Meetings and Symposium of the NCAA Faculty Athletics Representatives Association, where I heard a keynote address from Cedric Dempsey, who recently had retired as the NCAA's executive director. The theme of the speech was the five major turning points that had occurred during Dempsey's term from 1994 to 2003. The talk stirred me into thinking about what turning points I would identify as critical in the history of modern college sports, and I returned from the meeting excited about the project that resulted in this book. I thank Cedric Dempsey for his stimulation.

At the NCAA headquarters in Indianapolis, Ellen Summers, archivist and librarian; Betty Reagan, assistant archivist and librarian; and Lisa Greer Douglass, assistant director of research, were both gracious and generous in their assistance during my several visits to the archive. At the Brown University Library, Sarah Bordac, Steven Thompson, and Holly Snyder helped along the way. A former student, Katie Hyland, provided important research assistance, and I owe thanks to all the Brown undergraduate students, athletes and nonathletes alike, who have inspired my thinking in my courses on sports history. During my research and writing, several friends and colleagues generously offered critical input. I especially owe much to James

T. Patterson and Luther Spoehr, who critiqued every chapter and whose suggestions, criticisms, and comments have been welcome and valuable. Steven Mintz and Scott Eberle also offered useful insights during several conversations and e-mail exchanges. Because this book combines original and secondary research, I have mined the work of others whose publications provided valuable insights and information. The list of scholars and writers is long, but I especially acknowledge Joseph N. Crowley, whose comprehensive history of the NCAA, *In the Arena*, provided a much-appreciated overview. I also benefited from works by Keith Dunnavant, Mary Jo Festle, Michael Oriard, Allen Sack, Ronald A. Smith, Ellen Staurowsky, John R. Thelin, John Sayle Watterson, Ying Wushanley, and Andrew Zimbalist. Discussions with friends in the Brown University Athletic Department also helped expand my knowledge; I especially recognize Arlene Gorton, Michael Goldberger, Jack Hayes, and Sarah Fraser. Wendy Strothman helped when keener focus was needed. Jeffrey Orleans, former executive director of the Ivy Group, offered important insights, especially on matters of race and gender, and Kent Thaler has consistently provoked me to think about college sports in alternative ways. Thanks also go to Willis Goth Regier, editor of University of Illinois Press, and to Randy Roberts and Aram Goudsouzian, editors of the Sport in Society series. And, as always, my best editor and critic has been my wife, Nancy Fisher Chudacoff. I cherish all she has done for and with me.

Changing the Playbook

Introduction

It is a truism: College sports today is mass entertainment, a $16 billion-a-year enterprise. College football is the second-most-watched sport on television, behind only professional football, and each March, the "madness" of Division I championship college basketball dominates the television ratings. The number of networks airing college sports, sometimes around the clock, has mushroomed; not just NBC, CBS, and ABC, not just ESPN, Fox, and TBS, but countless local and regional ones—not to mention the Internet—feed ardent fans not only intercollegiate football and basketball, but contests in "nonrevenue" sports such as lacrosse, softball, and volleyball. Schools as disparate as Harvard and Ohio State finance three dozen or more varsity teams, and annual athletic budgets of several institutions top $100 million. Nearly every college and university, large and small, prides itself on the prowess of one or more of its varsity teams, and alumni/ae often remember more about the "big game" than the "big term paper" or "big exam." Passionate donors heap largesse—often millions of dollars—on athletic programs, though they sometimes have to share credit for their generosity with corporate sponsors. In the expanding quest for cash, conferences—even those of less-than-major status—have signed television deals, and the sale of team-related apparel, pennants, and memorabilia has become such lucrative a revenue source that the athletes are seeking ways to share in the booty.

For most of their history, college sports have been the front door of practically every major institution of higher learning in America. Most colleges and universities present athletics as a prominent link on their websites and promotional brochures, on equal footing with the other A's: academics, admissions, and administration. No wonder apologists and critics alike refer to college sports as an industry, and a corps of athletic directors, marketers, financial analysts, and lawyers refer to institutional names as brands and their teams as product. Those brands, those teams, that industry, are hosted by nonprofit, tax-exempt institutions dedicated to teaching and research, a relationship duplicated in no other country. And in spite of the fact that so much money flows around the industry, the vast majority of colleges and universities spend more on athletics than they make from athletics. During the past six decades or so, American institutions of higher learning and their athletic programs have increasingly found themselves living in an uneasy coexistence with sports; while the sports establishment pushes for every advantage, those in charge of higher education accept the glory but are embarrassed by their obsession with it.

How did all this come about? Who made the decisions and why? What decisions were not made? How did these decisions affect college life? What was at stake? Were the athletes winners or losers? Can the college sports enterprise endure in the way it has for the past 65 years? Have there been missed opportunities for reform? In other words, what is the dramatic story of modern college sports? This book tells that story by highlighting the major milestones, the new playbook from which modern college sports have emerged.

Over the years, journalists, historians, sociologists, economists, anthropologists, and more have exhibited various amounts of bedazzlement and cynicism in their analyses of intercollegiate athletics. Most published works have focused on specific sports and major episodes, usually in a triumphal way and featuring legendary teams, coaches, and seasons. Or they have been written in a disparaging tone, ranging from disappointment to outrage, emphasizing scandals, inconsistencies, and hypocrisies. I have chosen a different and broader perspective. By synthesizing the narrative of college sports history since 1950, I hope to convey a fuller understanding of how and why "game changers" have created today's intercollegiate athletic landscape.

American college sports emerged in the mid-nineteenth century from the efforts by male undergraduates to engage in out-of-the-classroom activity independent from the strict faculty control that governed their college lives. Those sports were commercialized from the start. The first intercollegiate competition, a rowing race between Harvard and Yale crews in 1852, was sponsored by a railroad to advertise its passenger service between Boston and Montreal. As rivalries in baseball, football, and track joined those in crew in the late 1800s, student control of teams and competition was replaced by institutional supervision, and the code of amateurism—sport for sport's sake, transferred from Great Britain—collapsed as an intensifying compulsion to win prompted schools to professionalize their teams by hiring coaches, attracting spectators, reaping ticket sales, building stadiums, and seeking alumni donations. The costs of victory included recruitment of athletes ill-prepared for college life, favoritism for star performers, hiring and paying athletes who were not students, and vicious on-the-field behavior. To quell the violence and sustain what remained of a tattered but unrealistic commitment to amateurism, sixty-two schools of higher education met in 1905 and formed what became the National Collegiate Athletic Association (NCAA). Though it initially served only as a body for discussing and passing rules for competition, in 1921 the NCAA began sponsoring national intercollegiate championships, the first being in track and field. Still, because it was an association of voting members, the NCAA's power depended on how much prerogative its constituents were willing to surrender and how much independent action those constituents wished to retain for themselves. (The retention of independent action was, and is, known as home rule.) Consequently, in these early years, the NCAA exercised little authority over recruiting or academic standards.

By 1920, it was becoming obvious that schools were still trying every means, fair or foul, to win. As a result, late in 1922 the NCAA membership adopted a ten-point code to reinforce principles of amateurism and fair play that had been established in 1905. The provisions included prohibitions on freshman- and graduate-student eligibility, restrictions on athletes who transferred from one school to another, a ban on gambling, and an encouragement for schools to organize and join regional conferences that would set and enforce rules. Nevertheless, aside from some agreed-upon conference rules, each school was to retain its authority to regulate the operations and finances of its own athletic program.[1] From that time forward, the tension in intercollegiate athletics between a regulatory body (the NCAA) and an institution's prerogative to do as it pleased (home rule) was set.

During the 1920s, college sports continued to capture more resources and attention, highlighted by major football events now played in huge, newly constructed stadiums. These conditions, especially the colleges' staunch autonomy over the recruitment and subsidization of athletes, prompted calls for reform because of the cheating and fraud that were occurring. In 1929, the Carnegie Foundation published results of a three-year investigation that revealed widespread abuses, especially in under-the-table financial awards being given to prospective football players.[2] Little resulted directly from the Carnegie revelations, and both the NCAA and its member institutions continued to pledge allegiance to a code of amateurism while sustaining the trend toward professionalism and commercialism.

As competition intensified in the 1930s, attempts to create a level playing field focused on efforts to more strictly enforce the NCAA's amateur code. This meant that the NCAA needed to exercise police power to enforce its rules and penalize violators. Easier said than done, because individual institutions were slow to surrender control over their athletic affairs. Though some reforms were established in the 1950s, chiefly standardizing of rules for athletic scholarships, it was not until the 1970s that the NCAA's members gave its infractions committee authority to investigate rules violations and assess penalties, ranging from probation to loss of scholarships and exclusion from postseason play, and, in one case, suspension of an entire team's ability to compete.[3] Yet, along with major changes, important continuities with the past survived. By the early twenty-first century, the reality of commercialism and professionalism within the idealistic realm of amateurism characterized college sports more than ever before. Today, the money to be made from media and donors has spawned challenges to the athletic enterprise and to the existence of the NCAA.

This book, however, is about more than just the NCAA, though the NCAA occupies a prominent position. The major issues—the game changers—of the ensuing chapters involve money, media, race, gender, and reform. Though "money sports," chiefly football and men's basketball, often take center stage, they do so in the broader context of the evolution of college sports generally. That evolution begins in chapter 1 with regularization of athletic scholarships and establishment of the NCAA as the principal arbiter of the college sports establishment. The marriage between sports and television, with the resulting impact on athletic budgets and the quest for media income, has fostered dilemmas and conflicts over who deserves the revenues and how much control should be surrendered to the networks. These matters dominate discussions in chapters 3, 4, and 7. The racial integration of college sports, along with the "revolt of the black athlete" and the twisted history of Title IX and women's sports, provide important turning points in chapters 2 and 5. As chapter 1 points out, scandal has been a constant in college sports, but chapter 6 reveals how an especially alarming spate of cheating and fraud in the 1970s and 1980s spurred efforts by the NCAA to restore academic respectability to the enterprise. The crises of the twenty-first century, fueled by litigation and a renewed effort by the largest sports schools to exercise more autonomy, dominate chapter 8, which concludes with some insights into reforms that I deem practical and achievable. Because the issues addressed in the book are situated most commonly and most dramatically in athletic programs at major colleges and universities, the bulk of discussion pertains to schools in Division I of the NCAA, but the phenomenon of intercollegiate athletics contains themes common to all who participate.

It often is too easy to forget that, in a sense, athletics is the largest honors program on campus. In each place, that program consists of hundreds of students specially recruited, with talents that others lack. These young people sometimes receive unfairly advantageous treatment and sometimes are exploited. But, often overlooked by those concerned only with scandal, the vast majority of college athletes work hard, go to class, graduate, and enjoy pursuing a passion they have harbored for a long time. Anyone who has attended a college softball game or a squash match has observed the spirit, intensity, and commitment the participants exhibit, qualities that are no different from those displayed by the more heralded competitors on the football field and basketball court. These qualities merge into a quest for excellence that, when pursued with dignity and honor, should be appreciated and nurtured.

1 Abolishing the Sanity Code and Launching the Modern College Sports Establishment

Harold C. "Curley" Byrd had a star-studded career in college football before becoming president of the University of Maryland in 1936. He excelled as an athlete while an undergraduate at Maryland. Then he made history in 1909 when, as a graduate student at Georgetown University, he became one of the first quarterbacks to master the forward pass. He subsequently served for two decades as Maryland's athletic director and football coach, winning 119 games and overseeing construction of a stadium that later was named after him. (Today, he shares the heading with a corporate sponsor; the place was renamed Capital One Field at Byrd Stadium in 2009.) As University of Maryland president—one of only a few former football coaches to be demoted to university president—Byrd raised substantial sums of money and expanded the campus. But not without dissent. Critics groused that many of his accomplishments, such as building a new basketball arena while keeping faculty salaries low (he once allegedly uttered, "Ph.D.'s are a dime a dozen"[1]) showed that he fancied athletics more than academics.[2]

So it is no surprise that President Byrd staunchly defended his school's football program against meddling by the NCAA, whose Sanity Code of 1949 proposed to enforce the principle that college athletes were amateurs who played sports as an "avocation" and should not be differentiated from other students. Almost from its inception, the NCAA had canonized this ideal of amateurism. According to article VI(b) in the NCAA's 1916 bylaws, "an amateur is one who participates in competitive physical sports only for the pleasure, and the physical, mental, moral, and social benefits directly derived therefrom." Paying college expenses of students for their athletic ability, the

NCAA feared, would make athletes professionals, attract individuals who had no interest in learning, and set apart athletes from the rest of the student body.

The Sanity Code was proposed to the NCAA membership in 1946 by reformers wishing to eliminate unsavory financial awards given to football players. It banned athletic scholarships and required college athletes in need to support themselves with jobs just as other students did. In 1948 a majority of NCAA members voted to accept this proposal, putting it into effect in 1949. Many colleges, however, eager to enhance their football prominence, saw the Sanity Code as a threat, and they sought to legitimize institutionally sponsored aid to athletes with no strings of need or academic merit attached. Curley Byrd assumed the role of spokesman for those who resented what they believed was an imposition conspired by Midwestern and Eastern schools whose gate receipts, wealthy benefactors, and statehouse allies provided sufficient income and jobs to make athletic scholarships unnecessary—he conveniently overlooked the practice at his and other schools whereby alumni surreptitiously funded athletes In a speech before the NCAA convention in January 1950, Byrd came to the defense of his neighbor, the University of Virginia, which at the time offered more than eighty football scholarships, from being expelled by the NCAA for defying the Sanity Code. Using as his foil Ohio State University, a member of the Big Ten Conference—in which athletic scholarships already had been banned—he asked convention delegates, "Does Ohio State want to vote for expulsion of Virginia when Ohio State has facilities (meaning resources) to take care of four or five times as many athletes as Virginia?" Adding a sarcastic reference to dubious state employment given to Buckeye football players in lieu of athletic subsidies, Byrd observed, "Ohio State has some rather unusual jobs."[3]

A critical test of wills had been set in motion a year earlier when the NCAA compliance committee threatened twenty institutions with suspension because they had disregarded the Sanity Code and awarded athletic scholarships. Later, thirteen of the twenty regained good standing, but the remaining seven—University of Virginia, University of Maryland, Virginia Tech, Virginia Military Institute, The Citadel, Villanova, and Boston College—warned they would withdraw from the NCAA rather than comply. Amid the swirl of dissension, the NCAA scheduled a vote on expelling these Sinful Seven at the association's annual convention in 1950. A vote to expel needed approval from 136 members—a two-thirds majority—but only 111 voted in favor. The Sinful Seven prevailed, thereby making the Sanity Code unenforceable. All the NCAA could do in consequence was to declare the seven "not in good standing."[4] Soon, other schools, mostly in southern states, ignored the Sanity Code and announced unrestricted subsidies to athletes. The funding of college students for their potential contribution to an institution's athletic endeavors rather than for their academic merit or financial need now had moved from under the table to the top. As long-time NCAA executive director Walter Byers later reflected, the decision to bury the Sanity Code marked what to him was "one of the three or four most important decisions in the history of intercollegiate sports."[5] The era of modern intercollegiate athletics had begun.

Abolishing the Sanity Code

The Sanity Code arose at a time when college and university enrollments were burgeoning. Aided by the Servicemen's Readjustment Act (GI Bill) that helped fund tuition and living expenses, hundreds of thousands of World War II veterans were streaming into higher education, and, with a portion of them joining rosters of varsity teams, it was important in an environment of intense competition to regulate how athletes were recruited and rewarded. Perhaps more important, by the postwar years, there was a long history of scandal in college sports, during which football players, especially, received illicit payments, special academic advantages, and other favors. As some schools upped their rewards and inducements to athletes, others complained about violations of the amateur ideal, sometimes jealous that they could not do so themselves. Oklahoma State, for example, accused rival Oklahoma of keeping a secret $200,000 payroll for its athletes. The Sanity Code was intended to end these practices. Though it failed, it was accompanied by an important structural change in the NCAA. Before 1946, the NCAA was a loose organization and served chiefly as an advisory and rule-making body, providing members with information, regularizing playing rules, and sponsoring championships in various college sports. The association had no official means to investigate abuse of its principles or punish violators. Enforcement and sanctions were left to individual institutions and conferences. Alongside the Sanity Code, however, the NCAA Executive Committee created a Constitutional Compliance Committee with authority to interpret the association's constitution and determine whether "stated practices, actual or contemplated, are forbidden by, or are consistent with its provisions." It also created a fact-finding committee to investigate possible violations.[6] For the first time, a nationwide system for regulating college sports was in place.

Moreover, in spite of the NCAA's failure to oust the Sinful Seven, the Sanity Code was still on the books; its prohibition on athletic scholarships remained lodged in Article III of the association's constitution. A survey in

1950 of 270 association members taken by Clarence Houston, president of Tufts University and chair of the Constitutional Compliance Committee, revealed three attitudes about the code: indifference, opposition, and approval. Institutions with small or nonexistent football programs and who offered no aid to athletes generally favored some kind of code but were otherwise on the fence. Schools with large football programs, however, scurried to redirect NCAA policy, either by compromising on some kind of acceptable code or erasing it completely. Generally, schools in the South, where athletic aid had been customary and sometimes substantial, wanted no restrictive code. They preferred institutional (self-regulation, known as "home rule") rather than NCAA control of subsidies and believed that money furnished to star football players by enthusiastic alumni and other fans represented a legitimate reality.[7] The region's three major conferences, the Southern, Southeastern, and Southwestern, even considered abandoning the NCAA and forming their own association if they could not have their way—not the last time such a threat would arise.[8] Third, conferences from the Midwest and West, chiefly the Big Ten and Pacific Coast Conferences, had previously outlawed athletic scholarships and backed some kind of associationwide restriction. Many schools in this group furnished work programs to athletes instead of direct subsidies, generous aid that President Houston's committee observed was "quite out of proportion to the importance of any athletic program."[9] The exception in this category was Michigan State University, which had joined the Big Ten in 1949 and whose ambitious president, John A. Hannah, was using athletics to achieve national prominence for his school and had created the Spartan Foundation to tap alumni and business supporters for funds to finance athletic scholarships.[10] Considerable discord separated these three groups, prompting Houston to remark that "we talk about individual integrity, yet individual institutions do not trust each other."[11]

As delegates gathered for the 1951 NCAA annual convention in Dallas, several proposed changes to the Sanity Code were on the agenda, reflecting these three stances. One set of proposals would permit aid to needy athletes, renewable on the basis of academic progress. Southern schools backed an alternative measure to allow unrestricted aid, with amounts determined by the institution without consideration of financial need or academic merit. A third scheme would enable schools to choose between honoring the present code and following a liberalized one. Debate on these options was passionate. University of Kentucky's A. D. Kirwan, another president who had formerly been his university's football coach, spoke against limiting subsidies to tuition, declaring, "If it is not morally wrong to grant a student his institutional fees so that he might be able to go to college and play football, why should it be evil to give him three meals a day and a bed to sleep in so that he may remain in college?" Gordon Gray, president of the University of North Carolina—a lawyer and former secretary of the army who was schooled on regulations—broke ranks with fellow southerners and sided with those northern schools that supported some sort of NCAA oversight. Gray charged that "the very integrity of American education is in some way threatened by excesses in the matter of handling intercollegiate athletics."[12]

Proponents of home rule, the third option, won the battle. Instead of regulating athletic aid, NCAA members opted for a hands-off policy. Convention delegates voted to abolish the Sanity Code by a vote of 130–60. A coalition of southern schools, who favored no or watered down restrictions on scholarships, were joined by a few eastern schools, who believed that purging the Sanity Code was the only way to keep the NCAA from dissolving. Delegates replaced the code with of a constitutional amendment stating that "control and responsibility for the conduct of intercollegiate athletics shall be exercised by the institution itself or, in the case of the institution having membership in a regional athletic conference, by such conference." The only vestige of the Sanity Code that survived was an agreement on a provision that NCAA member schools "cannot solicit athletes with the promise of financial aid—pay travel expenses of prospective students visiting campuses—or conduct a practice session or test for display of athletic abilities in any branch of sport." The vote marked a bitter defeat for the Pacific Coast and Big Ten conferences. Reacting to the Sanity Code's demise, the Big Ten commissioner snorted, "The southern schools want to finance players. Well, we have the money to whip them. It's a free for all."[13] How prescient that term "free for all" would be.

A crossroads had been passed. Schools of the South and Southwest, eager to build victorious football programs, felt they could not accept the Sanity Code's restrictions on athletic subsidies. Would these and other institutions have seceded from the NCAA with resulting chaos in intercollegiate athletics if the Sanity Code had been preserved? Unlikely. Rising college enrollments and the mushrooming popularity of college sports after World War II, especially as television loomed as both an attention-getting and income-producing entity, made surrender of at least some of an institution's sports autonomy inevitable. Yes, violations of the Sanity Code still could have occurred. As Curley Byrd intimated, schools with strong connections to wealthy alumni and other boosters were subsidizing college costs of star athletes through phony summer and afterschool jobs. Still, if twenty-five members had changed their votes on expelling the Sinful Seven, the NCAA might have found ways to enforce the Sanity Code to the grudging satisfaction of its membership instead of abolishing it in 1951.

Moreover, a viable alternative to the NCAA's Sanity Code already existed. In 1945, presidents of eight schools that became known as the Ivy Group—Brown, Columbia, Cornell, Dartmouth, Harvard, Penn, Princeton, and Yale—signed an agreement banning football scholarships at their institutions; in 1954; they extended that rule to all sports. Their intention was to ensure that athletes were academically representative of each institution's overall student body, a goal embodied in their declaration that "Athletes shall be admitted as students and awarded financial aid only on the basis of the same academic standards and economic need as are applied to all other students."[14] Initially considered unworkable, the model has survived to the present and prevails among the 450 institutions in Division III of the NCAA. Needless to say, schools in Division I, where big-time, revenue-producing sports serve as public entertainment, have continued to support a much different version of athletics.[15]

Purists Attempt Intervention

At the same time that the NCAA was embroiled in its fractious squabble over the Sanity Code, a startling scandal rocked college sports. New York City's Madison Square Garden, then the country's basketball mecca, stood at the center of a web of bribery and fraud. The dishonesty emerged from the point spread, the means by which bets may be placed on the number of points by which a team wins or loses, rather than on who might win the game. On January 17, 1951, authorities arrested two players from New York's Manhattan College basketball team, which played games at Madison Square Garden, and three professional gamblers and charged them with violating a state law making it a criminal offense to attempt to bribe a participant in any sporting event. The two players were accused of accepting several thousand dollars during the 1949–50 season to ensure that their team lost games by more than the point spread, thereby fixing or dumping games so that the gamblers could win by betting on the spread. (If Manhattan had won the games or lost by less than the point spread, gamblers would have lost their bets.) Then, in February and March 1951, five members of the national championship basketball team from City College of New York were arrested and charged with taking bribes and helping gamblers by intentionally manipulating point spreads in games at Madison Square Garden during the 1950–51 season.

Investigation into game-fixing by New York County District Attorney Frank Hogan soon implicated teams from other New York area schools and beyond. Hogan ultimately accused seven basketball programs and thirty-two athletes that also had played games at the Garden, including players from the universities of Toledo and Kentucky. A particularly egregious case was that of Bradley

University. Not only did three Bradley teammates plead guilty to accepting $500 each to dump a game in 1950, but the university's president also was accused by journalists of allowing boosters to subsidize players, enrolling athletes in sham courses, and advising a team member to ignore a court appearance when it conflicted with his basketball schedule.[16] Cynics snickered when the University of Kentucky, led by its haughty but highly successful coach Adolph Rupp who had indignantly—and disingenuously—claimed that gamblers could not "touch my boys with a ten-foot pole," was revealed to be so deep in corruption that the NCAA planned to enforce a "death penalty" by asking members to cancel all basketball games with Kentucky for the 1952–53 season. In reaction, the Southeastern Conference suspended Kentucky from conference basketball competition for the year. University officials accepted the punishment, avoiding a disruptive challenge to NCAA's and the conference's authority.[17] Of thirty-two college athletes accused, three served jail time, nineteen received suspended sentences, two got probation, four were tried and acquitted, and charges against four were dropped.[18] Lucre—for athletes, who otherwise had little or none, and for gamblers, who wanted more—was insinuating itself into what was presumed to be a pure endeavor.

Point shaving was only the most sensational of several scandals that erupted in college sports in 1951. At the U.S. Military Academy, eighty-three cadets, many of them football players, were expelled for academic cheating. At the venerable College of William and Mary, the basketball coach and the athletic director resigned as a result of grade and credential altering, and the school's president, who was blamed for not dealing with the improprieties forcefully enough, also stepped down. Ohio State's football coach was forced to resign after revelations that influential alumni and coaches had pressured faculty to give passing grades to "scholastically wobbly athletes. . . . even though they were physical education majors."[19] The scandals prompted critics to lament the way the quest for cash was contaminating college sports. The taint was palpable, stirring New York State Supreme Court Judge Saul Streit, who presided over trials of the City College of New York, Bradley, and Kentucky point shavers, to charge that commercialism in football and basketball was "rampant" and that as a result of an "athletic scholarship racket" there were "no longer amateur sports. . . . [A]thletes are bought and paid for."[20] The NCAA, supposedly the watchdog over college sports, seemed powerless to stem the dishonesty and greed, especially since its splintered membership had recently jettisoned reforms of the Sanity Code.

Into the breach stepped the American Council on Education (ACE), a Washington, D.C.–based organization that represented the needs of higher education across the country. Intent on repairing the damage to colleges and universities from the scandals, the ACE formed a special committee to study conditions in college sports and make recommendations. John Hannah, president of Michigan State University, was appointed committee chair, ostensibly an unusual decision in that he had recently used an alumnus's bequest to fund football scholarships and had actively engaged in recruiting to help build his school's football team. In 1948, after enlarging his football stadium and overcoming opposition from the University of Michigan, which did not want to compete with Michigan State for in-state football stars, he won an invitation to join the Big Ten conference. A shrewd politician, Hannah entertained local and state politicians and businessmen and gave countless speeches to alumni groups in which he touted the value of athletics at his institution. At the same time, Hannah had been outspoken about ending abuses from the "excessive desire to win" that pervaded college football.[21] Hypocritical or not, Hannah guided the special committee to a focus on football, rather than basketball, because most abuses the Sanity Code was intended to correct had occurred within football programs.

Once Hannah's committee began hearings, a long-standing conflict surfaced. On one side stood purists, including some college presidents and faculty, who clung to the notion that college athletes should be treated no differently from other students in admission, financial aid, and academic standing. These reformers found inspiration in conclusions reached by the Carnegie Foundation's investigation into college sports in the 1920s, which declared that the recruitment of college athletes had had "profoundly deleterious" effects on athletic programs and that the influence of athletic policies on "American higher education has been no less noxious."[22] On the other side were coaches and athletic administrators who insisted that recruitment of athletes and institutional support for teams, coaches, and facilities were vital for successful competition. This attitude was voiced by Harvard's Lloyd Jordan, head of the football coaches' association, who argued that "We must recognize that colleges are in the entertainment business. The only question is, How far shall we go? But if we do it at all, shouldn't we do it well?"[23] To this group, "doing it well" provided a mantra for victory at all costs, a logic that had developed long before 1951 and has persisted. The "entertainment business" label, though denied by college presidents, had also described big-time college sports in previous decades and it became increasingly relevant as the twentieth century wore on.

In the end, the ACE sided with the purists. The most notable recommendations it adopted were (1) athletes and athletic policy should be controlled by college presidents and faculty, rather than by alumni or other outside groups; (2) coaches should have faculty status and salaries not to exceed those of other faculty members; (3) athletes should be subject to the same admission and academic standards as other students; (4) freshmen should be ineligible to play varsity sports; (5) out-of-season practices should be prohibited. The ACE also proposed restrictions on recruitment methods; bans on bowl games and other postseason competitions; public disclosure of athletes' grades and academic standing; scholarships limited to room, board, and books; and aid based on financial need and academic performance instead of on athletic ability.[24] In other words, the ACE would restore the Sanity Code and more. Indeed, these measures would have radically altered the direction of big-time football and the future of all college sports. None of them, of course, exists today.

Recognizing that it lacked power to execute its proposals, the ACE's special committee turned to accrediting agencies. These are the regional bureaus that evaluate and enforce, through certification, academic standards of member institutions. Why not enlist them to help enforce athletic standards, the committee reasoned? Most accrediting agencies demurred, claiming that athletic policy should be the business of individual institutions, conferences, and the NCAA. The North Central Association of Colleges and Secondary Schools, however, the largest accrediting agency, waded in. At a meeting in December 1951, the North Central agency issued a report that recommended penalizing any of its members whose athletic program did not meet academic standards. The report contained six directives on those standards: (1) "snap courses," i.e., soft spots in the curriculum that abetted corruption in athletics should be eliminated; (2) the "public entertainment" of "athletic spectacle" was "alien to the true function" of higher education; (3) colleges should bankroll only "functions that bring a high educational return"; (4) an institution's chief administrator should be responsible for athletic policy; (5) "educational merit," not "athletic renown," should be the basis for securing public support; and (6) the "existence of an unsatisfactory athletic situation in an institution will be regarded as a serious enough weakness to justify the denial of accreditation."[25] North Central had thrown down the gauntlet. Would the athletic establishment, now entrenched in the NCAA, yield? The answer was a resounding "No."

Invention of the "Student Athlete"

By the end of 1951, the NCAA was reeling. Scandal had rocked intercollegiate athletics, and nonathletic interest groups such as the ACE and North Central accrediting association were threatening intervention. In an attempt to right its ship, the NCAA appointed Walter Byers as its first full-time executive director. Born in Kansas City, Missouri, and just thirty years old, Byers was a former sports journalist who always wore cowboy boots and (later) a toupee. He had previously worked in subordinate roles for both the Big Ten and the NCAA, but he had no formal background as an administrator. Nevertheless, he served as executive director for the next thirty-six years and built the NCAA into the most powerful—and well-heeled—force in college sports. As one journalist observed shortly after Byers retired, "If there wasn't much to the NCAA before Byers, there wasn't much else when he left."[26] Wayne Duke, former Big Ten commissioner, recalled, "The NCAA (has) prospered, in my opinion, because of three factors: enforcement, football on television, and the basketball tournament. And Byers was the architect of all of them."[27] When Byers became executive director, the NCAA was headquartered in a Chicago hotel room. One of his first acts was to convince the association to build a new headquarters outside Kansas City and give him a full-time staff. Newly ensconced, Byers ran his operation with stern efficiency. He required employees to work half days on Saturday, imposed a dress code, and banned smoking and coffee breaks. A critic once compared Byers to dictatorial, abusive personalities such as J. Edgar Hoover and Adolf Hitler, while an admirer gushed that he was "demanding, thorough, fair, witty, shy rather than arrogant, tolerant of disagreements and intolerant of incompetence."[28]

When Byers assumed control, the NCAA was still a loose, largely powerless federation consisting of several hundred members who distrusted each other and, as the handling of the Sinful Seven proved, were fervently protective of institutional independence.[29] But Byers had a passionate faith that NCAA rules could preserve all that was best in college sports, including amateurism, and he set out to put the house in order. He first garnered power from his ability to persuade the University of Kentucky to accept NCAA penalties resulting from its basketball improprieties. He then expanded the NCAA's enforcement staff to more effectively compel compliance with existing rules, and he bolstered his influence by stacking association committees with friendly appointees. At the time, the NCAA Council was the association's main decision-making body. It consisted of 44 members, half appointed by the various conferences and half elected from an NCAA-backed slate of delegates. By cajoling and bargaining, Byers stacked most of the Council with allies. And the act of opening a genuine headquarters in Kansas City signified a flow of power away from individual institutions and conferences toward the unified authority of the NCAA.[30]

Late in 1951, Byers and the NCAA launched a countermove against the ACE and North Central Association reform proposals by drafting a formal Amateur Code. Designed to "enlist the support of true lovers of wholesome college athletics," the code would strengthen the NCAA's ability to discipline cheaters. Adopted by the membership at the January 1952 convention, the measures created a new subcommittee on infractions to receive complaints, investigate rules violations, and recommend punishments. (Notably, however, the subcommittee could initiate investigations only in response to complaints that identified a "critical need" for action.) The NCAA, apparently satisfied with its own reforms, made no direct response to the ACE proposals, which quickly faded from public attention, relegated "to the scrapheap of well-intentioned reforms."[31] Meanwhile, initiative from the North Central Association sputtered. When North Central threatened Oklahoma A & M (now Oklahoma State), Missouri, and Bradley Universities with loss of accreditation in 1953 because of objectionable subsidies to athletes, the football powers of the Big Seven and Missouri Valley conferences rushed to aid their accused brethren. A number of conference members made it known that they would withdraw from North Central if it did not retreat, and the agency backed down, never again to meddle in athletics. Though Byers and the NCAA stayed on the sideline when North Central attempted its intrusion, in the aftermath the path had been cleared for the NCAA to rule undisputedly over the domain of college sports.[32] Another major turning point had occurred.

The reforms outlined in the ACE report of 1951–52 offered what might have been a reasonable resolution to the contention over the Sanity Code by preserving much of what was vital to the operation of intercollegiate athletics while stemming the drift of athletic departments away from the academic enterprise. The ACE, however, lacked power to carry out these measures and failed to galvanize necessary support from entities that could. Many presidents, eager for the glory that sports success might bring to their school, proved lukewarm at best to serious reform. Alternatively, accrediting organizations such as the North Central Association might have provided sufficient muscle to impose measures such as those proposed by the ACE. North Central boldly attempted to infuse athletic programs with academic integrity but got cold feet, and ultimately the NCAA made an end run around both it and the ACE by advancing its own watered-down version of reform.

Once Byers had solidified his position in the NCAA by mid-1952, two major issues occupied the athletic establishment: how or whether to regulate televised college sports and how or whether to award athletic subsidies. The former will be discussed in chapter 3; the latter still lingered in the wake of the Sanity Code's failure. The fork in the road was clear. One path led toward treating athletes no differently from all other college students, in admission, financial aid, and on-campus status. The other direction promised special considerations for skill and potential contribution to a school's athletic success. Significant interest groups, represented most powerfully by the relatively wealthy Big Ten schools, continued to oppose aid based on athletic ability, labeling the practice as "pay for play." Others, especially football and basketball coaches, led the way in advancing a provision that would allow financial aid to athletes for talents other than those in the classroom. Their attitude was couched in a statement made by Clair Bee, Long Island University's legendary basketball coach, who argued, "Just because a kid is big and strong and is able to play basketball, is that any reason for him to be offered any less help than another kid who is good at music or math?"[33] This point of view drew backing from athletic administrators, especially from newer and less well-endowed southern schools, who came to believe that some form of regulated subsidization would halt illicit payments from alumni and booster groups. Consequently, in 1952 the NCAA took a first step toward regularizing athletic scholarships when it replaced the Sanity Code with a constitutional provision allowing individual schools to establish and administer their own financial aid policies for athletes.[34] This home-rule arrangement, however, proved highly unsatisfactory because it permitted wide disparities that depended mainly on how much aid a given institution was willing to furnish.

In addition, a nagging question loomed: If colleges were to give athletes, who were enrolled students, anything that resembled "pay for play," they would face what Byers called the "dreaded notion that NCAA athletes could be identified as *employees . . .*" (his emphasis).[35] He warned that athletes, like regular college and university staff, would be subject to federal labor regulations, state labor commissions, and the courts, thus calling into question the principle of amateurism ensconced in the NCAA constitution and in every panegyric to intercollegiate sport. Struggling to prop up its amateur standard, the NCAA tabled action on institutional aid and made concerted efforts to penalize violators of rules banning external subsidies. In 1953, for example, the NCAA infractions committee imposed probation and censure on Arizona State for illegal payments made to football players by a booster foundation. Then, in 1956, the committee handed out harsh penalties to the University of Washington, UCLA, and the University of Southern California, including exclusion from televised football games, for booster payments to football players, and it censured the football program at University of California–Berkeley. It was becoming clearer that something was needed to stem the tide of illicit payments to athletes. Perhaps athletic scholarships were the answer. If so, Byers's fear about "employees" needed to be overcome.

Conflicting court decisions complicated the situation. In 1953, in the case of *University of Denver v. Nemeth*, the Supreme Court of Colorado held that a college football player injured during practice was to be considered an employee of the university and therefore entitled to protection under workers' compensation statutes. The complaining athlete in this instance had not received a football scholarship; rather, his campus job was one reserved for a member of the team, and instead of monetary compensation he received a ticket for free meals. Because the plaintiff's employment and meals were contingent upon his playing football, the court concluded that an accidental injury sustained during the course of a football activity entitled him to workers' compensation benefits.[36] Shortly thereafter, the same court reversed itself and disallowed the Colorado Industrial Commission's award of death benefits to the widow of a Fort Lewis A & M (now Fort Lewis College) football player, whose husband had died from a head injury received during a game in 1955. Ray Dennison, the deceased footballer, had received a tuition waiver for playing football and a job on the college farm. In this case, the court determined that there was no evidence of a contract involved in Dennison's participation on the football team or that his job was contingent on his playing football. Moreover, said the judges, the college did not profit from Dennison's football activities because Fort Lewis did not intend its football program to operate as a business.[37] Victorious in court, Fort Lewis A & M memorialized Dennison by renaming its football stadium Ray Dennison Memorial Field.

In spite of this blurry landscape, advocates of the athletic scholarship, or "full ride," pushed ahead and induced the NCAA to pass landmark reforms. In 1956, NCAA members established a system of financial aid that allowed institutions to award athletes financial subsidies to cover educational expenses without a necessary requirement of need. This provision was elaborated the next year when the association defined expenses to include tuition, fees, room and board, books, and fifteen dollars per month for laundry and other personal necessities during the school year. At the same time, the NCAA passed bylaws that regulated recruiting of high school athletes: (1) schools could pay for only one two-day campus visit per recruit, (2) booster groups were forbidden to cover any recruiting costs, (3) coaches could not contact a potential recruit without permission from the recruit's high school coach, (4) athletes would be required to sign a letter of intent to enroll at a school that had recruited him, and (5) an institution could not offer a recruit financial aid beyond that permitted by the NCAA—meaning that subsidies by boosters or alumni were outlawed.[38] The 1957 legislation also mandated that if an athlete voluntarily left a team or a coach removed him because he was not performing to expectations, the athlete's financial aid could not be reduced or canceled. (At this point in time, all athletes eligible for scholarships were male.)[39]

The purpose of these measures was twofold: (1) to level the playing field by standardizing the award of financial aid to college athletes and theoretically removing the advantage that more affluent schools had held, and (2) to forestall the payments made by alumni and booster groups that undermined the amateur ideal of college sports. To demonstrate to all observers, including state and federal governments, that athletes were not paid to perform, the NCAA regulations stipulated that athletic aid should cover no more than normal college expenses; that a school's financial aid process, not that of the athletic department, would fix the amount of aid; and that a coach could only recommend that an athlete receive aid, not promise it. In other words, the process of awarding "grants-in-aid," as the newly defined subsidies were labeled to differentiate them from employment compensation, would now be completely aboveboard. And to further ensure that the connotation of these grants was and would remain clear, Byers invented a new label for the recipients. As he subsequently explained, "We crafted the term *student athlete*" (his emphasis), and soon it was embedded in all NCAA rules and interpretations as a mandated substitute for such words as "player" and "athlete." Furthermore, Byers instructed that additional language be used to distinguish the amateurism of college sports: "We told college publicists to speak of 'college teams,' not football or basketball 'clubs,' a word common to the pros."[40]

Byers believed that the reforms enacted in 1956 and 1957 "would lead to a better day."[41] Indeed, the abandonment of the Sanity Code and the creation of the concept of grants-in-aid signaled the creation of a new playbook for college sports. Acting in the name of amateurism, the association fashioned rules that were intended to prevent the cheating and financial chicanery of the past. The new system also aimed to establish competitive equity among schools that wished to provide athletic scholarships. By promulgating Byers's concept of the student athlete, the college sports establishment could tighten the link, however deceptive that link might have been or become, between athletics and education. Moreover, with the formation of new enforcement mechanisms, the NCAA had stronger tools with which to compel rules compliance and penalize transgressors.[42]

Three decades later, Byers looked back with a rueful eye, labeling the practice of awarding athletic scholarships as a "nationwide money-laundering scheme."[43] What he meant was that the 1956 rules, while outlawing direct, private payments to athletes or their parents, did not prevent interference from outside groups; rather, alumni and boosters evaded restrictions by donating money to colleges that then funneled it to athletes. As Fritz Crisler, football coach and athletic director at the University of Michigan, predicted, "a lot of good programs are going to mortgage their integrity by raising money from alumni to pay for grants-in-aid."[44] By the 1970s and 1980s, critics had adopted these same sentiments. More important for the history of college sports, the legitimization of athletic scholarships and propagation of the term "student athlete" consigned college athletes to a select category within the student body, separate, and in the minds of many, unequal.[45]

Failed Challenges to the Grant-in-Aid

Whether to stave off competing groups such as the ACE, which wanted to rein in college sports, or to sustain genuine commitment to the amateur ideal, the NCAA has largely stood by its reforms of 1956. The question of whether the athletic establishment endorsed pay-for-play continued to resurface, however, as several lawsuits challenged the NCAA contention that college athletes were not employees. One of the first such cases involved the death of Edward Van Horn, a football player at California State Polytechnical College, who died in a plane crash while returning from a game in 1960. Van Horn had received a scholarship that came from boosters whose donations to Cal Poly had been intended to subsidize athletes. Van Horn's family, arguing that his football participation constituted employment, sued the school for death benefits. In 1963, a California district court supported this claim, determining that because Van Horn's grant-in-aid was dependent on him being a member of an athletic team, his scholarship was an employment contract.[46] The decision prompted Walter Byers to hire a noted tort lawyer, who sent a memo to NCAA member institutions with advice on how to word grants-in-aid awards to avoid legal challenges arising from workers compensation issues.[47]

It was at this point that the judiciary might have altered the direction of college sports by following up on the Van Horn decision and determining that athletic subsidies indeed constituted employment. But the NCAA managed to rebuff intrusion by propounding its peculiar definition of amateurism. At a critical juncture, the courts ultimately declined to define an athletic scholarship as a contract subject to workers compensation for injury on the job. A different decision in the Dennison case and broader acceptance of decisions in the Nemeth and Van Horn claims might have induced the NCAA and its members to restore need-based scholarships tied to academic criteria rather than athletic performance. Subsequent lawsuits brought courts to the brink of knocking down the façade of amateurism that has sheltered athletic scholarships. But ultimately, judges retreated. In 1984, for example, the Supreme Court of Indiana overturned a state appeals court decision awarding workmen's compensation benefits to an Indiana State University student, Fred Rensing, who held a football scholarship and in 1975 had suffered a debilitating back injury that resulted in pneumonia and paralysis. Using twisted logic in determining that Rensing's scholarship did not constitute employment, the judges rooted their decision in the NCAA bylaws that outlawed pay for play. According to the majority opinion, an athlete was not an employee because the NCAA said he was not; and because Indiana State and the NCAA did not consider free tuition, room, board, laboratory fees, and book allowance as "pay," a student on athletic scholarship did not receive compensation for playing a sport. Also, the court endorsed the university's defense that when accepting the scholarship Rensing and his parents did not explicitly consider the aid as pay, and as a recipient Rensing did not report the benefits for income-tax purposes. So Rensing's claim was void.[48]

More consequentially at the time, rising costs stirred new efforts to change aid policies. By the late 1960s, institutions seeking to outdo rivals in inter-collegiate competition had increased the number of grants-in-aid awarded, hired more coaches, spent lavishly on recruitment, and provided ancillary benefits for athletes such as separate dorms and training tables. Football especially was eating up resources, largely as a result of a 1965 rules change that restored two-platoon style of play with unlimited substitution, meaning that squad sizes and coaching staffs expanded markedly. As a result, in 1971, an NCAA Special Committee on Financial Aid proposed to limit the number of scholarships an institution could hand out and make grants dependent on financial need. Schools struggling to finance their ever-sprawling athletic operations backed the measure, but opposition, especially from major foot-ball schools, was loud and emblematic of how central athletics had become to U.S. higher education. Rev. Edmund Joyce, Notre Dame's executive vice president and the era's leading proponent of big-time college sports, argued that aid limits would only tempt alumni to evade the rules in order to give their schools an advantage. Other opponents of reform advanced the notion that the traditional American value of merit would be undermined; talented athletes, they claimed, deserved the same assistance as talented scholars.[49] These and other contentions prevailed. In both 1972 and 1973, Division I members of the NCAA voted down need-based athletic scholarships, just as they had done twenty years earlier. The votes were very close, but the major football powers carried the day, voting in the opposition by a 4–1 margin.[50]

Not to be undone, reformers, including those concerned about new com-mitments to women's sports required by Title IX (See chapter 5), reintroduced need-based aid to the NCAA convention in 1977. This measure included an exemption for football and men's basketball, but it went down to defeat, as did similar measures in 1978 and 1979.[51] Then, in a last gasp by cost cutters, another need-based measure was introduced in 1981. Once again, Father Joyce spoke for the opposition, defending special treatment for athletes in revenue-producing sports because their contributions both enhanced a school's reputation and helped pay for nonrevenue sports. Such athletes, Joyce argued, make "a major contribution toward balanced budgets in athletic departments."[52]

Cost reduction did prevail to some extent. Before 1975, there had been no restrictions on the number of coaches a football program could hire or the number of scholarships it could provide. In the early 1970s, the University of Alabama, for example, employed seventeen football coaches, and the University of Pittsburgh funded eighty-three grants-in-aid just to freshmen football recruits. A Special NCAA Convention in 1975 created new rules for Division I (major sports) members, limiting total football coaches to eight, freshman football scholarships to thirty, and total football scholarships to ninety-six. (The scholarship numbers eventually were reduced to twenty-five and eighty-five, respectively.) Also, men's basketball grants were restricted to fifteen per team, and total grants for all other teams, aside from football and basketball, could not exceed eighty. Lawsuits protesting this loss of institutional control lost either in their original courts or on appeal.[53]

One other vital turning point in the saga of athletic scholarships was passed in 1973. Once grants-in-aid had become formalized and regulated, coaches, particularly those in football and men's basketball, worried that some recruited athletes might accept a scholarship as a means of getting admitted to college but then decide not to participate on the team for which they were recruited. The result would be a lost scholarship for the coach. How could this loophole be closed? If, as a remedy, a grant included a stipulation that the recipient must play the sport for which he was recruited, it could be construed as a contract, a consequence that Byers and the NCAA had done acrobatics to avoid in 1956. Though few athletes actually manipulated the system in the way coaches feared, during the tumultuous 1960s rebellious behavior by athletes who, like other college students, dressed, grew hair, and spoke out in ways objectionable to coaches, moved coaches and athletic directors to seek a change in scholarship policy that would enable them to more closely control team members and the aid they received.[54] Consequently, the NCAA at its convention in 1967 considered legislation that would create one-year athletic scholarships and tie their renewal to continued team participation and "good behavior," essentially meaning deference to a coach's code of conduct. The one-year scholarship failed to attract the necessary two-thirds vote, but a provision enabling cancellation of aid for "misconduct" passed.[55]

Proponents of the one-year scholarship continued to press their case, and in 1973 the NCAA, by a simple show of hands, approved one-year grants renewable on the basis of performance and behavior. The previous year, the association had authorized freshman football and basketball players as eligible for varsity play, making them more vulnerable to the demands of their sport. (Four years previously, freshmen in "minor" sports already had been made eligible.) A coach now had powerful command over team participants and could easily replace anyone who failed to live up to expectations on the field of play, whose attitude or conduct could be construed as unacceptable, or who suffered an injury that could reduce future athletic contribution. The new NCAA rules linked financial aid to athletic performance, toppling the association's pre-1952 philosophy, and completed the transformation of the student-athlete into an athlete-student.[56]

The Fateful Turn

The evolution of intercollegiate sports took a fateful turn between 1950 and 1956, and by 1973 athletics and athletes had become virtually separate from the rest of the institution in which they resided. Varsity sports, especially football, had made heavy demands on athletes and differentiated them from other students long before the mid-twentieth century. But after 1956, an athletic scholarship and the time demands of competition often forced many "student athletes" to make their academic commitments secondary to their athletic ones. Dave Meggysey, a lineman at big-time football school Syracuse University from 1968 to 1971, observed in his memoir that he and his teammates were told as scholarship recipients "to be grateful for the opportunity we were getting," but that in reality they were semi-professionals whose welfare would suddenly evaporate once their athletic usefulness expired. Meggysey noted that he found it "next to impossible to be a legitimate student and a football player too, and that of twenty-six freshmen in his class who received football scholarships, only three graduated.[57] With almost full authority over who got a scholarship and for how long, a coach assumed prerogatives that even legendary coaches of the past—Knute Rockne, Amos Alonzo Stagg, for example—did not have. Moreover, the recruitment of highly sought after prospects by schools eager for success in football, basketball, and other sports took on a distinct character, one quite different from the enrollment of ordinary students. Fully paid visits to campus with tours of lavish athletic dorms constituted just the tip of the recruiting iceberg that prospects could experience. At the same time, athletic departments populated by head coaches, assistant coaches, trainers, administrators, business staff, tutors, and more burgeoned and operated outside the budgetary and administrative constraints that applied to academic departments. As time went on, the gulf between athletics and academics deepened, especially at institutions with high-profile, revenue-producing sports.

Walter Byers had made sure that intercollegiate athletics could develop along a sheltered path by transforming the NCAA into a preeminent power, supervising and regulating all aspects of an ever-widening enterprise. And by coining the term "student athlete," he packaged young men (and eventually young women) as a unique breed with a label that has persisted in current vernacular until it is rarely questioned. Only a few critics have pointed out that there is no equivalent, such as "student musician" or "student journalist." It is impossible to ascertain whether another person would have pulled the NCAA in a different direction and either accommodated to home rule or encouraged policies that integrated athletes and athletic departments more snugly into an institution's academic enterprise. There is no doubt, however, that Byers built a wall around the NCAA and college sports that became increasingly difficult to penetrate.

Whether disingenuous or not, Byers publicly confessed in his 1995 memoir that much had gone wrong in college sports. He blamed college administrators and accrediting agencies for countenancing curricula that enabled academically weak athletes to retain eligibility by taking "soft" courses and majors. Regarding establishment of the full-ride athletic scholarship in 1956, Byers admitted, "I thought it would lead to better days, but the record shows the full ride was an act of administrative convenience for college management and a recruiting bonanza for coaches, It encouraged a separation of the student-athlete from the student body, promoted self-government for the athletic department, and sanctified an industry-wide, common pay scheme based on athletic skill."[58] And it made young athletes into pawns, exploited by their coaches and schools and excluded from the huge sums of money that they earned for their schools, a situation unshaken until it was challenged by litigation a half century later. (See chapter 8.) Byers absolved himself of responsibility, saying he and the NCAA were overwhelmed by "big-timers" bent on building "a national entertainment business" and wanting "great players on the field, whether or not they met customary academic requirements."[59] Regardless, the die had been cast.

What happened to college sports between 1950 and 1956 formalized the operation of what Harvard's Lloyd Jordan had called an "entertainment business." The major turning point had been passed, and Jordan's question of "How far shall we go?" has vexed institutional CEOs, the fraternity of coaches and athletic directors, faculty, journalists, and the public ever since.

2 Integrating the Team

It was just an ordinary handshake, one that always occurs between opponents meeting at center court at the start of a basketball game. Jerry Harkness, a 6′3″ guard who had been born in Harlem, who played for Loyola University of Chicago; and Joe Dan Gold, a 6′5″ forward from a small rural town in Kentucky, who played for Mississippi State University (MSU), lined up, facing each other. Leaning in, each clasped the other's right hand, pulled back, and crouched for the jump ball to begin the opening contest in the Mideast Regional bracket of the NCAA Division I Men's Championship Basketball Tournament, on March 16, 1963, in East Lansing, Michigan.

In the game's opening moments, the favored Loyola Ramblers did not get off to a good start. Using a control-type strategy to befuddle Loyola's customary fast-paced style, the MSU Maroons scored the first seven points, holding the taller, faster Ramblers scoreless for almost seven minutes. Then the Chicago team began to click. Harkness, already an All-American, and his teammates Les Hunter, Ron Miller, Vic Rouse, and John Egan rallied, and Loyola took command of the game. MSU came within three points in the fourth quarter, but their star, Leland Mitchell, fouled out with six minutes left, and the Ramblers pulled away to win 61–51.[1]

The outcome paled in comparison to something else about the game and the days preceding it. Before that night, neither that all-white MSU team nor any of its MSU forerunners had ever competed against an opponent with even a single African American player. In 1963, the Maroons had won the Southeastern Conference championship and garnered the right to compete for the national title. Their first opponent in the NCAA tournament would have to be Loyola. But in Mississippi, an unwritten law—a "gentlemen's agreement"—blocked all college athletic teams in the state from competing against any opponent that had a black player on the roster. Just the year before, the University of Mississippi had rejected an invitation to the NCAA basketball tournament for fear that the Ole Miss team might have to contend against an opponent with black players. Loyola boasted not one but four African American starters—Harkness, Hunter, Rouse, and Miller. Could MSU break the gentlemen's agreement and accept an invitation to travel to East Lansing and play Loyola? Many of the school's students and alumni, eager for a chance at a national championship, strongly favored doing so, and MSU president Dean W. Colvard eventually agreed with them. Local and state segregationists reacted bitterly. The civil-rights movement was in full swing, and just a half year earlier, after a long and contentious struggle, U.S. marshals had enforced a Supreme Court order that the University of Mississippi must admit its first African American student, James Meredith, an event that soured white supremacists who now vented their anger against MSU's decision to play an integrated northern team. A Jackson, Mississippi, newspaper editor charged that Colvard's consent would subject "young Mississippians to the switch-blade knife society that integration inevitably spawns."[2]

The day before the Maroons were to depart for Michigan, opponents of the trip convinced a county court to enjoin the basketball team from leaving Starkville, the home of MSU. Coach James "Babe" McCarthy decided to defy the court. McCarthy, who hailed from the town of Baldwyn in northeastern Mississippi and who was known as "Ole Magnolia Mouth" for his syrupy thick southern accent, was intent on elevating his team to national prominence, so he entered into an elaborate ruse to realize his desire. On the day of the scheduled flight, Coach McCarthy and the MSU athletic director drove 165 miles to Memphis, and from there flew to Nashville. At the same time, a group of MSU freshman basketball players, not on the varsity team, drove to the Starkville airport as decoys to impersonate the team while the active players hid in the athletes' dormitory. If the sheriff tried to serve the injunction on the ersatz team that showed up at the airport, the varsity players would sneak away to a private plane that was ready to take them to Nashville, where they would join McCarthy and fly on to Michigan. When no one arrived to serve the court order, the "real" team hurried to the Starkville airport and left for Nashville. Later that day the Mississippi Supreme Court overturned the injunction.[3]

So the game went on as scheduled, and when Joe Dan Gold's white hand clasped Jerry Harkness's black fingers ahead of the first jump ball, a momentous turning point in the history of intercollegiate athletics took place. (After losing to Loyola, MSU beat Bowling Green University in the consolation contest, at the end of which MSU's captain Leland Mitchell shook hands with another African American opponent, Bowling Green's Nate Thurmond.) An athletic contest had enabled a team representing the Deep South to make an important symbolic step toward accepting interracial activity on a level playing field. Other firsts in the racial integration of college sports had already taken place by March 16, 1963, but there was something special, as well as adventurous, about the Loyola–MSU game because, in traveling to East Lansing, the MSU team broke free of the restraints that the region's formal segregation had placed on its college sports and brought the team into a truly national arena. As Leland Mitchell later recalled, "It was much more than a basketball game. We were making history. We were ambassadors for the south, though none of us realized it at the time."[4] A milestone had indeed been passed, though not just the MSU team, but much of the college sports establishment did not fully realize what African American college athletes gained, what they lost, and what this turning point fully meant.

Pioneers in the Arena

In 1896, the year that the U.S. Supreme Court handed down a decision in *Plessy v. Ferguson*, the case credited with establishing the principle of "separate but equal" public facilities in support of racial separation, Preston Eagleson completed his career as the first African American on the Indiana University football and baseball teams. He also was the only African American on those teams. For many years, this singularity—one per team—was the standard among college varsity squads that had integrated rosters. Other notable pioneer athletes of color before World War I who were the sole blacks on their football teams were George Jewett (University of Michigan), Robert Wells "Rube" Marshall (University of Minnesota), George Flippin (University of Nebraska), and Frederick Douglass "Fritz" Pollard (Brown University).[5] Though many of these individuals were stars and usually accepted, if only grudgingly, by their teammates, their lives on campus were a challenge, if not a misery. Racial taunts and discrimination followed them everywhere, and they had to endure attitudes exemplified by no less a highbrow than Harvard University's venerable president Charles W. Eliot, who in 1909 wrote that there should be "separate schools for Negro children" and that matters of equality should be left "to the people of a hundred years hence."[6]

When Eliot wrote these words, a racial divide characterized almost all of U.S. higher education. Northern land grant institutions established under the first Morrill Act of 1862, which included many state universities, were almost exclusively white. The second Morrill Act (1890), which funded institutions in the South, resulted in separate schools for whites and people of color. Between 1854 and 1866, several institutions that would become known as historically black colleges and universities were founded: for example, Lincoln University (Pennsylvania), Wilberforce College (Ohio), Fisk University (Nashville), and Morehouse College (Atlanta). The second Morrill Act assisted many of them, including Tuskegee University (Alabama) and Prairie View A&M (Texas).

By the early twentieth century, most of these schools boasted a football team, and in 1912 and 1913 two athletic conferences of historically black colleges and universities were established, the Central Intercollegiate Athletic Association and the Southern Intercollegiate Athletic Conference. In 1920, six Texas historically black colleges and universities founded the Southwestern Athletic Conference (SWAC). Most of the Texas schools eventually dropped out of the conference, but the league added institutions such as Grambling State, Jackson State, and Southern and evolved into the most elite athletic association of historically black colleges and universities. Football was the premier sport at all these universities, and the first bowl game among them, the Orange Blossom Classic, was held in Miami, Florida, in 1933, where host Florida A&M defeated Howard University 9–6.[7] By the 1950s, the Orange Blossom Classic had become the most important game of the year for historically black colleges and universities, offering a chance to expose African American football stars to the wider world—meaning the white world. NFL teams had begun scouting the game and signing black players to contracts.[8] There remained a belief among white coaches and athletic directors, however, that a black football team could not beat a white team, and in the South that belief masked a fear that a black team might win such a game.

Although football occupied top position for male athletes at all-black schools, basketball became the most popular varsity sport for women, particularly at all-female historically black colleges and universities in the 1920s and 1930s. For example, at Bennett College in Greensboro, North Carolina, founded by the Methodist Episcopal Church in 1873 as coeducational but transformed to all-female in 1926, basketball, as well as general physical education, were seen as a means to inculcate moral values, self-expression, and leadership skills in women of color, all with the goal of advancing the race. By the late 1930s, however, Bennett and other historically black colleges and universities began to succumb to the white-influenced belief that competitive sports for women were unladylike and physically dangerous. Black women's basketball programs first shifted from the fast-paced five-player-per-team style that men played to the less physically demanding six-player-per-team game that had been adapted for white women. Then, as the 1940s began, schools such as Bennett dropped varsity basketball and substituted noncompetitive "play days," which, according to a female physical educator at Howard University, were intended to develop "beauty of movement, poise, (and) femininity by affording each individual who participates an opportunity to play in an atmosphere of dignity, courtesy, and refinement."[9] This goal fit with white middle-class values, and it delayed the expansion of varsity athletics for black female college students.

From the 1920s to the year of the MSU–Loyola basketball game, African American athletes at historically black colleges and universities seldom captured national attention, but black athletes—especially football players—at integrated northern and western schools both excelled and suffered under a spotlight. Sometimes, they were prohibited from competing, even if they made the team, even if they were stars. When a northern football squad that included black athletes was scheduled to play a game against a southern team, it regularly agreed to the opponent's demand for compliance with the gentlemen's agreement and benched its African Americans. In 1934, for example, legendary University of Michigan football coach Fielding Yost agreed not to play one of his premier ends, Willis Ward, the school's second black footballer, against Georgia Tech, even though the game took place not in Atlanta but in Ann Arbor, Ward's hometown. Facing student demonstrations against his decision and a threat (not carried out) from team member and future president Gerald Ford to quit the team in protest, Yost, the son of a Confederate soldier, hired a Pinkerton detective and several husky undergraduates to thwart any trouble from both fans and mutinous footballers, and Ward sat out the game. In 1940, New York University left behind its star fullback, Leonard Bates, when the football team traveled to play at the University of Missouri. Two weeks before the game, NYU activists petitioned to cancel the game if Bates was not allowed to play, but president Harry W. Chase, formerly president of the University of North Carolina, held fast, claiming that denying the gentlemen's agreement would impede whatever slow progress was being made in race relations. The "Bates Must Play" movement then sputtered, ironically to be replaced by protests over the deflating record of NYU's once successful football team.[10]

After World War II, the gentlemen's agreement weakened somewhat, paralleled by the influx of a few African Americans onto professional baseball, football, and basketball teams. In 1947, with Charles Eliot long gone (he died in 1926), Harvard successfully insisted that its African American lineman, Chester Pierce, be on the field when its football team visited the University of Virginia. The Virginia team, which included several war veterans, played the game without incident, but spectators peppered Pierce with vicious verbal abuse. Harvard players stood by their teammate, electing to be housed in the same segregated facility where Pierce was forced to stay. In 1950, a black football player for the University of Pittsburgh participated in a game against

Duke University in Durham, North Carolina, and in 1948 an integrated University of Nevada team played against the University of Tulsa in Oklahoma's first interracial football game. These contests remained exceptions, however. In 1946, Penn State canceled a game against the University of Miami when the southern host refused to allow the team to bring its black halfback, Wally Triplett. And in 1947, the same year that his pioneer recruit Jackie Robinson broke Major League Baseball's color line, Brooklyn Dodgers president Branch Rickey failed to convince Rollins College of Winter Park, Florida, to reverse its decision not to play a scheduled football game against Rickey's integrated alma mater, Ohio Wesleyan.[11] Southern schools were not alone in excluding black athletes. Yale's football roster did not contain an African American until the late 1940s, and Princeton's football roster was not integrated until the mid-1960s.[12]

In 1951, the year that the college basketball point-shaving scandal was exposed, an act of on-field racial violence erupted in Oklahoma and graphically displayed how ugly racism in sports could be. The previous year, the U.S. Supreme Court had ruled that the University of Oklahoma had violated the rights of George McLaurin, a black man admitted to the university's Ph.D. program in education. At first the university denied McLaurin admission under state law, but then allowed him to enroll, but required him to sit in the hallway outside his classroom, study on a separate floor of the library, and eat in the cafeteria at a separate table at different times from white students. The Supreme Court ruled that these provisions violated McLaurin's rights under the equal protection clause of the Fourteenth Amendment, reasoning that a public institution of higher learning could not deny a student equal treatment solely on the basis of race.[13] The decision did not sit well with prosegregation politicians, citizens, and athletes, some of whom brought their hatred with them when the Drake University football team from Des Moines, Iowa, came to Stillwater to play Oklahoma A&M (now Oklahoma State) on October 20, 1951.

The Drake Bulldogs and Oklahoma A&M Aggies were members of the Missouri Valley conference, which had voted in 1947 to end racial discrimination by 1950. By 1951, all conference members had complied except the University of Tulsa and Oklahoma A&M. When Drake brought its African American quarterback, Johnny Bright, to the game against the Aggies, rumors spread that he would be a marked man. Malice exploded early. In the first play from scrimmage, Bright handed off the ball and as he looked downfield afterward, an Aggie lineman dove into him, smashing Bright in the head and breaking his jaw. Bright stayed on the field and threw a touchdown pass on the following play. The next time Drake had the ball, the same lineman attacked Bright again, injuring him so seriously that the Drake star had to be carried from the field. The *Des Moines Register* published a six-sequence photograph of the attack that broke Bright's jaw and ten days later reported that some students had overheard an A&M coach shout "Get that nigger" when the team was practicing to play against Bright. In protest against the incident, Drake, along with Bradley University, withdrew from the conference, after Missouri Valley officials refused to take any disciplinary action. Sports and race had become a volatile mixture.[14]

The Walls Buckle

During the 1950s and first half of the 1960s, as the nationwide civil-rights movement pushed for racial integration in schools, lunch counters, and public transportation, integration of college sports in the South and its neighboring states occurred in a piecemeal fashion, full of fits and starts. In Oklahoma, after the attack on Johnny Bright, teams remained all white for another five years. Then, in 1956, less than a year after Rosa Parks refused to yield her seat to a white bus passenger in Montgomery, Alabama, the University of Oklahoma football team, coached by the legendary Bud Wilkinson, featured its first African American player, running back Prentice Gautt. Born in Oklahoma City, Gautt had starred at all-black Douglass High School and in 1955 became the first African American to play in the Oklahoma High School All-State football game, sufficiently impressing Wilkinson to make himself a desirable recruit. When racist football boosters pressured Wilkinson to deny Gautt an athletic scholarship, a group of black physicians and pharmacists raised funds to finance his first year at the university. Thereafter, there was no reason to refuse Gautt full university-sponsored financial aid, because he proved his worth. He won All–Big Eight awards twice, garnered Most Valuable Player at the 1959 Orange Bowl, and made Academic All-American his senior year. During Gautt's career at the University of Oklahoma, the team won the third of its three national titles under Wilkinson, and Gautt's early college career coincided with the final games of the university's forty-seven consecutive victories (1953–57). After graduation, Gautt played professionally for eight seasons and then earned a Ph.D. in psychology at the University of Missouri. He later became an administrator for the Big Eight and, after that, the Big 12 Conference.[15]

In the post–World War II era, the major bowl games, most of which were hosted by deeply segregated southern cities, became a testing ground for the integration of college football. In 1947, the Cotton Bowl invited Penn State to play Southern Methodist University in Dallas and allowed the northern team to bring its black players as long as the entire team was housed not in Dallas but at the naval air station, fourteen miles away. The next year, bowl officials invited another integrated team, the University of Oregon, but on the condition that Oregon's three African American players stay at the home of a local black physician and not at the team's hotel. And in 1952, an integrated team from College of the Pacific was allowed to play in the Sun Bowl in El Paso, Texas.[16]

As the mauling of Johnny Bright proved, however, there was no consensus on whether or how to extend white southern hospitality to northern teams that contained blacks. Among groups enraged by the landmark school desegregation case in 1954, *Brown v. Board of Education*, were those who opposed interracial athletics. Some of this contingent in Georgia angrily protested in 1955 when the Sugar Bowl invited Georgia Tech (formally, Georgia Institute of Technology, a public university) to play the University of Pittsburgh, with its one black player, in New Orleans, on January 1, 1956. They petitioned Georgia Tech's coach, Bobby Dodd, to renege on his acceptance of the invitation and goaded Governor Marvin Griffin, an archsegregationist, to urge the Georgia Board of Regents to force the Georgia Tech football team to remain at home. After first staying out of the controversy, Griffin decided to play to the racist crowd, fuming that no difference existed between "compromising the integrity of race on the playing field than to do so in the classroom. One break in the dike and the relentless seas will rush in and destroy us." A band of Georgia Tech students, however, expressing their desire to see their team play on a national stage, marched through downtown Atlanta and hung Griffin in effigy. As the mob became rowdier, state police were called in, and Griffin blamed Georgia Tech's president for the students' insolence. Subsequently, the regents allowed Georgia Tech to play against Pitt, but they followed up with a ban against interracial competition in Georgia. The dike had cracked, but the fissure was patched.[17]

Soon, the power of money and quest for prestige opened larger gaps in the dike. In 1958, just three years after the Georgia Tech fiasco, Philadelphia's Liberty Bowl invited the University of Alabama to play Penn State on January 1, 1959. For the tenth-ranked Alabama Crimson Tide and its second-year coach Paul "Bear" Bryant, the game offered a chance to play on a national stage against the twelfth-ranked Penn State Nittany Lions, guided by Head Coach Rip Engle and his assistant, Joe Paterno. The bowl also provided a $150,000 payout, a strong inducement for Bryant to take his team north to play an opponent whose roster included one African American, even though a Tuscaloosa (home of the university) citizens council had expressed bitter opposition, stating, "The (Crimson) Tide belongs to all Alabama and Alabamians favor continued segregation." In contrast, an editorial in the Tuscaloosa newspaper reflected how big-time college sports were beginning to override social traditions. "It is a fact of life," the newspaper stated, that

> the young men who play on Alabama's football team—or in any other sport—will meet players of other races if they enter a professional career. In sports centers of the East, Midwest and Far West sports attractions and teams are not segregated. This year's Alabama team can help the cause of the Tide and the University if it goes to Philadelphia, plays a hard, clean game of which it is capable, and demonstrates sportsmanship at its highest level.[18]

Alabama lost the game in a snowstorm, 7–0, and a decade would elapse before Bryant would integrate his Crimson Tide team, but for one brief moment he had put his ambitions for his team above the old gentlemen's agreement.

The bowl games made southern coaches, educators, and politicians realize that if they wanted national recognition for their athletic programs—and their schools—they would have to play integrated teams somewhat routinely. And eventually, they themselves would have to recruit African American players, principally in football and basketball. For some southern coaches, playing against blacks was easier to do than playing with them. Alabama's Bryant epitomized that attitude. Though he had agreed to compete against teams with black players, his own squad remained lily-white throughout the 1960s—as did the entire student bodies at the University of Alabama and all other southern state universities, at least until the mid-1960s—while Bryant's stature as one of football's premier coaches soared. He supposedly claimed that he would like to recruit African Americans but could not find any that were acceptable. Some critics have concluded that Bryant, like other Deep South coaches, simply was making an excuse to obscure his racism. Others, however, have surmised that in a state led by a governor who represented the virulent backlash against civil rights and desegregation—George C. Wallace—Bryant had to tread gingerly even if he sincerely intended to integrate his team.

Whatever his motives, Bryant and Alabama passed a milestone in 1970. For that year's football season, Bryant invited powerhouse University of Southern California to Birmingham to play the Crimson Tide on September 12. The USC roster featured an all-black backfield, including Sam Cunningham, a bruising sophomore fullback from Santa Barbara. Cunningham's performance during the contest startled fans attending the game and viewers watching on television. Standing 6'3" and weighing 230 pounds, Cunningham overpowered the Alabama defense with long runs from scrimmage and helped USC crush the Tide 42–21. After the game, Bryant allegedly escorted Cunningham into the Alabama locker room and lectured his downcast players, "This is Sam Cunningham. This is what a football player looks like."[19]

Did Bryant try to use the USC game to prove that competing at the high-est level could no longer be successful with only white players? That is the myth, and it is at least partly accurate. The previous year, the Tide's record had slipped to 6-5, a mediocrity intolerable to Bryant. The university now had a small number of black students, and in 1969 its African American student association filed a lawsuit, charging the football program with racial discrimi-nation. So maybe Bryant was trying to avoid public embarrassment by finally recognizing the value of an outstanding black athlete. Alternatively, Bryant might have realized on his own that he had waited long enough. Perhaps Bryant, who had not wanted to be the first Southeastern Conference coach to integrate, decided not to be the last. The true reason remains blurred.[20] Whatever the Bear's true motives, he soon made a more concerted effort to bring African Americans onto his squad. Already in 1969, he had offered a scholarship to Wilbur Jackson, a highly touted running back and end from Ozark, Alabama. Jackson only watched the game against USC because fresh-men were ineligible to play in 1970. But between 1971 and 1973, he starred for a Crimson Tide team that lost only four games in three years.

Adolph Rupp provides an example of a coach whose recalcitrance on integrating his team left him even more embarrassed than Bryant after a landmark game. Born in rural Kansas to Mennonite German immigrants, Rupp was nine years old when his father died in 1910. As a child, he played basketball with his older brothers, and when he sprouted to 6'2" as a teen-ager, he became a high school standout. He then attended the University of Kansas, where he played and learned under Forrest C. "Phog" Allen, the "Father of Basketball Coaches," who won 746 games in a fifty-one-year coaching career that ended in 1956. (Rupp eventually won 876.) Rupp was hired as head basketball coach for the University of Kentucky Wildcats in 1930, when he was just twenty-nine years old. He remained at that post for forty-two years, winning 82 percent of his games, twenty-seven South-eastern Conference titles, and four national championships. Moon-faced, heavyset, and amiable (when he wasn't coaching), Rupp earned a reputa-tion for quick quips and quick play. As desirous of acclaim as Bear Bryant, Rupp was willing to temper his aversion to integrated play if it would help his team's standing. Twice before 1963, though his team finished second in the Southeastern Conference, he took Kentucky to the NCAA tournament when first-place MSU refused to compete against a team with black play-ers. But Rupp steadfastly held to the color line. He once vowed that a black would never play for Kentucky, and in 1960, he refused to recruit Connie Hawkins, the foremost high school basketballer in the country, allegedly because Hawkins was African American.[21]

Rupp's devotion to white superiority butted head first into Texas Western University's (now the University of Texas–El Paso) basketball team in the championship game of the 1966 NCAA tournament. Whereas Loyola of Chicago had started four African Americans against MSU in the breakthrough regional game in 1963, the Texas Western Miners boasted five blacks in its starting lineup—seven total on the team—the first time any tournament team featured such a composition. Miners coach Don Haskins, a former pool shark from Oklahoma, was upset that the Kentucky team was heavily favored and vowed to do anything possible to undercut Kentucky's confidence. In pregame warm-ups, Haskins let his players dunk to intimidate the Wildcats. Once the game began, he used a patterned offense and tight defense to counteract Kentucky's quickness. The game's tone was set early. The Miners' David "Big Daddy" Lattin blocked the first shot attempted by Kentucky's star, Pat Riley; then, on the other end of the floor, Lattin dunked the ball over Riley and was said to have muttered, "Take that, you white honky."[22] Behind by three points at halftime, Rupp reputedly exhorted his team to beat the "coons," but their efforts failed. Texas Western won, 74–65. Afterward, Rupp refused to shake hands with the Miners team.[23]

No national network televised the Texas Western–Kentucky game, so few people saw it live. Yet, because the game occurred two years after passage of the historic Civil Rights Act of 1964 and featured an unknown team of African Americans beating an all-white Goliath, it has passed down through history as a momentous event, the subject of uncountable media references and a feature-length Hollywood film, "Glory Road." (2006). [24]

Several months after the fabled Texas Western–Kentucky basketball game, a less heralded but equally groundbreaking event occurred. Perry Wallace, a 6'6" African American basketball star and valedictorian at Nashville's all-black Pearl High School, had agreed to accept an athletic scholarship at Vanderbilt University. In fall 1966, he became the first African American basketball player to compete for a team in the Southeastern Conference. (Steve Martin, a baseball player at Tulane, had become the first African American to compete in any sport in the Southeastern Conference earlier that year.) Alone and reviled everywhere he played, Wallace exhibited extraordinary commitment and fortitude. During his first year, on the freshman team, the University of Mississippi canceled its game against Vanderbilt when it discovered that blacks were on the roster—it had suddenly discovered "scheduling conflicts." The next year, Vanderbilt, with Wallace on the varsity team, traveled to Oxford, Mississippi, home of Ole Miss, for a game, and ugly jeering began during warm-ups. During the game, the crowd laughed boisterously at every mistake Wallace made, and the Mississippi players pummeled him, at one point injuring his eye. Still, he returned to the lineup and led his team to a resounding victory. The abuse at opponents' arenas continued until the last game of Wallace's senior year, also against Ole Miss, when Wallace, who refused to give in, made his final shot, an illegal slam dunk that symbolized his feelings of release and revenge. He graduated from Vanderbilt in 1970 with a degree in engineering, then earned a law degree from Columbia University in 1975, served as a trial attorney for the U.S. Department of Justice, and then became a law professor.[25]

Perry Wallace's career at Vanderbilt was a landmark, but in a way, it resembled the enrollment of James Meredith as the first African American undergraduate at the University of Mississippi in 1962—a pioneering but unique accomplishment against vituperative racism. By 1966, in college basketball, a major turning point had already occurred in 1963, when MSU snuck out of Starkville to play Loyola, bringing its all-white team to the integrated North. But the turn toward integrated sports at major schools was slow. Southeastern Conference football teams, for example, first began to integrate their rosters in 1967, with Nat Northington, a football player at Kentucky who stayed on the roster for only a year. He left school unable to recover from the death of his black teammate, Greg Page, who had died from an injury during preseason practice. Tennessee played its first black footballer in 1968, followed by Auburn and Alabama in 1970. Even when these schools tried to recruit star athletes from all-black high schools, they did so halfheartedly or lost out to schools that appeared more welcoming to blacks.

Two important developments affected the recruitment of African American athletes. For one thing, exposure of college football and basketball on television and in the print media expanded in the 1960s. Although *Sports Illustrated*, for example, began publishing in 1954, its circulation and profitability did not boom until the 1960s. Seeking the kind of media exposure successful teams could bring, schools widened their search for premier players. And as athletic scholarships became increasingly available for blue chip athletes in football and basketball, an increasing number of recruited African American high school stars from the South and North opted, courageously, to play in the big time instead of at historically black colleges and universities, even if it meant integrating an all-white roster. Black athletes from Kentucky, a state that in the 1960s was known for producing some of the nation's top basketball prospects, provide an example. Wes Unseld, who excelled in basketball at two-time state champion Seneca High School in Louisville, opted in 1964 to attend hometown University of Louisville, which had integrated its football team just two years previously. The next year, Butch Beard, from Hardinsburg, also joined the previously all-white University of Louisville basketball team. In 1967, Jim McDaniels, from Scottsville, began playing basketball at Western Kentucky University, as did fellow black Kentuckian Jerome Perry.[26] Some of the most celebrated black basketball college stars of the late 1950s opted for northern integrated institutions. Oscar Robertson, born in Tennessee and raised in segregated Indianapolis, attended the integrated University of Cincinnati. Elgin Baylor, who was born in Washington, D.C., as much a southern place as any, went first to the College of Idaho, then to Seattle University.

The enrollment of outstanding black athletes in integrated northern colleges and in integrating southern schools left the athletic scene at historically black colleges and universities in somewhat of a limbo. Lacking financial resources to offer the scholarships—and, as often happened in big-time athletic recruitment, the illegal inducements—that major integrated schools could employ to attract standout athletes, historically black colleges and universities could not keep pace. During the 1950s and 1960s, some historically black colleges and universities were able to focus resources on one or two sports—football at Grambling State, track at Florida A&M, for example—and reap occasional publicity from the accomplishments of a single star, such as Willie Davis in football at Grambling and Bob Hayes in track at Florida A&M. But most historically black colleges and universities were forced to rein in whatever ambitions for athletic renown they might have had. As a consequence, historically black colleges and universities could not attract the television revenue and booster money that have flowed into majority schools during the past several decades. At the same time, the limited scale of varsity sports at most historically black colleges and universities meant that the schools have invested as much as possible in sustaining academic standards.[27]

By the late 1960s, the walls that had blocked African American athletes—and nonathletes, for that matter—from attending major southern colleges and universities had only buckled, not crumbled. Across the country, outside historically black colleges and universities, blacks were mostly tokens in white-dominated higher education, and those who were accepted, grudgingly or not, onto athletic teams were a lonely few, part of a team part of the time, isolated and discriminated against the rest of the time. A five-part series by Jack Olsen in *Sports Illustrated* in summer 1968 highlighted their plight in "The Black Athlete: A Shameful Story." Olsen, a former crime reporter, became senior editor for the fledgling magazine in 1961. His series linked the exploitation of black athletes in colleges and the pros to the poor treatment of African Americans generally in American society. Olsen exposed college coaches and administrators who praised blacks in one breath and referred to "nigger athletes" under that breath, and he revealed that low graduation rates and the isolation of black athletes in campus housing and campus activities burst the myth that "sports has been good to the Negro." Olsen concluded with a warning that black athletes were becoming restless. "Almost to a man," he wrote, "they are dissatisfied, disgruntled and disillusioned."[28] His prophecy already was coming true.

Black Athletes in Revolt

It was February 1969, off-season for college football, and Fred Milton, a promising linebacker at Oregon State University, decided to grow a mustache and goatee. As he was walking on campus one day sporting his new hirsuteness, Milton, an African American, by chance encountered his white coach, Dee Andros, a roly-poly white man dubbed "The Great Pumpkin" because, as one journalist described him, he packed "250 pounds on a 170-pound frame." Andros ordered Milton to shave. A popular, fairly liberal coach, Andros had one hard-and-fast rule off the field: no hair over the ears or collar, no sideburns below mid-ear, no facial hair. It was, of course, the 1960s, when protests over the Vietnam War and the generation gap rent by youths challenging adult authority made daily headlines. Andros was one of those adults who saw excess hair as a symbol of disrespect. "I will not tolerate a player who will embarrass me or the university," he proclaimed.[29]

Not just young people were rebelling in 1969. Also African Americans of all ages, freshened and frustrated in their quest for civil rights, were asserting race pride and militancy. Three years earlier, Stokely Carmichael, new chairman of the Student Nonviolent Coordinating Committee (SNCC), had made his famous "Black Power" speech, urging people of color to unite and oppose white dominance more aggressively than they had previously and to exclude whites from top roles in activist civil-rights organizations. In addition, by 1969, the nation had already experienced five "long hot summers" of urban violence and near race war, putting many white people on edge. On campuses as diverse as the Ivy League's Cornell University and the historically black Howard University, black students were demonstrating, sometimes violently, for redress of discriminatory practices on and off campus, for more admission of black applicants, and for new curricular programs in African and African American studies. So a higher-than-normal degree of tension ensued when Milton refused to shave, saying his beard was a symbol of racial identity, and when Andros responded by kicking him off the football team. More than ever before, national issues were intruding into college sports, and the innocent encounter of a black man seeming to flout team rules imposed by a white coach who believed in the prerogatives of authority burst into a conflict that stretched beyond the sidewalk and the locker room.

At Oregon State, the Milton case escalated quickly. The Black Student Union, representing the university's forty-seven African American students—out of a total enrollment of 14,500—called for a boycott to protest Milton's treatment and then claimed widespread discrimination in various kinds of treatment and practices across the campus and the city of Corvallis, Oregon State's home. Campus rallies ensued, and many white students, alumni, and community people rushed to Andros's side. One hundred seventy-three athletes signed a letter in support of the coach, while the Black Student Union, including all eighteen black football athletes, staged a walkout. In response, Oregon State president James Jensen took the safe path of ordering an investigation and then created a Commission on Human Rights and Responsibilities. After weeks of deliberation, the commission conceded the need for team discipline but offered a compromise that facial hair need not be regulated off-season and that "neatly groomed mustaches" should be acceptable in season. Andros rebuffed the measure, grumbling, "The way the resolution stood, they were giving the hippies license to walk naked at graduation." Soon, however, the controversy cooled, not least because Milton withdrew from Oregon State—along with seven other black athletes and a majority of the Black Student Union—and Andros was given a new five-year contract. Two black footballers remained, and one of them, Bryce Huddleston, showed up for spring practice with a mustache. Andros immediately dismissed him from the team, but then accepted Huddleston back after he shaved off the mustache. "He was a real gentleman about the matter," Andros reported.[30]

The Fred Milton case exemplified a string of events that splintered campus athletics across the country during the late 1960s. The era of open rebellion by black athletes began in 1967 when Harry Edwards, an instructor of sociology at San Jose State and former track and basketball star, formally presented grievances suffered by the school's fifty-nine black students, including discriminatory treatment of black athletes by white coaches. Tall (he stood 6'8") and imposing (he weighed more than 250 pounds), Edwards adopted direct action and inflammatory language to get his points across. When he threatened a sit-in at an impending football game with Texas–El Paso, San Jose State's president canceled the contest. Edwards soon left San Jose to enter Ph.D. work in sociology at Cornell, but the hornets' nest had been stirred, and the athletic establishment at San Jose State scurried to a stance of self-defense. When seven black San Jose State football players boycotted a game against Brigham Young University over the Mormon Church's discriminatory policies that barred blacks from the church's priesthood, they were dismissed from the team.

The unrest spread. In 1968, African American athletes at the University of California, the University of Kansas, and Michigan State University staged or threatened boycotts over racial biases, prompting the NCAA at its January 1969 convention to pass a resolution permitting coaches and athletic directors to revoke scholarships from disruptive and disobedient student athletes.[31]

Later that year, a coach's prerogative came under more heated attack. At the University of Iowa, sixteen black football players boycotted the first day of spring practice over the lack of a black advisor and black assistant coach. Head coach Ray Nagel allowed the dissidents to return to the team only if their teammates agreed to accept them back. The team approved only the least militant seven of the twelve who petitioned for reinstatement. In October, another protest occurred when fourteen African American members of the University of Wyoming football team, supported by the school's Black Student Alliance, resolved to wear black armbands in their upcoming game against Brigham Young University in protest of antiblack Mormon policies. Wyoming's coach Lloyd Eaton warned the players they would be dismissed if they carried through with their plan. The protesters refused to back down, even after a marathon meeting with the school's president and the state's governor. Neither did Eaton yield. The game went on, with Wyoming trouncing BYU 40–7, but the fourteen black players watched the game from the stands. Most spectators, including the few who flew a Confederate flag, voiced support for Coach Eaton, but in the days after the game, the Wyoming Student Senate and Faculty Senate voted for reinstatement of the fourteen. They failed. Nevertheless, the Iowa and Wyoming incidents showed that the integration of sports at schools outside the South, which had brought much-desired success on the playing field—Wyoming had won the Sugar Bowl in January 1969—also was creating a critical mass of black athletes who were willing to take risks and assert themselves to advance their cause against discrimination.[32]

That cause took center stage as it spread to more schools. Football coaches—all of them white—at big-time universities such as Indiana, Washington, and Syracuse, who had histories of recruitment of African Americans but also were accustomed to unquestionable authority, suddenly found themselves confronted by fractious athletes who threatened and carried out boycotts over alleged racial slights. The Syracuse case took place within campuswide racial tensions. There, in 1970, Coach Ben Schwartzwalder suspended seven black players who had demanded the hiring of a black assistant coach and had boycotted spring practice. Schwartzwalder, like others of his kind, had a reputation for being both lovable and tough. He also was eccentric. A former college athlete and decorated World War II paratrooper, Schwartzwalder once conducted a practice while wearing pajama bottoms. Not averse to recruiting academically challenged athletes, he also used athletic scholarships to good advantage and coached several academically qualified African Americans who became legends of the National Football League, including Jim Brown, Ernie Davis, and Floyd Little. The racial protests at Syracuse targeted both Schwartzwalder and the university. As a result of the football boycott, the chancellor appointed a special committee, who concluded that the school was infused with "institutional racism." After the racial protests, which discouraged black recruits from enrolling, Syracuse's football prowess, already on the decline, did not recover, and Schwartzwalder retired in 1973 after winning only two of eleven games.[33]

By the early 1970s, the so-called Revolt of the Black Athlete had calmed. As more teams included more African Americans, and as sensitivities on controversial matters of race and culture became more accepting nationwide—though negative actions and reactions never disappeared—coaches managed to retain their power on the field and in the arena while making at least some concessions to the demands of their athletes. Athletic departments, both northern and southern, hired more black assistant coaches—though hardly ever promoting them to head coach—and white coaches accepted—within limits—goatees, Afro hair styles, and soul music in locker rooms. At least one school—Stanford—stopped scheduling games against Brigham Young, and many bowed to demands from black student groups and instituted black history courses. A head coach still, however, controlled who made the team and who received and who kept a scholarship. No revolution was going to change those facts of life.

History does not move in a linear fashion, and the present is not an inevitable consequence of the past. When Jerry Harkness and Joe Dan Gold shook hands on the basketball court March 16, 1963, it would have been difficult to predict what the future of integrated college sports would be like—or whether there would be a future at all. After all, resistance and violence still were common reactions when African Americans tried to enter the white-controlled mainstream, whether the move involved housing, schools, jobs, or sports. The outrage wreaked upon Johnny Bright revealed that, except at historically black colleges and universities, racist coaches and politicians viewed college sports as an exclusively white domain. In the North and West, a few athletes of color were granted entry to that domain prior to the 1960s, but only if, like Perry Wallace, they proved capable both of absorbing mistreatment of all sorts and at the same time propelling their team to victory.

Nevertheless, the MSU–Loyola basketball game of 1963, and other historic contests involving athletes of color, demonstrated the power that sports have had to propel social change and alter the course of history. After all, athletes and fans wanted winners more than they wanted to preserve or alter an artificial racial order. At MSU, students, alumni, and the school president put aside racial prejudice and allowed the basketball team to sneak away to play against a northern team laden with African Americans because the quest for a championship and national esteem overrode long-institutionalized racist attitudes such as the gentlemen's agreement. And recognition by coaches, athletic administrators, college presidents, students, alumni, and fans that athletes of color could often be important, even vital, to a team's and a school's success became a matter of fact in the South as well as the North. But that recognition came haltingly across the South and not much less so elsewhere in the intercollegiate sports landscape. True, the achievements of black college athletes in the 1960s who were some of the greatest stars ever to play in the college ranks—Gale Sayers (Kansas) and OJ Simpson (Southern California) in football; Lew Alcindor (UCLA) and Elvin Hayes (Houston) in basketball— earned respect and even adulation from white Americans as well as lucrative professional careers for themselves. And they paved the way for countless others who followed.

Issues of unfair treatment and lack of toleration for racial differences consequently fueled the outbursts of protest that dotted the late 1960s, the movement called Revolt of the Black Athlete. The combined effect of the civil-rights movement—and its evolution into race pride and Black Power—along with the cultural and political alternatives raised by the era's college students in their protests against the Vietnam War and against authority in general, created a context for black athletes like Fred Milton to display their alternative personae and to protest against discrimination. Moreover, during the 1960s, many northern colleges and universities began actively recruiting students of color, not just athletes, and though they remained a distinct minority on campus, the nonathlete black students nevertheless provided support groups that legitimized the athletes' protests. Thus, the walkouts over a lack of black assistant coaches and against the Mormons as represented by Brigham Young University became viable because the Black Student Union and other African American student bodies backed and even encouraged the athlete-protesters.

Aside from the critical issues involving race pride and assertiveness, the Fred Milton affair, plus many other controversies over the status of black

athletes, illustrate an important aspect of intercollegiate athletics that was
perhaps overshadowed by the boycotts and demonstrations. By the 1960s
and 1970s, coaches and their athletic departments had reached such a level
of influence within colleges and universities and were generating so much
revenue that they could operate independently in a way that practically no
other wing of higher education could act. When, for example, Oregon State's
Faculty Senate declared that students, including athletes, had the right to
represent their own cultural values in the way they dressed, and Oregon
State University's Committee on Human Rights and Responsibilities stated
that "neatly groomed mustaches" should be allowed on the football team,
coach Dee Andros rejected the proposal by saying, "I'm not just fighting
hair on the face; I'm fighting for a principle of education—the right to run
my department. . . . If they beat you on one issue, they'll keep right on."[34]
Significantly, Andros linked the "principle of education" with the "right to
run my department." That "right" allowed him to ignore the bodies whose
recommendations and authority every other department of the university
presumably accepted. Not so the athletic department and not so the football
team. They had become semiautonomous, enterprises that conducted their
own affairs by their own rules.

The 1960s, then, were momentous for the world of college sports just as
they were for college life in general, but not always in the same way. The
racial integration of teams, accelerating in the North and beginning in the
South, altered the quality of games as well as the composition of rosters.
By the 1970s, football and track squads contained two dozen or more black
athletes, and on some basketball teams blacks constituted a majority. To a
considerable extent, the opening up of these rosters spelled the decline—or
at least inability to compete at the highest levels—of historically black college teams. Meanwhile, coaches, though they lost some of the battles against
assertive black athletes, and though their sensitivities on race matters were
raised, most often emerged with their authority not only intact but enhanced
by control of scholarships and by increasingly independent athletic departments. The college athletic enterprise was opening a new playbook in which
money and media would be involved as never before.

3 Television and College Sports as Mass Entertainment

A publicist dubbed it the Game of the Century, a landmark college basketball contest between two top-rated and undefeated teams, on Saturday night, January 20, 1968. On one bench sat the powerful UCLA Bruins, coached by the renowned John Wooden and boasting a forty-seven-game winning streak. On the other side, the upstart University of Houston Cougars, coached by Guy Lewis, whose last loss had come at the hands of UCLA at the NCAA Championship Tournament in March 1967. Hatched in the mind of Lewis at the end of the 1966–67 season, the idea of Houston playing UCLA was sold to Judge Roy Hofheinz, owner of the Houston Astros and the Houston Astrodome, the first domed sports stadium. A Houston official contacted UCLA's sports information director, who then persuaded Coach Wooden that facing the Cougars at the Astrodome would give college basketball a major boost. As soon as news of the game reached the public, its appeal skyrocketed. During summer 1967, thirty thousand tickets were sold, and requests for media credentials flowed in from across the country. The TVS Television Network bought broadcast rights for $27,000 and signed up 120 stations in 49 states, most of whom canceled their regular prime-time programming to air the game.[1]

The contest itself fulfilled expectations. UCLA's star center, Lew Alcindor (who later changed his name to Kareem Abdul-Jabbar), had suffered a scratched cornea a week earlier and played the poorest game of his college career, but his Houston counterpart, Elvin Hayes, sparkled, scoring 39 points, grabbing 15 rebounds, and blocking 8 shots. Nevertheless, UCLA kept the game close, tying the score with 44 seconds left. Hayes then sank two free throws and the Bruins subsequently lost the ball out of bounds twice, missing a chance to tie or win and extend their winning streak. The final score: Houston 71, UCLA 69. As the game-ending horn sounded, ecstatic Houston fans leaped over press tables and stormed the court. Both teams went undefeated for the rest of the season and met again in the semifinals of the NCAA Tournament. This time, UCLA got revenge, swamping the Cougars 101–69, and two days later beat the University of North Carolina to collect the national championship. The NCAA title carried great prestige, but the UCLA–Houston matchup two months earlier brought an economic windfall to both universities. For the game at the Astrodome, each school received $125,000, four times the 1968 NCAA tournament payout of $31,781 that each received, and more than the Houston basketball team had earned in the entire previous season.[2]

Other numbers from the Astrodome game had historic significance well beyond what took place on the basketball court. In addition to the 52,663 spectators at the Astrodome—the largest number at that time ever to watch a basketball game in person, a record that lasted until 2003—the broadcast drew a vast television audience. An estimated 12 million fans viewed this first national telecast of a regular-season college basketball game. At a time when the nation was embroiled in the Vietnam War and was apprehensively recovering from a summer of its worst racial violence, a hyped sporting event provided welcome distraction. Today, many times more viewers tune in to the NCAA's March Madness and other big games, but in the 1960s 12 million was unprecedented. Moreover, the game on January 20, 1968, launched college basketball as an entertainment product on television. Football had first given intercollegiate sports televised exposure, but the UCLA–Houston contest demonstrated to officials in commercial broadcast media and to college athletic directors that an avenue paved with gold led out from this fork in the road. The rise of television created a turning point at which both the NCAA and American higher education made fateful decisions. The choices made in pursuit of the gold, however, deepened rifts within the college sports establishment with resulting rancor that rocked the NCAA.[3]

The Beginning of College Sports on Television

On September 30, 1939, Waynesburg College (now Waynesburg University) in southwestern Pennsylvania entered sports history when its football team, the Yellowjackets, played the Fordham University Rams at New York City's Triborough Stadium. That day, four months after RCA inaugurated regular television transmission, when it aired speeches by President Franklin

D. Roosevelt and Albert Einstein at the opening of the New York World's Fair, an RCA camera mounted on the stadium's forty-yard line sent images to NBC station W2XBS, which then broadcast this first televised college football game. Fans watching on an estimated one thousand television sets saw Waynesburg's Bobby Brooks run sixty-three yards for a touchdown on the game's third play, promising an upset of Fordham, the preseason pick for the nation's number one team. But the Rams recouped, scoring in every quarter and winning easily, 34–7.[4] More important, W2XBS brought the game into people's living rooms. The day was dry but cool, and football fans with memories of the previous September, when a destructive hurricane raced past New York City and brought massive destruction to southern New England, appreciated the ability to watch the game indoors. One viewer remarked that he could see the ball better than if he had been at the game, and Orrin Dunlap, a *New York Times* reporter, raved, "When the players gallop directly in front of the camera the televiewer feels that he is plunging through the line." Aided by a knowledgeable announcer, a fan watching at home did not have to be unsure about who carried the ball, who made a tackle, or how many yards were needed for a first down. As Dunlap concluded, "Science has scored a touchdown at the kickoff of football by television."[5]

Dunlap suspected that there could be a downside to the wonderment, however. To be sure, inclement weather mattered little to fans watching in the dry comfort of their living rooms. Nor did they have to battle postgame traffic. But televising a game posed challenges. For one thing, in an age before color broadcasts, how could television viewers distinguish between similarly colored uniforms, such as Harvard crimson and Cornell red? Many school colors included green, blue, and black, all of which looked alike on the screen. Also, early television reception was not always dependable; "snow" could enshroud a game on the set as much as from the stands. Most of all, televised games gave viewers what historian Keith Dunnavant has called "an unlimited supply of free tickets."[6] College football, which at the time depended on revenues from tickets sold, faced financial loss if fans stayed home to watch on television. "[I]t is no wonder," Dunlap observed, "that the telecasters report that they are encountering resistance all along the line in trying to arrange with college athletic associations to pass football forward to the home."[7]

At midcentury, the American home was increasingly becoming the site of those free tickets. In 1948, 172,000 homes had televisions; four years later, the number mushroomed to 15.3 million and four major networks—ABC, CBS, NBC, and Dumont—were overtaking the entertainment industry with coast-to-coast programming. By 1955, 32 million television sets were in use, and an estimated three-fourths of households owned at least one TV set.[8] In the late 1940s, American television broadcasting, unlike the British Broad-casting Corporation, was already a fully commercial enterprise rather than a public service, meaning that networks and stations were in business to make money, and they sold air time to advertisers as their means of generating revenue. Indeed, by 1952, television advertisers spent $288 million (about $2.5 billion today), an increase of 39 percent in just one year.[9] The impact of this commercialization on college sports would be considerable.

Broadcast media had long posed dilemmas to college sports, starting with football on the radio. The airwaves created opportunities for publicizing a school, as well as its team, to a large audience, but there was always fear that fans would stop paying to see a game in the stadium if they could hear it at home. During the 1930s and 1940s, attendance at college football games declined, because of the Depression and World War II. College officials, however, blamed radio coverage, and in 1935 the NCAA appointed a com-mittee to assess whether radio broadcasts of football games were reducing live attendance and the revenues on which teams depended. After a year of study, the committee could not reach a conclusion and the NCAA decided to allow each school and conference to determine for itself what its broadcast policy should be.[10]

This policy of autonomy initially was applied to television when broadcasts of football games expanded after World War II. But TV had a more damag-ing effect than radio; attendance at college football games plummeted by 1.4 million between 1948 and 1950. At the NCAA convention in January 1951, Tom Hamilton, athletic director at the University of Pittsburgh and chair of the NCAA television committee investigation, asserted that when his com-mittee examined the falloff in attendance at football games, it was "appalled at the size of the problem" of television's impact on college sports.[11] Reacting to the committee's alarm, the NCAA first declared a moratorium on football telecasts for the 1951 season and then instituted a plan for limited broadcasts.[12] By a vote of 161–7, the membership approved an NCAA-controlled TV con-tract with Westinghouse Corporation for $680,000 to telecast one football game each week, with proceeds paid to those schools whose games appeared on television, after the NCAA took a portion for itself. (Just minutes later, the same members refused to oust the "Sinful Seven" and consequently dis-mantled the Sanity Code. See Chapter 1.) Westinghouse, in turn, picked the 52-station NBC network to broadcast the games and advertise Westinghouse products during games.[13] If the TV fees had been divided among the twenty schools whose games were telecast, they would have amounted to about $34,000 apiece; after the NCAA skimmed its share, each school received about $14,000 per game, not much money, but a little snowball that would expand rapidly as it rolled forward.[14]

The University of Notre Dame, whose football team had occupied national prominence since the 1920s, and the University of Pennsylvania, led by its ambitious president Harold Stassen, already were reaping their own returns from televised sports. A Chicago station began telecasting Notre Dame football games in 1947, and in 1949 the school contracted for its games to be broadcast over the Dumont Television Network. In 1950, Penn, which had begun televising its football games in 1940, sold broadcast rights to ABC for $75,000. Both schools envisioned television as a vital future revenue source.[15] These initiatives, however, made rivals nervous. The Big Ten conference, many of whose members competed for attendance in the same Midwestern market where Notre Dame games were broadcast, and eastern schools, who were losing ticket sales, pressed the NCAA to respond to Notre Dame's and Penn's independence by establishing greater control over football telecasts.[16]

Notre Dame's president, Father John J. Cavanaugh, held his ground as complaints against Notre Dame and Penn mounted in 1951, grumbling, "If these [limitations by the NCAA television committee] are permitted, what would prevent some future committee from telling a school how many games it might play or where it might play them or to levy a 60 percent tax on the proceeds from ticket sales?"[17] Cavanaugh had graduated from Notre Dame in 1921 and become a successful salesman for the Studebaker Corporation, rising to assistant sales manager at age 27. Tired of hawking automobiles, he returned to Notre Dame to study for the priesthood, stayed on to be appointed the school's vice president and then served as president from 1946 to 1952. In his brief tenure, he bolstered the university's research stature and expanded undergraduate and graduate enrollments. Father Cavanaugh also worked to increase his institution's endowment from outside sources of income. One of those sources was television, and when other schools balked at his contract to televise Notre Dame football, Cavanaugh countered by threatening a plan to create a superconference of a dozen or so football powers who, independently of the NCAA, would ally with a television network to broadcast football games and, eventually, other athletic contests to the benefit of the conference and the "public demand." Presidents of prospective members, however, were leery of such a bold scheme and declined to sign on.[18]

Stassen was a former governor of Pennsylvania and perennial, but never successful, candidate for the Republican Party's nomination to run for president. His ambitions for Penn matched those of Cavanaugh for Notre Dame. Stassen and his energetic athletic director, Francis (Fran) Murray, also opposed limitations on their television ambitions. Reacting to the moratorium passed at the 1951 NCAA convention, Murray proclaimed what now seems a truism, disregarded at the time but presciently keen: "This very dramatic part of our educational picture which is college football has now gotten to a point where it is more than just the sports department of the university. It now becomes part of the public relations division of the university."[19] Stassen and Murray promoted their own alternative to NCAA limitations; their plan would allow schools to make unfettered television contracts but voluntarily limit televised games to five per season. Like Cavanaugh's superconference, the Penn proposal elicited little support. Especially vehement in their opposition were presidents from schools coalescing into what in 1954 formally became the Ivy Group (League), who objected to the commercialization a TV contract represented; they threatened to refuse to play football against Penn if Stassen maintained his obstinacy. The NCAA also weighed in against Penn, deeming it a member "not in good standing" for its renegade action and threatened a boycott of all Penn football games. Stassen backed down and cancelled his contract with ABC. At this point, Notre Dame joined with Penn in seeking an opinion from the U.S. Justice Department on whether NCAA control of television contracts would constitute a restraint of trade under federal antitrust law. Though unsuccessful, this challenge to NCAA authority over televised games, ahead of its time in 1952, would climax thirty-two years later.[20]

By the time the 1951 football season began, turmoil reigned in matters of television policy, pushing college sports toward a new crossroad. The networks were eager to capture Saturday afternoon football audiences. Notre Dame and Penn were striving to put their own games on air as often as possible, while their immediate opposition—Big Ten in the case of Notre Dame, incipient Ivy League in the case of Penn—tried to rein them in. At the same time, the NCAA and its new executive director, Walter Byers, were attempting to establish and broaden the NCAA's power, especially after failure of the Sanity Code a few months earlier. The Westinghouse contract approved by the NCAA television committee early in 1951 had been deemed experimental, and as the association's January 1952 convention approached, anticipation for a more permanent policy intensified.

Ultimately, Byers and the NCAA television committee prevailed, at least for the time being, with momentous consequences. The 1952 convention approved a new plan that provided for eleven football games, one each week, to be broadcast nationally, with the stipulation that no team could be telecast more than once and, in an effort to fend off antitrust charges, allowed for games of regional interest to be broadcast so long as the NCAA could black out a national game when it appeared that a regional game's tickets were not going to be sold out. Byers then approached Tom Gallery, an NBC executive, about televising the NCAA game of the week concept. According to Byers, Gallery bubbled with excitement, "Oh, my gawd. It'll be wonderful!"[21] Gallery signed up sufficient advertisers and NBC paid $1.14 million for broadcast rights. Initially, the NCAA proposed that the fee be shared equally among all association members, but Notre Dame still chafed at the NCAA's imposition on its independence. Father Theodore Hesburgh, who had replaced John Cavanaugh as Notre Dame's president, and Hesburgh's tough-minded athletic director, Edward "Moose" Krause, voiced strong displeasure. Drawing from Cold War rhetoric prevalent in the 1950s, Hesburgh called the NCAA contract "socialistic," while Krause went a step further, labeling the contract "communistic." So the committee backtracked and decided that most of the money would be distributed to schools whose games were televised.[22]

Nevertheless, the NCAA had traversed a major turning point. With its control over the television contract, the NCAA transformed from an advisory body mainly concerned with creating rules and sponsoring tournaments into a powerful central authority that enforced rules and distributed TV revenues. Guided by the shrewd Walter Byers and backed by a new and potentially lucrative revenue source, the NCAA now was capable of using its power over television appearances as a stick to punish a transgressing member. Thus, in 1956, when the NCAA found Auburn University in violation of recruiting rules in its football program, the punishment, meekly accepted by Auburn and supported by the NCAA membership, included a two-year ban on television as well as a two-year ban on bowl appearances.[23]

Television and the Expanding Number of Free Tickets

The NCAA's 1952 contract with NBC made national telecasts of a college Game of the Week a regular Saturday afternoon home entertainment event, and it was not long before colleges discovered that the "unlimited supply of free tickets" to football games had wide-ranging repercussions. The exposure and prestige a school could secure from having its football team play on TV began to replace fear of lost revenue from empty stadium seats, and confidence grew among major conferences that gate attendance and television exposure could coexist. The conferences were right; beginning in 1954, attendance rose, doubling over the next seventeen years.[24] Fans increasingly eager to see their alma mater on a Game of the Week clamored for a policy that would allow more regional telecasts of games and were joined by a host of unaffiliated nonstudent football-enthusiasts. Even politicians got into the act. When the NCAA blacked out a Notre Dame–Michigan State game in the Midwest, Gerald Ford, Michigan's congressman and a future president, joined the public outcry and helped force the NCAA to partially reverse its decision and allow the game to be aired in Michigan and the District of Columbia.[25] And once again, Notre Dame and Penn joined forces to resist the NCAA. At the NCAA's convention in January 1953, Notre Dame's new vice president, Father Edmund P. Joyce, protested all regulation, asserting that television created good advertising for football, good advertising for a university, and an illegal restraint of trade if controlled by the NCAA. Penn's Fran Murray supported Joyce with the prophecy that "in all too few a number of years, those among you sitting here who are attempting to stay out of television, will be struggling to get into it because it will have established itself as the medium for providing even greater, widespread interest in football."[26]

A loud chorus of objectors prompted the NCAA to consider revising its television policy to include more regional games. The Big Ten and Pacific Coast (PCC) conferences, especially, pressured the NCAA television commit-tee to allow more regional telecasts. The NCAA voted down such expansion at its 1954 convention, largely because dissenting southern members still numbered among those who blamed television for shrinking game atten-dance. Thus the lineup of sides replicated the recent conflict over the Sanity Code, with southern schools resenting the wealth and power of midwestern and western schools and fearing that regional telecasts would only make the rich richer. In 1955, however, after threatening to secede from the NCAA, the Big Ten and PCC got their way when a new NCAA plan permitted regional telecasts on five of the thirteen weeks of games.[27] And Notre Dame, still maneuvering for broadcast independence, opened a new path in 1953 when Father Joyce convinced the NCAA television committee to permit member schools to negotiate individual contracts with theater television and pay TV companies. Consequently, Notre Dame signed with Box Office TV, Inc., for theater broadcast of all its home games.[28] Untapped at the time, cable televi-sion loomed on the horizon.

Over the next few years, the NCAA continued to debate television policy. Still nervous about the effects on attendance and the division of television revenue, most members would only accept a middle course of moderation and reasonableness. This meant limits on the total number of games that were telecast and on the number of appearances of any one institution's team. Byers and his television committee were able play networks off against each other in a bidding war for the annual football television contract, but this road proved bumpy. In 1954, ABC outbid NBC and paid $2 million for TV rights, 14 percent higher than what NBC had paid the previous year, but it was unprepared for the task and lost on its investment when advertising revenues failed to cover network expenses. NBC regained the contract the next year, paying only $1.25 million. Holding the rights for the next four years, NBC slowly increased its bids, reaching $2.2 million in 1959.[29] Though some NCAA members, especially Notre Dame, continued to grouse about the way the money was distributed, the cut that the NCAA took from annual contracts helped put it on sound financial footing. Once dependent on membership fees, the NCAA could now use football television rights income to expand its staff and facilities, fund postgraduate scholarships, and subsidize championships in nonrevenue sports that helped all institutions develop their athletic programs.[30] Television money and college sports were now inextricably linked.

During the 1960s, both turnstile revenues and football TV contracts increased. Game attendance grew by 50 percent, and the bidding contest among networks intensified. Between 1960 and 1966, the television rights ping-ponged between ABC, CBS, and NBC. But in 1966, ABC, now guided by sports broadcasting pioneer Roone Arledge, recaptured the contract, paying $15.5 million for 1966 and 1967, $20.4 million for 1968 and 1969, and $24 million for 1970 and 1971. By this time, a team appearing on a Game of the Week could earn hundreds of thousands of dollars. As Byers later reflected, "I felt we [the NCAA] were on an express elevator ride up with no top floor."[31] Meanwhile, fans at home benefited from enhanced technological features. NBC and CBS both telecast some games in color, and in 1963 CBS innovated what possibly was the most consequential boon to television sports audiences when it premiered instant replay at the Army–Navy game, a technology that, according to Dunnavant, "gave the viewer an edge over the fan in the stands: a second look."[32] College football, like the professional counterpart, the NFL, was creating an unprecedented fan base.

In 1966, NCAA television policy collided with fan demand. In November of that year, fourteen months before the UCLA–Houston television watershed, Notre Dame and Michigan State, the nation's top two football teams, were scheduled to play each other on November 19. With the national championship potentially at stake, the matchup stirred nationwide anticipation and seemed capable of attracting a record television audience. There was a hitch, however. According to NCAA rules, each collegiate team was restricted to one national and two regional TV appearances per year; Notre Dame already had played on one nationally televised game and Michigan State had appeared on a regionally broadcast game. When the NCAA initially sanctioned only a regional, not a national, telecast of the Notre Dame–Michigan State game on ABC, fans revolted, flooding the network with angry letters, telegrams, and phone calls; one enthusiast even sued the NCAA. The television committee then compromised, allowing the game to be broadcast live in the Northeast and Midwest, with a taped rebroadcast to the rest of the country after the regularly scheduled Kentucky–Tennessee national game.[33] The incident revealed how commercialized televised football had become, and the fallout made the NCAA yield greater control to ABC over which teams' games would be telecast, the date and time when televised games would be scheduled, and how many ads would be included during games.[34] Television was flexing its muscle.

At the same time debates over football telecasts rumbled, the NCAA paid little attention to what was to become its most lucrative revenue source: televising its national basketball championship. The association began sponsoring a men's basketball championship in 1939 but derived nothing from radio broadcasts and only minor income from tournament attendance revenues: $52,000 in 1951 and just under $178,000 a decade later. The NCAA kept half the proceeds and divided the rest equally among the sixteen participating teams.[35] The tiny Sports Network Incorporated, which broadcast baseball games, golf tournaments, and other sports events that major networks did not want to cover,[36] paid the NCAA a nominal fee to broadcast the Final Four semifinal and final games to its 120 stations between 1963 and 1968, but few television executives yet saw college basketball as an alluring popular entertainment.[37] One of the most exciting games in tournament history, the University of North Carolina's triple-overtime victory over Wilt Chamberlain and the University of Kansas in 1957, wasn't even on national TV .

Then, in 1968, came the epic UCLA–Houston clash. The game, as mentioned, demonstrated that big-time college basketball, featuring big-time stars, could become a major television event, drawing a larger viewing audience than any football game. But even though Byers and a few athletic officials foresaw the benefits, they dithered over how to package games. Colleges played many more basketball than football games, making it difficult for the NCAA or a network to determine how many games to televise nationally and what days to broadcast them. Moreover, by the 1960s, conferences and individual schools already were involved in telecasting basketball games locally, and incomes from these broadcasts were rising. To protect their own basketball broadcasts, many schools and conferences rebuffed an NCAA-sponsored national basketball television contract. Consequently, the NCAA focused on contracting telecasts only of its national basketball championship, chiefly the Final Four games, rather than on regular season contests. NBC secured these broadcast rights in 1969, gradually upping its payments to the

NCAA from $550,000 in 1970 to $4.0 million in 1977.[38] The real boom in televised basketball—and real boon to the NCAA—lurked just around the corner. Meanwhile, cable television was beginning to surface as a weighty influence on college sports.

Cable television, initially called Community Antenna Television, or CATV, arose in the late 1940s. Unlike commercial television, cable television at first was not regulated by the Federal Communications Commission (FCC), and when the FCC imposed a moratorium on new licenses for commercial stations between 1948 and 1952, demand for cable TV increased. Once CATV began transmitting signals in the 1960s and 1970s, a larger variety of programs were broadcast over a proliferating number of cable stations to a greater number of customers. According to one source, by the mid-1960s there were 1,325 cable systems serving 1.25 million customers, and in 1969 only about 6 percent of the 60 million American homes with television sets subscribed to cable service.[39] By this time, however, the FCC had begun to restrict cable operations, mostly in large metropolitan areas, in response to complaints from over-the-air stations.[40]

Early on, the college sports establishment realized there was potential in cable and related pay-for-view television. Wary about possible Justice Department objections over restraint-of-trade issues in its television policy, the NCAA in the late 1960s began to permit telecasts of "exceptions" to its TV restrictions—mainly allowing a station to broadcast a sold-out football game to the home institution's region and to the market of the visiting team as long as that market was more than 400 miles away. But when cable stations expanded the number of exception games, they threatened the exclusive contracts the NCAA negotiated with major networks. The situation was further complicated in the 1970s when the Home Box Office (HBO) cable network offered to broadcast twelve weeks of college football games not covered by the NCAA contract with ABC. Though Walter Byers found the offer appealing, the NCAA television committee agreed to permit HBO to telecast only three games in the 1978 season.[41]

As cable television stations began to utilize new microwave and satellite technology to deliver movies and sports to subscribers, their popularity and profitability grew. So too did their resolve to restore their former freedom from FCC restraints. HBO, which by the mid-1970s had developed an extensive national presence, sued the FCC, claiming undue limits on its programming options. In 1975, the District of Columbia Court of Appeals sided with HBO, saying that FCC regulations were unjustifiable. More important, the court determined that cable television service was less of a broadcasting enterprise and more like newspapers and therefore entitled to broader free speech prerogatives than commercial television. As a result, cable networks had liberty to air any programming they desired (including films and programs that contained nudity and profanity prohibited on commercial broadcasts).[42] The industry now mushroomed. From 3,500 systems serving 10 million subscribers in 1975, it grew to 6,600 systems and 40 million subscribers by 1985. With their court-authorized autonomy, cable companies now broadcast sports events, including college games, that NCAA television policy barred local stations from carrying, and a cable station could telecast games beyond regional limits.[43] The way was paved for the Entertainment and Sports Programming Network, better known as ESPN, in 1979 to begin broadcasting a variety of sports contests, including college football games and early rounds of the NCAA men's basketball tournament.[44]

In his memoir, Walter Byers noted that by the 1980s, the commercial television networks that previously had dominated sports broadcasting were under attack from the cable industry. One result was that more and more money was becoming available to schools whose football and basketball games might be broadcast, both within and outside the NCAA television contracts. The other result was that TV money had opened the floodgates of avarice. As Byers wrote, "Greed was gnawing at the innards of college athletics. Rich schools within conferences increasingly rebelled at sharing their television and other revenues with less affluent conference relatives. Blood is thicker than water, but there has been many a bloodletting among kinfolk when a substantial inheritance is divvied up."[45] Television lucre now separated haves from have-nots, with the latter becoming increasingly uncomfortable about the benefits accruing to the former.

The Debate over Who Gets What

John Stephen Horn had strong impulses that he could not always hold in check. A political scientist by trade, he represented California's Thirty-eighth Congressional District between 1993 and 2003 as a moderate Republican, championing both a balanced budget and funding for the arts, humanities, and science. But before he entered politics, Horn lofted a bomb at the NCAA. Between 1970 and 1988, Horn served as president of California State University–Long Beach (Long Beach State), a fast-growing new public institution that needed money to foster its academic and athletics aspirations.[46] Shortly after Horn became president of Long Beach State, the NCAA, under pressure from big-time football schools, split its membership into three divisions, relegating schools sponsoring fewer than twelve sports programs to Divisions II and III and allotting most of the power within the association to bigger schools in Division I. (Division II schools offer athletic scholarships; Division III schools do not.) Long Beach State joined Division I, but it, along with a number of other lower-level programs in the division, were deprived of television money because their football teams rarely if ever appeared on a Game of the Week, and only those schools whose games were televised shared income from the NCAA television contract. President Horn bristled at this policy. He believed that institutions such as Long Beach State should receive a portion of TV revenue. After all, they were paying members of the NCAA, and their participation in association business was just as important as that of any other school. So in 1974, Horn sent a letter to college and university presidents advocating more equitable revenue sharing and urging them to become "more familiar with what is going on in their own intercollegiate athletic programs."[47]

The high-profile football schools countered angrily that Horn's recommendation was unacceptably radical—some called him a Robin Hood—adding that the NCAA television policy was actually unfair to them. They wanted more: more television exposure for themselves and more money from the TV contract that by 1974 was bringing in $16 million from ABC. And there was another finger in the pie: the NCAA wanted and needed more revenue, not just to fund its headquarters, staff, championships, and other operations, but also for its expanding litigation and lobbying activities, including its battle against the Title IX gender equity provision. (See Chapter 5.) Consequently, within the NCAA, discussion of television football money became increasingly heated.[48]

The debates might have been less rancorous if not for another factor: College sports had become a very costly operation. National inflation, caused by the government's leftover dual commitment to the Vietnam War and domestic spending in the 1960s, soaring energy costs exacerbated by the Arab oil embargo of 1973–74, and a declining stock market, threw the nation into economic crisis. In higher education, institutional budgets were creaking under the weight of costly obligations for student aid, salaries, facilities, and more. Varsity sports felt the crunch. To economize, some schools eliminated teams and cut back on scholarships, especially for so-called minor sports. Football posed the thorniest dilemma. For many schools, especially those in Division I, football generated substantial revenues, but it also required huge outlays for recruiting, travel, staff, equipment, and scholarships. Since the 1950s, the NCAA had never limited the number of athletic scholarships a school could award, and those in major conferences each handed out between twenty-five and thirty-five scholarships annually just to freshman football players and often upwards of one hundred to the whole team. Reacting to the hard times, Byers urged the NCAA to set limits on scholarships and salaries, but coaches objected angrily, even threatening to secede if forced to make reductions.[49] Nevertheless, cost cutting became a major theme in college sports in the 1970s, Division I included. But this wing of the NCAA was divided internally. Of its 237 members, about 120 sponsored a football team, and of those, about 80 played big-time football. Slightly over 50 members of this last group—such as Notre Dame, Oklahoma, and Michigan—profited from televised games, while the others, including Long Beach State, were shut out from the benefits. Thus Horn's letter stirred a hornet's nest. Not only did he propose a dramatic redistribution of TV money—5 percent to the NCAA, 40 percent divided among Division II and III schools, 40 percent divided among all Division I members, and only 15 percent to those appearing on television—he also recommended that to save money, each football team be restricted to a total of fifty-five scholarships. Horn also would split bowl game revenues among all NCAA members, not just the participants.[50]

Though Horn denied financial problems, Long Beach State was, according to one report, "awash in red ink," and he likely was seeking to repair his athletic program, which had suffered after recent NCAA penalties for rule violations by its basketball and football teams.[51] Nevertheless, Horn's ideas offered a means to rein in the stampede by high-profile football schools toward super-commercialized sports that in the minds of some was trampling the image of higher education and turning stately universities into money-grubbing combatants. Revealing that the horses had already left the barn, however, Don Canham, athletic director at the University of Michigan, reacted to Horn's scheme by snarling, "Hell, that's socialism, and we're not in a socialist state. Why should Michigan play for $40,000 rather than $450,000?"[52] Others in Canham's camp suggested that Horn ought to butt out of Division I football affairs and remove Long Beach State to Division II where it could better afford to compete.[53] Byers tried to persuade Horn to move slowly, but the Long Beach State president plunged ahead and submitted his proposal to a vote at the January 1976 NCAA convention. The association, influenced by the football elite, defeated it easily in a voice vote.[54]

Though the NCAA dismissed Horn's "socialistic" plan, the combination of thirst for revenue with the threat of radical change in the distribution of television football money sounded an alarm to Division I athletic powers. Late in 1975, even before Horn's measures flopped at the 1976 NCAA convention, representatives of seven major athletic conferences—Atlantic Coast, Big 8, Big 10, Pacific 8, Southeastern, Southwestern, and Western—formed a steering committee to discuss how they and their members might protect their present and future interests. One possibility involved reducing or splitting Division I so that big-time football schools could occupy a class by themselves—a Division I-A—and prevent smaller schools, who might support another Horn-type reform, from interfering with the affairs of larger schools.

When the NCAA convention in January 1976, where all members large and small had one vote, nixed a plan to separate Division I into I and I-A, the mood of rebellion among big-time sports schools intensified. In April 1976, representatives from five of the seven conferences involved in the earlier steering committee (the Big Ten and Pacific 8 refused to join), plus independents Notre Dame and Penn State, met and drafted a manifesto asserting that the NCAA had become too large to accommodate the needs of major football-playing schools. The solution, the group repeated, was formation of a new division of elite institutions. Lurking behind these discussions were television revenue and the limits that NCAA TV contracts had imposed, but at the time this issue remained obscured by the rhetoric of organizational change.[55] Though the rebels did not yet seek independence from the NCAA, their commitment to more autonomy had hardened. After further meetings, the group drafted Articles of Association and at a meeting in Dallas on December 20, 1976, the College Football Association (CFA) was born, a step that fomented momentous developments in both the structure of the NCAA (realized more fully in 2014) and, more important, inaugurated a new era in the commercialization of college sports.[56] That era, previewed by the UCLA–Houston game of 1968 and challenged by the Horn proposals of 1974, was opened to full view by a landmark Supreme Court decision in 1984, to be discussed in the next chapter.

What Television Hath Wrought

John Wooden, UCLA men's basketball coach, once remarked, "I think television is one of the worst things that ever happened to intercollegiate [sports]. . . . It's made showmen out of the players and that hurts team play. . . . There's always the other side, though, and that's that it provides income that has been the savior of many women's sports and the non-income-producing sports."[57] This two-sided coin was minted in the 1950s, 1960s, and 1970s. In this era, Walter Byers and the NCAA television committee pursued deals worth millions of dollars with commercial, for-profit networks instead of broadcasting football and, eventually, basketball games on nonprofit, public radio and television where the link between athletics and higher education might have been maintained and the commercialism of intercollegiate athletics restrained.[58] But this alternative never was considered. The college sports establishment opted for an economic playbook that promised direct benefit to athletics and to the institutions in which that establishment operated. Televised football increased the visibility of a few privileged schools, but the bulk of money an institution derived from TV appearances went to support athletics, as John Wooden observed. The schools themselves were not victims of the television policy; they willingly complied with it so they could use television revenues and the booster contributions inspired by TV exposure to pay for sports rather than to fund them from the educational budget. Thus the commercial route was the one taken.[59]

The NCAA may have exerted control over who played football on television, but the networks found ways to use dollar appeal and flex their muscle to stretch television policy in their favor. In 1964, for example, NBC took over the contract for broadcasting the Orange Bowl and moved the game time from New Year's Day to New Year's night in order to attract a larger viewing audience. The NCAA, which lacked control of bowl games, offered no resistance. More significantly, when ABC regained rights to telecast the football Game of the Week in 1967, the network influenced competition more powerfully. Roone Arledge chafed at the NCAA's control over the advance schedule of who would play live on television, because a game scheduled in May might have little viewer appeal in November. First, Arledge convinced the NCAA to allow some flexibility so that a key game could be rescheduled for broadcast even after the season was in full swing. Then, in summer 1969, Arledge had a premonition that Southwest Conference rivals Texas and Arkansas might contend for the national title, and he persuaded them to schedule their game against each other at the end of the season rather than the middle so ABC could capitalize on the potential drama. The gamble paid off when more than 30 million people watched in late November as Texas pulled out a dramatic victory. Subsequently, Arledge strong-armed the NCAA into accepting network demands for more commercials during televised games, including beer ads.[60] Thus, early in the history of televised college sports, media moguls infringed on the prerogatives of the NCAA and its members to exercise control over scheduling and broadcast decisions.

The newfound riches that accrued to big-time college football and, later, basketball teams not only enabled them to expand facilities and coaching staffs but also had a notable effect on recruiting. The publicity a team acquired from playing on TV put stars in the eyes of standout high school athletes eager for a chance to perform before a national audience. Moreover, television publicity, combined with the new ease of air travel—jet passenger service expanded rapidly from 1958 on—transformed recruiting from a local and regional process into a national one as the elite powers, flush with dollars, could afford to send coaches to distant venues to assess and attract potential athletes and to fund campus visits for those recruits. According to Byers, the jet airplane and coast-to-coast television "shrank the recruiting map" and "turned an extracurricular activity into big business."[61] The result was that the athletes, increasingly drawn from a national pool, became a more distinct class, disconnected from those who watched them, a detachment exacerbated by the remoteness between viewer and viewed created by television.

College sports might have adopted a different playbook had Stephen Horn's share-the-wealth scheme—or some variant—created some form of television revenue distribution beneficial to every institution that sponsored intercollegiate athletics. By the early 1960s, one alternative model already existed for distributing proceeds from televised football. In 1961, Pete Rozelle, farsighted commissioner of the National Football League, then a struggling association of professional teams, persuaded team owners to share equally in a $4.65 million contract with CBS to televise league games. He also convinced the U.S. Congress to grant the league legislative exemption to protect the revenue-sharing plan from judicial challenge on grounds of antitrust violation. Each of the league's fourteen members received $332,000 from the TV contract, a sizable amount worth $2.5 million today and an amount that exceeded each team's payroll expenses, so that when combined with gate receipts the total virtually guaranteed each team a profit.[62]

To be sure, the NCAA at the time of Horn's insurgency consisted of far more than fourteen members. And any form of television revenue-sharing in college sports would probably necessitate a congressional immunity from antitrust prosecution similar to what the NFL received. But unlike Rozelle, Horn did not propose that each NCAA member share equally in television income, only that distribution include at least some cut for all schools that sponsored sports, not just a favored few. He wanted schools appearing on television to receive only a 15 percent portion of the TV contract rather than the 80-to-90 percent they actually split up. Under Horn's plan, a team appearing once on a nationally televised game would receive roughly $60,000 from the $16 million ABC contract of 1974, worth about $285,000 today and probably enough to fund the majority of a football team's annual scholarships at the time.

Would a wider dispersal of television revenues have checked the acquisitiveness of teams aspiring for greater and greater success on the national stage, symbolized by Don Canham's blunt assertion that he wanted $450,000 for University of Michigan athletics while dismissing shares for others? It would be naïve to conclude so. Still, a scheme of more liberal distribution, negotiated and imposed at a time when the really big bucks remained on the distant horizon (see Chapter 7), may have tempered ambitions and enabled college and university CEOs to bind their athletic programs more tightly to their academic missions. Moreover, a more egalitarian distribution of television money might have had a mitigating effect on the less salutary features of college sports. Income from television, plus booster and alumni donations, provided funding for ever higher coaches' salaries, making coaches assume that their jobs depended on the highest forms of success—conference championships, bowl games, national ranking, and so on. How could they compete with others seeking the same goals? Temptation for indulging in illicit tactics had always lurked inside big-time college sports. But by the 1970s, the sordidness seemed both more prevalent and more exposed. With the scale of finances reduced, this consequence might also have been checked.

Again, a caution against naïveté and the simple solution is in order. There never were innocent times in intercollegiate athletics. Even before televised sportscasts were envisioned, perceptive observers foresaw the direction in which things were headed. In 1929, Harvard historian Albert Bushnell Hart noted, "The Greeks made [sports] a cult; the English a spectacle; the Americans made it a business."[63] Supporters of college sports aver that the money from that business has made it possible for thousands of young people—men first and women later—to attend college who might never have had the opportunity. The normalization of the athletic scholarship discussed in Chapter 1 propelled the racial integration of higher education discussed in Chapter 2 and opened doors to young men and women from low-income groups of all races and ethnicities. But the business that Americans created out of intercollegiate athletics expanded dramatically because of the pot of gold that some colleges found and that others sought behind the flickering screen that transmitted images to eager viewers. As that pot grew bigger, the quest for its contents became ever more fervent.

4 "Earthquake": *Board of Regents v. NCAA*

A sportswriter nicknamed him "Whizzer," a moniker that, to his displeasure, stuck with him all his life. His given name was Byron White, and long before his twenty-nine-year service as associate justice of the Supreme Court of the United States, he was one of the country's biggest college football stars. An all-American halfback at the University of Colorado in 1937, White held the record for highest per-game average of all-purpose yards—runs from scrimmage, from pass receptions, from kickoff and punt returns, and from interceptions[1]—until 1988. After spending a year in England as a Rhodes scholar, White became professional football's first big-salary player, with the Pittsburgh Pirates (later renamed the Steelers), then with the Detroit Lions, while also earning a law degree from Yale.[2] After a stint in the U.S. Navy during World War II cut short his professional career, White clerked for U.S. Supreme Court justice Fred Vinson, then entered private law practice in Denver. In 1960, White chaired John F. Kennedy's presidential campaign in Colorado and was rewarded with an appointment as U.S. deputy attorney general. Shortly thereafter, Kennedy nominated him to the Supreme Court, where he served until 1993.

At the University of Colorado, White exhibited a firm commitment to academic as well as athletic accomplishment. Thus, his attitude about college sports derived from balanced and idealized experiences, free from the celebrity status that football stars of later generations would carry. By the 1980s, White's qualities made him a throwback, who prized college life and college sports the way he had known them, not the way they had become. So when a landmark case involving the new culture of college sports came before the Supreme Court in 1984, White found himself defending his views from a minority position. The case involved the three-decades-old question of how much control the NCAA should wield over television broadcasts of college football games. It pitted bygone ideals against the growing commercialism of big-time intercollegiate sports. White defended tradition, lamenting in his dissenting opinion to the case that a desire to win at all costs had created "a wide range of competitive excesses that prove harmful to students and institutions alike." He lionized the NCAA's defense of amateurism by asserting, "By mitigating what appears to be a clear failure of the free market to serve the ends and goals of higher education, the NCAA ensures the continued availability of a unique and valuable product, the very existence of which might well be threatened by unbridled competition in the economic sphere."[3] But the times had passed the former halfback by; the new playbook for college sports was undercutting the NCAA's old way of doing things.

A formidable alliance of big-time sports universities won the case against the NCAA. Byron White occupied a minority of only two dissenting justices, and the failure of his viewpoint revealed a reality that even the NCAA had to accept. Indeed, the NCAA soon tried to capitalize on it. No event has had greater influence on the direction of college sports as an entertainment industry than this 1984 U.S. Supreme Court decision in *National Collegiate Athletic Association v. Board of Regents of the University of Oklahoma*. Not only did the decision free big-time college sports schools—and lesser ones too—to pursue and accumulate media dollars on their own terms, it also propelled a wider separation of athletics from academics that revenues from televised major sports, chiefly football and men's basketball, enabled. The road leading to the decision, however, was more than rocky; it was strewn with boulders. And the road leading out from the decision held hazards that neither the winners nor losers of the case had fully anticipated.

Flexing Muscle: Rise of the CFA

Try as it might, the NCAA could not appease its most powerful members. By the mid-1970s, it had separated into divisions, subdivided its Division I, crafted a television policy that slowly eased restrictions on whose games could be broadcast, and negotiated contracts that brought more money to schools whose football teams appeared on TV. Nevertheless, the football powers harbored a number of grievances against both NCAA management and smaller members of Division I, some of which did not sponsor football programs and which the major schools thought interfered with their ambitions. Mostly, the major schools sought reforms in two basic areas: (1) a greater voice in association policymaking, including more appointments on important committees and more participation by coaches in the legislative process; and (2) a release from NCAA's restrictive television policy so they might independently reap the benefits of broadcast fees.[4]

During 1976, representatives from the seven major conferences—Big Eight, Southeastern, Southwestern, Atlantic Coast, Western, Big Ten, and Pac 8—plus independents (no conference affiliation) such as Notre Dame, Penn State, and Pittsburgh—met to discuss strategy. Secession from the NCAA was not an objective, at least not initially; rather, the schools favored a fourth division within the NCAA that better reflected their needs. As Father Edmund Joyce, Notre Dame's chief financial officer and one of the group's leaders, described their efforts, "It was not some conspiracy to take over college athletics. . . . We just needed to be able to talk among ourselves to see what we could accomplish."[5] Notre Dame would go its own way a decade later, but for now Joyce sought solidarity with those who agreed with him.[6] By December, the rebels were ready to act, and they drafted Articles of Association that formed the College Football Association (CFA).[7]

The CFA, which its members insisted was a lobbying group not an insurgent body, confronted two problems from the start. For one, the two most powerful and prestigious conferences—Big Ten and Pac 8 (shortly to become Pac 10)—refused to affiliate with the CFA. University presidents in these conferences argued that the CFA too starkly symbolized big-time athletics over big-time academics. Behind the scenes, however, these CEOs knew they traditionally had exercised strong influence over NCAA policymaking, and they did not want to diminish that influence by appearing to be bolting the association. Their effort to distance themselves from the CFA provoked resentment from other major football schools that accused the holdouts of elitism and arrogance. Penn State's head football coach Joe Paterno voiced the antipathy, grumbling, "From the beginning, they (Big Ten and Pac 8) pointed to us like we were a bunch of troublemakers, and I resented that."[8]

The second dilemma for the CFA was Walter Byers, the NCAA's executive director. Byers had managed to solidify the NCAA's authority by obtaining members' acceptance of vigorous rule enforcement and by expanding staff and resources through the share the NCAA skimmed for itself from football television fees, which in 1977 totaled $29 million per year. Also, in 1978, Byers maneuvered the less prominent members of Division I into accepting assignment to a separate subdivision, I-AA, in return for a nationally televised football championship for their subdivision. The split left 105 major football schools in Division 1-A and 139 smaller ones in Division 1-AA, only about 40 of which sponsored a football team.[9]

The realignment had been neither easy nor agreeable. Even before the creation of Division I-A, the CFA schools found themselves fighting off challenges from NCAA members outside their orbit. Suffering like the rest of the country from the economic downturn of the mid-1970s, financially strapped schools proposed at the NCAA annual conventions in both 1976 and 1977 to replace the full-ride athletic grant-in-aid with grants based on financial need, an echo of the Sanity Code that had been jettisoned in 1951. As before, the major schools managed to defeat the measure. Then, in 1978, an attempt by the majors to whittle down Division I-A to include only schools with strong football schedules, large stadiums, and heavy attendance was beaten back by an amendment from the Ivy League that allowed schools that sponsored at least twelve sports to qualify for Division I-A.[10] These and other efforts to curtail big-time sports stirred those potentially most affected to voice the threat that many had been harboring all along: the threat of secession. Thus, Indiana University's athletic director Paul Dietzel warned that future attempts to restrict athletics could force the "75 or so major powers" into their own organization.[11]

By 1980, in spite of their threats, money kept rolling into the major schools. Basketball now joined football as a vein to be mined. Lacking NCAA controls, the televising of college basketball generated significant revenues without the drama that characterized football television policy. Cable companies especially filled winter nights with countless games. The landmark telecast of the regular season UCLA–Houston game in 1968 had shown that college basketball could draw millions of viewers, and the NCAA's three-week Division I championship tournament, soon to be called "March Madness," became a national TV event. The highly anticipated 1979 March Madness final game, which pitted the era's two biggest stars against each other—Earvin "Magic" Johnson of Michigan State and Larry Bird of Indiana State—in what proved to be an anticlimactic Michigan State victory, nevertheless fueled fan fascination with the tournament. Because the NCAA sponsored the tournament, it controlled television rights and Byers encouraged competing networks to escalate offers to air March Madness games. Early in 1981, CBS submitted a winning bid of $16 million a year to telecast the tournament for the years 1982–84, a fee 60 percent higher than what NBC had paid to air the 1981 tourney.

The NCAA used some money from the basketball contract to fund administrative costs, but distributed most of the revenue to participating schools in proportion to how many rounds they survived in the competition. In 1982, as a result of the CBS deal, a team losing in the tournament's first round made $150,000, and a team reaching the semifinal and final rounds received more than $600,000, a payout larger than a football team would receive from playing on television in any but the top four bowl games. These sums would increase at an accelerating rate over the next three decades, with the NCAA negotiating a multinetwork deal for $10.8 billion in 2010.[12] Though network fees for televising March Madness enriched the big-time schools, football and television remained at the center of the power struggle between those schools and the NCAA, and the disgruntled members began looking outside the NCAA for recourse.

The Antitrust Issue

In his 1995 memoir, Walter Byers wrote he was convinced that by 1981 "the CFA wanted to destroy the NCAA."[13] But if he looked back a few years, he might just as easily have accused the U.S. Congress of the same intention. Concerned that the NCAA was enforcing its rules selectively, the House Subcommittee on Oversight and Investigations began a probe in October 1977. Early in 1978, the subcommittee heard from J. Brent Clark, a former member of the NCAA enforcement staff, who accused the NCAA of ignoring rule violations at major institutions and running roughshod over due process when investigating schools it wanted to punish. Clark also claimed that Byers meddled in enforcement procedures and that athletes were intimidated and bribed to give the NCAA information it wanted.[14] At the same hearing, witnesses from Michigan State and Mississippi State alleged that the NCAA had punished their football programs excessively.[15] In consequence, the NCAA reformed its most objectionable procedures, but the door was now open to further congressional investigation, and the politicians were about to find a powerful instrument to bring with them: the Sherman Anti-Trust Act.

In 1976, the NCAA had accused the basketball program at the University of Nevada at Las Vegas (UNLV) and its popular coach, Jerry Tarkanian, of numerous rule violations, including gifts to players, improper cash allowances, and free airline tickets to players and their families. It penalized UNLV with a two-year ban on television appearances and ordered the school to suspend Tarkanian for two years. UNLV accepted the measures, but Tarkanian sued the NCAA, claiming he was denied due process and won an injunction that lifted his suspension. Unhappy with the NCAA's procedures and penalties, Nevada's congressional representative James Santini pressed the House Subcommittee on Oversight and Investigations, of which he was a member, to determine whether the NCAA was in violation of federal antitrust laws. Vowing to expose the association's "arrogance and intransigence," Santini accused the NCAA of being "indisputedly a monopoly."[16]

Meanwhile, other universities besides UNLV were emboldened to use antitrust arguments in lawsuits against the NCAA.[17] The University of Oklahoma was particularly aggrieved. When the NCAA issued a two-year television ban against the university's football team as a penalty for rigging a recruit's academic transcript, Oklahoma sued in federal district court in 1974, arguing that NCAA's power over television was an illegal restraint of trade that violated the Sherman Anti-Trust Act. The court decided against the university, determining that because as a nonprofit entity the NCAA had no commercial objectives in its TV contracts, it was not liable to court action.[18] In another case, a federal district court ruled that the NCAA could legally define the number of football and basketball coaches a school could employ and was not subject to antitrust law because it was a "nonprofit, voluntary organization whose activities and objectives are educational."[19] Nevertheless, major athletic schools, especially Oklahoma, resolved to press their contention that the NCAA's interference in their aspirations violated antitrust and property rights law.

Heading for a Showdown

In spring 1980, Charles "Chuck" Neinas began a fateful term as first commissioner of the upstart College Football Association. Tall and broad-faced with a half-ring of silver hair surrounding his crown, Neinas had assembled a long résumé in college sports. A graduate of the University of Wisconsin, he first worked in radio and television, and then became assistant executive director of the NCAA in 1961. After ten years under Byers, he applied to become commissioner of the Big Ten Conference and lost out, but he accepted an appointment as commissioner of the Big Eight Conference. Byers later claimed that Neinas resented the Big Ten for the rebuff,[20] but Neinas found another outlet for his ambitions with the CFA, where he soon put his television experience to use.[21] Concerned about falling TV ratings for college football games, in contrast with rising ratings for NFL games, Neinas and other CFA leaders wrote a report criticizing the NCAA for limiting television coverage and for negotiating a contract with only one network. Moreover, CFA schools chafed because their share of TV appearances under NCAA television contracts had shrunk from 66 percent in 1976 to 55 percent in 1979, which they contended was a cause of the ratings decline. At first, Neinas proposed working within the NCAA to liberalize the television policy, but the CFA's most powerful members were growing increasingly impatient.[22]

Two forces within the CFA reflected the restlessness. One was Notre Dame, which had already defied the NCAA's original television policy in 1951 before eventually backing down. As the school's advocate for athletics, Joyce continually sought ways to benefit from telecasts of Notre Dame football and seethed over an NCAA penalty against Michigan State that prevented the lucrative Notre Dame–Michigan State game from being televised in 1979. Second, several southern coaches and university presidents had grown bitter because the NCAA structure, in which each member institution had one vote on association matters, enabling smaller schools and the Big Ten and Pac 10 to outvote them. The southerners' spokesman was Fred Davison, president of the University of Georgia and also president of the CFA. Like Joyce, Davison considered televised football games an institution's own property right, which should be free from NCAA regulation. A former veterinarian who held multiple doctorate degrees, Davison took particular pride in his university's football team. He once stated, "Athletics and primarily football at the University [of Georgia] is the one focal point that gives cohesion to all our members, both students and alumni; it brings them back."[23] In contrast, the NCAA's position, as voiced by its president, James Frank, head of Lincoln University in Pennsylvania, was that the "law of voluntary associations" and majority rule meant that NCAA members had no right to pursue independent actions in their own interests. Countering Frank's assertion, Davison expressed the CFA position: "The football television issue is an example of folks not on our level determining what we can do."[24]

By 1981, the CFA, still hoping to reform NCAA football television policy without taking independent action, nevertheless initiated talks with the three major TV networks plus cable's ESPN to design a contract that would benefit CFA members more profitably than the NCAA's deal with ABC, which was due to expire in 1982. In response, Byers took a multiple-network path that Neinas and others had desired. He negotiated four-year contracts with both ABC and CBS plus a two-year contract with the Turner cable network for a total of $281 million and raised the limit on the number of annual broadcast appearances by any one team from two to three.[25] The contract had the support of the Big Ten and Pac Ten, which steadfastly refused to join the CFA. In a mail ballot sent out in April 1981, NCAA members overwhelmingly endorsed the two-network contract, 220–6.[26]

The contract did not satisfy the CFA, which contended that many of its 62 member schools had abstained from the vote, believing that the outcome would be stacked by votes from smaller schools. The CFA issued a resolution in June that "until further notice, the C.F.A. members reserve the right to determine the best use of their property rights to broadcast, telecast and cablecast their institutional football contests."[27] Then, in August, the CFA moved closer to direct confrontation with the NCAA when Neinas signed a separate four-year,

$180 million football deal with NBC that would guarantee each CFA member at least $1 million per year and up to seven television appearances every two years. When CFA members voted in favor of the contract on August 21—the tally was 33–28 with one abstention—they put the NCAA's two-network contract in jeopardy because that contract stipulated that if the NCAA could not provide football games involving all its major schools, the terms would have to be renegotiated. The CFA negotiation outraged Byers, and the NCAA issued a statement threatening to expel any member that agreed to a TV deal different from that negotiated by the NCAA.[28] A revolt seemed close at hand.

Byers, however, scrambled to make peace. He hinted to the *New York Times* that a policy granting Division I-A schools more authority over television policy "could evolve." Also, the NCAA Council called a special convention for December 1981 to consider constitutional changes that would reduce the size of Division I-A from 139 schools to 95 and allow major schools more autonomy in matters of their own interest. To the CFA, the effort was too little, too late. Neinas already had begun to consider organizing separate championships in a few sports in the event the CFA was banished from the NCAA. And shortly after the NCAA Council approved plans for the special convention, three of the most outspoken CFA members—the universities of Georgia, Oklahoma, and Texas—filed class-action lawsuits seeking judgments on their ability to control television property rights to their football games. The Georgia and Oklahoma suit was filed in federal district court in Oklahoma City; the Texas complaint went before the Texas State Court in Austin. Both complaints requested a restraining order to prevent the NCAA from expelling or penalizing CFA members for honoring their prospective contract with NBC. President Davison of Georgia, speaking on behalf of the plaintiffs, announced, "In view of the N.C.A.A. position [threat of expulsion] and the resulting confusion, it was determined that the question of ownership of a university's athletic program could best be decided in a court of law."[29]

The situation remained tense but not explosive—not yet. Even though the NCAA announced that the special convention in December would discuss only reorganization of Division I-A and omit dealing with television property rights, the CFA nevertheless opted for conciliation, at least initially. Trying to avoid a direct confrontation with the NCAA, the CFA delayed its contract with NBC, and the three litigants delayed their court cases. As the special convention opened December 3, Neinas expressed "optimism that there will be a satisfactory move to head in the right direction in the area of TV property rights and contracts."[30] The convention recommended a reduction of Division I-A from 137 schools to 92, assigning the Ivy League and other small Division I schools to Division I-AA, and gave CFA members a majority of votes within the division. The television property rights issue was left to be taken up by the regular NCAA convention in January 1982.

After the special convention ended, CFA schools faced a quandary: proceed with the NBC contract or abandon it and go along with the multinetwork NCAA television deal. A majority of CFA members, including most from the Southeastern and Atlantic Coast conferences seemed resigned to accept the NCAA contract, while some dissidents—namely Clemson, Notre Dame, Georgia, Oklahoma, and Texas—still favored the CFA contract. Clemson president William Atchley was heard to boast, "The NCAA can't afford to kick us out!"[31] Within a few days, however, too few CFA schools had expressed outright willingness to sign the NBC contract and the deal fell through.[32] As planned, the NCAA convention in January 1982 took up the television issue, and when the dust cleared, Byers had won a major victory. By a landslide vote of 631–179, the delegates reinforced the NCAA's exclusive prerogative to negotiate network television contracts for football as well as future deals with cable television and other potential forms of telecasts. All 61 CFA schools voted in opposition.[33] The NCAA had prevailed for the time being, but the courts had not yet had their say.

Showdown in Court

The University of Oklahoma and its president, William Banowsky, now took the lead in the CFA's case against the NCAA. (The state court dismissed the Texas lawsuit on procedural grounds.) Banowsky was an intensely religious person who as a young man showed talent on the playing field and in the pulpit. He had attended David Lipscomb College, a Bible-based school in Nashville, Tennessee, on a baseball scholarship but began his career as a minister in the Church of Christ, first in Nashville, then in Albuquerque. In the early 1960s, he continued preaching while completing an advanced degree in speech communications at Pepperdine College before accepting the ministry at the two-thousand-member Broadway Church of Christ in Lubbock, Texas, in 1963. Five years later, Banowsky returned to Pepperdine to help raise money for the school's new campus on prime acreage above Malibu, California. Then, in 1972, at age 34, he became Pepperdine's president and was hailed by *Time* as one of America's two hundred leaders of the future. After a term of six years, Banowsky left Pepperdine in 1978 to become president of the University of Oklahoma, where he applied his religious fervor to fund-raising and sports. He established a highly successful private giving program and accommodated football coach Barry Switzer, who was in the midst of restoring Oklahoma's team to the prominence it had held under the legendary Bud Wilkinson in the 1950s. When the issue of television property rights arose, Banowsky took the position that his institution should be able to exercise its own "market and business judgment."[34]

In April 1982, Banowsky received a pledge from Chuck Neinas that the CFA would reimburse Oklahoma for its early expenses in the lawsuit against the NCAA. President Davison agreed that the University of Georgia also would share costs, and soon afterward CFA members contributed to the TV Legal Defense Fund.[35] The NCAA, though not overflowing with cash, had substantially more funds for a court battle than did the CFA. For one thing, the CFA, still without a TV contract, lacked the resources the NCAA could draw upon from its television deals. Moreover, because, the Big Ten and Pac 10 persisted in their refusal to join the CFA, the plaintiffs could not count on contributions from the two wealthiest conferences.

The case of *Board of Regents of the University of Oklahoma v. National Collegiate Athletic Association* went before Judge Juan Burciaga of the Federal District Court for Western Oklahoma in late spring 1982. Arguments before the judge centered less on property rights than on whether the NCAA was acting illegally under the Sherman Anti-Trust Act of 1890 by monopolizing all college football television contracts. The NCAA offered a three-pronged defense against the antitrust charges: that its TV plan was intended to protect and promote live attendance at games, that it was promoting "athletically balanced competition," and that its restrictions were "justified by the need to compete effectively with other types of television programming."[36] This contention did not succeed. In September, Judge Burciaga decided in favor of the plaintiffs, concluding that the NCAA was a "classic cartel . . . exercising almost absolute control over the supply of college football which is made available to the networks, to television advertisers, and ultimately to the viewing public." The NCAA, concluded the judge, violated antitrust law by acting in restraint of trade in three ways: fixing prices of telecasts; creating boycotts of networks excluded from its contracts and threatening boycotts of its own members that might engage in alternative television contracts; and placing an artificial limit on televised college football.[37] Burciaga noted also that "college basketball has done quite well without the interference of the N.C.A.A., and there is no reason to believe college football would not."[38] The NCAA appealed the decision to the Tenth Circuit U.S. Court of Appeals, which in a 2–1 ruling in the spring of 1983, upheld Judge Burciaga's decision, confirming that the NCAA could not impose its television contract on schools as an obligation of membership.[39] The NCAA then took the case to the Supreme Court, obtaining a stay from Justice White to enable the multinetwork contract to continue through 1983 while the plaintiffs and defendant awaited the high court's decision.[40]

From the outset, two legal principles as applied to antitrust law were involved in the deliberations. Under "rule of reason," even if an action such as the NCAA TV contract qualified as a restraint of trade, a court could determine that such a restraint enhanced competition, and thereby was not necessarily unreasonable. Against this principle stood the "per se" rule, which assumed that a certain act of restraint was inherently unreasonable with no beneficial results. Judge Burciaga had concluded that the NCAA's power over televised football prevented many games from being telecast and thereby constrained competition among networks and unreasonably controlled the price a network had to pay for television rights. The Appeals Court concurred that the NCAA's policy was inherently unreasonable and constituted a per se violation. Still, the NCAA hoped that the Supreme Court would overturn the decision by applying a rule of reason argument because the dissenting judge on the Appeals Court had opined that even though the NCAA's television policy was anticompetitive, it was necessary "to maintain intercollegiate football as amateur competition."[41]

After hearing testimony in March 1984, the Supreme Court rendered its decision on June 27—a major turning point. Historian Michael Oriard has proclaimed, "More than any other single date, this one marks the beginning of the college football world we have today."[42] By a 7–2 vote, the Court upheld verdicts of the District and Appeals Courts. The decision, written for the majority by Justice John Paul Stevens, stated that the NCAA did not convincingly prove a rule of reason defense for any of its arguments on the protection of live ticket sales or the objective of maintaining competitive balance in college football. Rather, the NCAA's controls over the contract and number of televised games were anti- rather than procompetitive. According to Justice Stevens, the NCAA's television plan constituted "horizontal price fixing and output limitation." Because the plan

> places a ceiling on the number of games member institutions may televise, the horizontal agreement places an artificial limit on the quantity of televised football that is available to broadcasters and consumers. By restraining the quantity of television rights available for sale, the challenged practices create a limitation on output; our [precedent] cases have held that such limitations are unreasonable restraints of trade.

Stevens, who had been a respected antitrust specialist before becoming a federal judge, concluded that though the NCAA's goal of preserving amateurism in college sports was laudable, its television policy "restricted rather than enhanced the place of intercollegiate athletics in the Nation's life."[43]

In his dissenting opinion, Justice White, the former college and professional halfback, accused his colleagues of erroneously "treating intercollegiate athletics under the NCAA's control as a purely commercial venture in which colleges and universities participate solely, or even primarily, in the pursuit of profits." White admitted that "it would be fanciful to suggest that colleges are not concerned about the profitability of their ventures." Nevertheless, he accepted the NCAA's fundamental principle "to maintain intercollegiate athletics as an integral part of the educational program and the athlete as an integral part of the student body and, by so doing, retain a clear line of demarcation between college athletics and professional sports." To White, the NCAA served a public good because it prevented its member schools from engaging in activities that would undermine ideals of amateurism. In the name of amateurism, said White, the NCAA limited compensation to student athletes, restricted the number of coaches an institution could have, controlled the number of athletic scholarships and the academic standards of scholarship recipients, and regulated recruitment. Each of these, he noted, was necessary to prevent economically successful programs from skewing competition and to thwart "profit-making objectives from undermining educational objectives." [44]

Control of football telecasts, White argued, was no different from the NCAA's other regulations: It was intended "to advance the overall interests of intercollegiate athletics." He pointed out that Appeals Court and Supreme Court judges recognized that the NCAA was entitled to some authority over television, such as prohibiting broadcast of football games on Friday nights in competition with high school games and limiting the number of times one team could appear on television. But he disagreed with the opinion that the NCAA's TV contract was unreasonable. Contending that his colleagues had erred in applying purely economic analysis to the case, White instead emphasized the noneconomic importance, concluding that antitrust law did not apply because the NCAA and its members were nonprofit educational institutions, distinct from business entities. This factor made NCAA television policy "eminently reasonable" because it fostered "the goal of amateurism by spreading revenues among various schools and reducing the financial incentives toward professionalism." Like the NCAA's ban on compensating college athletes, the TV plan helped "students to choose their schools, at least in part, on the basis of educational quality," it ensured "the economic viability of athletic programs at a wide variety of schools with weaker football teams," and it promoted "competitive football among many and varied amateur teams nationwide." The majority of White's colleagues, however, decided that NCAA policy was anticompetitive and, in Justice Stevens's words, "unresponsive to consumer preferences."[45] And against White's sentimentalism, those justices thrust college football television into a free market and recognized that big-time college sports was indeed big-time business.

The Scramble for Television Contracts

The Supreme Court decision put televised college football in disarray. Could the NCAA retain some kind of control, or would a free-for-all ensue? Several pathways opened. In one, the NCAA would design a plan acceptable to all members and to the courts. In another, a coalition of big-time football conferences—the Big Ten and Pac 10 plus those of the CFA—would negotiate a new television contract for themselves. Or the CFA might negotiate one contract while the Big Ten and Pac 10 might negotiate another. What independents Notre Dame and Penn State would do remained uncertain. In fact, almost immediately after the Supreme Court announced its decision, rumors began to circulate that Notre Dame was about to sign an exclusive contract for rights to telecast its home games. A Notre Dame spokesman denied the rumors, and the school reportedly turned down a $20 million deal.[46]

Early in July 1984, the NCAA called a special meeting of its Division I-A members to consider a proposal for a liberalized television policy. The plan called for a three-and-one-half hour slot for televised college football each Saturday afternoon during the season in which networks, cable companies, and individual stations could bid for games to be telecast. More than one game could be televised nationally at the same time, along with various local and regional contests. Teams appearing on each national game would split 80 percent of the TV revenues, and the NCAA would receive 20 percent, 80 percent of which would be placed in a pool and divided among schools that did not appear on television at all. But on July 10, the Division I-A members rejected the plan by a vote of 66–44. Those who opposed the plan claimed they did so because of uncertainty that the courts would accept it, but the vote split almost completely between non-CFA schools in favor and CFA, Big Ten, and Pac 10 schools against, reflecting the intensifying minor powers–major powers division within the NCAA. Afterward, Byers gave in, stating that the NCAA would no longer attempt to impose a football television plan "unless there is a feeling the members want one."[47] About the same time, Congress began hearings on whether to grant the NCAA a limited antitrust exemption on television issues similar to what it had given the NFL in the Sports Broadcasting Act of 1961. But now, in the midst of the Reagan-era mood for deregulation of business, the government declined to act.[48] The thirty-three-year era of NCAA control of college football telecasts was over.

Shortly after the NCAA meeting, the CFA negotiated a contract with ABC and ESPN for telecasts of 35 games. Not to be left out, the Big Ten and Pac 10, plus a few independents, signed with CBS for 15 games, and several minor conferences made arrangements with cable companies. No windfalls resulted, however. The CFA contract was signed for $4 million less than the now-vacated NCAA deal with NBC would have paid.[49] Individual schools, accustomed to bolstering their athletic budgets with television revenue, suffered. The University of Alabama's television income in the first year of deregulation dropped from $1.9 million to $764,000. UCLA's declined from $1.3 million to $735,000. Ironically, Oklahoma, the lead school in the lawsuit to win TV autonomy, saw its television revenues fall from $1.3 million to $753,000.[50] Fans were the main beneficiaries, as the stock of weekly football games on TV kept expanding. Numerous conferences and schools partnered with television production companies to create ad hoc networks that broadcast some of their football games—those not televised by regular networks—on regional stations. Notre Dame, for example, worked with Chicago's superstation WGN to air its games that were not in the CFA package, and the Southeastern Conference signed with WTBS, the big Atlanta-based cable network, to broadcast some its games not covered by the CFA package. All the new television deals meant that Saturday football games began entering viewers' living rooms around noon and continued on multiple stations late into the night.[51]

The wide-open situation brought unintended consequences beyond reduced earnings. For example, once schools and conferences were free to enter their own television arrangements, disputes arose over whose contract applied when games took place between teams with different deals. In August 1984, the Big Ten, Pac 10, and CBS filed suit in federal district court against ABC because the CFA contract with ABC barred CBS from televising games of visiting CFA schools Nebraska and Notre Dame when playing non-CFA schools—in this case, the home teams of Pac 10 schools UCLA and Southern California (USC). A judge issued a restraining order to allow CBS to televise the UCLA–Nebraska and USC–Notre Dame games, and in 1985 the parties reached a settlement that granted the home team's network the right to broadcast crossover games.[52] Moreover, where previously the NCAA had limited telecasts mostly to a single weekly blockbuster, now there not only were a flood of games on several channels, but also two games featuring major rivalries sometimes were telecast in the same time slot. As a result, viewer ratings for individual games tumbled. Meanwhile, ratings for NFL games, exempted from antitrust rules by the 1961 act of Congress, rose.

Post-1984 conditions also bared the CFA's weakness. Ironically, the lure of television, which had underlain dissension between the NCAA and the CFA, soon threatened to fragment the latter organization because the CFA had no way to prevent its members from acting independently. Then, the inevitable happened. In 1987, the Southeastern Conference, once a steadfast member of the CFA, negotiated a tentative four-year contract with ABC to carry its schools' football games, a deal that signaled the willingness of a CFA segment to go its own way in the same fashion that the CFA had asserted its autonomy against the NCAA a decade earlier. CFA commissioner Neinas, taking the stance against the SEC that Byers had previously taken against the CFA, scrambled to hold his coalition together. Eventually, the SEC schools canceled the ABC deal by a vote of 6–4. In return, Neinas had to increase the number of SEC games to be televised under the CFA contract with CBS. Internal dissension now infected the CFA.[53]

Notre Dame remained the 800-pound gorilla in the room. The most nationally publicized and ardently followed football team, the Fighting Irish were the core of the CFA. Yet, ever since the 1950s, the school had thirsted for its own, separate television deal. By 1990, it could wait no longer. Just before retiring, Joyce negotiated a $35 million contract with NBC to televise all Notre Dame football games, home and away, for five years. Notre Dame's defection diminished the value of the CFA television contract, and the renegade coalition began to break apart. When the CFA TV deal was about to expire in 1994, the SEC signed an $85 million contract with CBS with no opposition from Neinas or other conferences, and shortly thereafter, the Big Twelve (formerly the Big Eight), Atlantic Coast, and Big East Conferences went their own way as well. The CFA, no longer able to control its component parts, announced that it would go out of existence in 1997, a casualty of its own success. As one writer pointed out, after the *Board of Regents* decision, "there was no such thing as a little freedom." Emancipated from the NCAA monopoly of televised football, schools and conferences could flee any television package, whether NCAA or CFA, that did not fit their desires.[54]

The Supreme Court's deregulation of televised college football created a situation that paralleled televised college basketball and reflected the atmosphere of deregulation nationwide prevalent at the time. In the early 1970s, the NCAA had explored the idea of creating a TV package for basketball similar to that for football, but the association's membership was cool to such a plan. Instead, the NCAA kept control only of the Division I "March Madness" championship tournament, whose public appeal skyrocketed after the dramatic championship matchup in 1978 between Michigan State and Indiana State. Between 1973 and 1981, NBC, which held the contract to televise March Madness, expanded its tournament coverage from fourteen hours to twenty-one and a half. CBS, which took over the contract in 1982, began with twenty-eight hours of coverage and expanded to more than forty-seven by 1990. At the same time, ESPN cut deals with major conferences to broadcast basketball games that progressively expanded coverage and eventually reached six nights a week and both weekend days during the winter months.[55]

The first year of deregulation resulted in an estimated decline of 60 percent in college football's combined income from network television. Cable broadcasts contributed some extra dollars, but the total revenues still fell $25 million short of what CFA schools would have netted from the now-vacated NBC contract. The number of televised games tripled, meaning that advertising opportunities also expanded, but that did not mean more revenue. The price paid for a thirty-second commercial on a network-televised game dropped from $57,000 to nearly $15,000.[56] Moreover, the *Board of Regents* case left college football without a single governing agency to supervise college sports on television. In an admission of the NCAA's defeat in the war against the CFA, Byers remarked in summer 1984 that the "real power in college football television now belongs to the networks."[57] That power came in the form of irresistible cash. Not only did individual schools and conferences negotiate separate TV contracts for their football teams; conferences also made organizational decisions to put themselves in advantageous positions for more money. Thus when the Big Ten added Penn State to the conference in 1990, it did so for an obvious reason: grafting Penn State's lucrative eastern television market to the Big Ten's (now eleven) Midwestern realm. The move started a fevered game of musical chairs in the 1990s, with more than forty schools changing conference affiliations so that they could organize football and basketball championship playoffs, all to milk the television cash cow. On-air exposure and new revenues made even bigger celebrities of coaches, especially those of football and men's basketball, and gave them opportunities to cash in. In the mid-1980s, salaries of major football coaches averaged around $150,000; by the mid-1990s, several coaches made close to $1 million.[58]

Television had an effect on its audience as well as on colleges and universities. The multiplication of games broadcast weekly captured a new breed of viewers: fans who watched and became followers of teams not because they were students or alumni, but because they had been lured by the new commodity that was televised college sports. The telecasts, with close-ups and slow-motion replays, and the on-air commentary from so-called expert analysts, who added human interest insights into the athletes' lives, enhanced viewers' knowledge of the games, making them ever more emotionally involved. Their devotion often got carried away. In 1984, for example, the lawyer for a Columbus, Ohio, client convicted of manslaughter, robbery, and drug charges demanded a new trial for his client when the jury apparently rushed its deliberations so that they finished in time to watch the Ohio State–Michigan football game on TV. One of the jurors signed an affidavit, claiming he had been pressured to change his vote from innocent to guilty.[59] Supreme Court decisions notwithstanding, the promotional tentacles of television had come to have a far-ranging reach.

Fallout: Who Won?

The Supreme Court's decision in the *Board of Regents* case represented a major turning point. For the previous thirty-three years, the NCAA had dictated the terms of, and returns from, network telecasts of college football games. Meanwhile, the NCAA began to reap burgeoning revenues by auctioning off rights to televise its Division I March Madness basketball championship. By the 1970s, however, the broadcast field for all sports, including college sports, had broadened, as national cable networks, especially ESPN, capitalized on fan interest, and a panoply of networks and channels were eager to add college competitions to their programming. *Board of Regents* freed schools and conferences, especially the CFA, to negotiate their own football TV packages, undercutting a pillar of the NCAA's dominance. The NCAA retained considerable authority over college sports, as it continued to establish playing rules, manage championship tournaments, pass and enforce bylaws, distribute income from the March Madness contracts, and more. But autonomy was now the standard for televised football, and the conflict between the NCAA and the CFA portended more efforts by major schools and power conferences to flex their muscle, either within or outside the NCAA.

In 1981, just as the CFA's legal maneuvers against the NCAA were coalescing, University of Oklahoma football coach Barry Switzer, never one to mince words, disclosed the growing impatience that big-time athletic programs were feeling, and his sentiments remain in the minds of some athletic interests today. Contending that about forty of the most prominent football-playing universities needed to ally in their own interest, Switzer candidly told the media, "We could set our own rules. Maybe give the players $50 a day [he meant a month]. Get rid of the 95 [NCAA overall football grant limit]. We sign 30 [recruits] every year, so let's educate [provide scholarships for] the whole 120. I don't care how many coaches Missouri has. If they want 20, let them have 20. . . . If we're expelled from the NCAA, it could enable us to do some things that are realistic."[60] The CFA was not expelled from the NCAA in 1984, nor did it carry out Switzer's and Chuck Neinas's threats to secede. But its members continued to smolder under the NCAA lid. Organizational reforms in the 1970s had split the NCAA into three divisions and created a subunit of Division I—Division I-A—to placate major football schools. The NCAA crafted a further realignment, reducing the size of the Division I-A by removing smaller football-playing schools to Division I-AA. In addition, Division I representatives were given greater presence on the all-important NCAA Council and other committees.

Still, some CFA members remained unsatisfied. Though by 1984 they were no longer obliged to abide by the dictates of NCAA football television policy, they desired what Switzer fantasized: a small coalition of schools with super-elite athletics schools that had greater autonomy over their affairs. Moreover, the continued unwillingness of the Big Ten and Pac-10 conferences to affiliate with the CFA against the NCAA during and after the court battle rankled CFA leaders. Byers and some historians believe that Neinas propelled CFA maneuvering, at least in part because of his own personal resentments. At the time of the CFA–NCAA conflict, Neinas was both CFA president and Big 8 commissioner. His ambition to become commissioner of the prestigious Big Ten had earlier been thwarted, and Byers had opposed him when he (Neinas) had tried independently to persuade ABC to televise more Big 8 games.[61] Nevertheless, the turmoil of the 1970s and 1980s entailed motivations beyond those of a single individual. Presidents Davison and Banowsky of the Universities of Georgia and Oklahoma respectively, for example, harbored sentiments for independent action extraneous to Neinas's career ambitions.

Suppose, then, that a united CFA had adopted Switzer's idea and formed a superconference in the wake of the *Board of Regents* decision? In all probability, such a path would have had to be taken within the NCAA's domain. That is, a full secession to create an entirely separate association would have required personnel and financial resources that would have made such a move overly daunting. In the 1980s, the NCAA's long-established ability to organize competition and championships in sports beyond just football and basketball—ranging across the alphabet from archery to wrestling—most likely would have deterred the CFA from becoming independent if its members wished to sponsor a full gamut of championship sports. Another deterrent at the time was that the CFA schools showed no willingness to assume responsibility for women's sports, already impelled by Title IX and which were taking root more firmly on college campuses. Moreover, without full allegiance from the Big Ten, the Pac-10, and important independents such as Notre Dame and Penn State—allegiance that did not exist in 1984—a separate confederation would have had considerable difficulty competing with the NCAA for national stature. The legal wrangling that resulted over which network would televise crossover football games between a CFA school and a non-CFA school, such as when Nebraska wanted to play UCLA, suggests how messy situations could become if multiple associations of big-time athletic institutions existed. Thus, talk of CFA independence was probably just that—talk.

What might have been an alternative to a lawsuit against the NCAA and CFA separation would have been some kind of Congressional exemption from antitrust prosecution of the NCAA television policy. Such immunity would have enabled the NCAA to retain control over televised football but also concede to the CFA schools more acceptable opportunities for television appearances and revenue. In his majority opinion to the *Board of Regents* case, Justice Stevens noted that although the court's decision favored the CFA plaintiffs, he appreciated the NCAA's historic role in regulating college sports. Stevens wrote that "the great majority of the NCAA's regulations enhance competition among member institutions. Thus, despite the fact that this case involves restraints on the ability of member institutions to compete in terms of price and output, a fair evaluation of their competitive character requires consideration of the NCAA's justifications for the restraints."[62] This admission might have served as a signal for Congress to consider a bill that would apply to the NCAA in a manner similar to that of the Sports Broadcasting Act of 1961. That measure protected from antitrust prosecution "any joint [broadcasting] agreement by or among persons engaging in or conducting the organized professional team sports of football, baseball, basketball, or hockey, by which any league of clubs participating in professional football, baseball, basketball, or hockey contests sells or otherwise transfers all or any part of the rights of such league's member clubs in the sponsored telecasting of the games of football, baseball, basketball, or hockey, as the case may be, engaged in or conducted by such clubs."[63] This path, however, was never taken. Byers had declined to seek such protection in 1979, apparently confident that the courts would support the NCAA's television policy, and neither Byers nor his successors seemed eager to pursue congressional relief after the *Board of Regents* decision.[64]

On the other hand, a different outcome certainly would have ensued if the Supreme Court had decided in favor of the NCAA. If Justice White's interpretation had been accepted by the majority of judges, the NCAA might then have had unfettered prerogative to regulate televised college sports, and antitrust exemption would have been unnecessary. In his minority opinion to the *Board of Regents* case, White noted that the NCAA's authority to distribute TV revenues and to prevent one or more schools from attaining an "insuperable advantage" from overly frequent appearances on television was essential "to maintain a system of competitive, amateur athletics." He also chastised the lower courts, as well as the plaintiffs, for subordinating the NCAA's educational goals to "competitive commercialism." He added as well that the Sherman Anti-Trust Act was not intended to apply to organizations such as the NCAA, which he contended had other-than-commercial objectives. Thus, White concluded, the NCAA television plan did not constitute an antitrust violation because it "fosters the goal of amateurism by spreading revenues among various schools and reducing the financial incentives toward professionalism," and "the restraints upon Oklahoma and Georgia and other colleges and universities with excellent football programs insure that they confine those programs within the principles of amateurism so that intercollegiate athletics supplement, rather than inhibit, educational achievement."[65]

White's understanding of the 1984 version of college sports nevertheless appears unrealistic. When he wrote "in my view, the television plan reflects the NCAA's fundamental policy of preserving amateurism and integrating athletics and education," he overlooked the complexities that defined the commercial landscape of big-time intercollegiate athletics. "Amateurism" might have been the applicable term for so-called nonrevenue sports such as swimming, wrestling, and softball, but the athletic budgets of many Division I institutions in 1984 reached into the tens of millions of dollars, bolstered in large part by revenues from ticket sales and media fees. Equally important, athletics had drifted well apart from academics. Division I athletic departments had become quasi-independent entities; coaches' statuses—and salaries—differed from those of faculty, athletic revenue streams derived from sources entirely different from revenues of academic departments, the athletic department and even individual teams often had separate endowed funds, and in some cases an athletic director operated with little or no supervision from an institution's CEO. The athletes were amateurs in the sense that they did not receive salaries, but their access to special training and practice facilities and other amenities such as tutors and lounges unavailable to other college students brought them close to being professionals. Much had changed since "Whizzer" White's glory days at Colorado, and restoring his idealistic vision of college sports would have entailed an impossible task of turning back the clock.

The only way that clock might have turned back from 1984 would have been if the NCAA had implemented a reform reinforcing a principle that all members participated in a common athletic-academic enterprise and should therefore share more equally in the rewards accruing to that participation. Such a principle would be sustained by some kind of something-for-everyone distribution of revenue from NCAA television contracts along lines suggested by President Steven Horn of Long Beach State a decade earlier. This was the proposal discussed in the previous chapter, the one that University of Michigan athletic director Don Canham labeled socialism, the one that the CFA and every other big-time athletic school ardently opposed. But expecting the major schools and conferences to accept any kind of revenue sharing in 1984 would have been even more fanciful than it had been in 1976. After all, just the opposite was the reason that Oklahoma and Georgia went to court against the NCAA. So as the dust from the *Board of Regents* case settled and new dust from the quest for more TV revenue and autonomy rose, intercollegiate athletics entered a new era, one that would ironically feature increased power among both the big-time athletic schools and the NCAA.

5 The Civil Rights Restoration Act and Enforcement of Title IX

On April 1, 1987, Lezlie Leier, a nineteen-year-old sophomore at West Texas State University, sat before the U.S. Senate Committee on Labor and Human Resources and read her prepared statement. A varsity volleyball player, Leier spoke in support of a measure to restore what she believed to be the equal rights of female college athletes, rights established by Title IX of the Education Amendments of 1972. In spite of the law, those expectations had not been fulfilled at West Texas State or at other colleges and universities. Comparing varsity sports for women in 1987 at her school to those for men, Leier recounted how her team endured lower funding, inferior equipment, and inconvenient practice hours. "For example," she stated, "men's basketball, with a total team size close to ours, travels with three coaches, a manager, a sports information person, statisticians, trainers, and all players. We travel with one coach, trainer, and statistician, and our coach decides which players to leave behind." She concluded, "Unless Congress acts soon to make Title IX clearly applicable to athletic programs like mine, college athletics will have been, for me, a second-class experience."[1]

The Education Amendments passed by Congress in 1972 included a provision in its Title IX that "no person in the United States shall on the basis of sex be excluded from participation in, be denied the benefits of, or be subjected to discrimination under any education program or activity receiving federal financial assistance." The act emerged during a resurgence of feminism that marked the 1960s and 1970s. Inspired by Betty Friedan's book, *The Feminine Mystique,* published in 1963, a number of American women, especially educated middle-class women who were restless about their circumscribed status in society, engaged in a quest for equal rights. In 1966, the National

Organization for Women formed to work for legislation and court decisions to remove barriers to women's economic and political rights, and by 1967, all fifty states had established commissions to promote women's equality. By the early 1970s, women were making gains but still found doors had opened only slightly in many fields, including sports.

Though Title IX did not specify athletics, supporters of competitive women's sports in high schools and colleges deemed the law to mandate that women's athletics be treated equally with men's. After 1972, the number of women's teams and female participation in intercollegiate athletics expanded, but many colleges and universities, whose athletic policies were dominated by male coaches and administrators, dithered on making significant commitments—or whether to make commitments at all. Moreover, the Department of Health, Education, and Welfare proceeded slowly in issuing regulations for how Title IX applied to women's sports. Women's teams, like the West Texas volleyball team, remained underfunded and understaffed. Meanwhile, the administrations of Presidents Richard Nixon, Gerald Ford, and Jimmy Carter, beset by problems of enforcing racial integration in schools and conscious of a growing sentiment against big government, paid little attention to gender issues flowing from Title IX.[2]

In February 1984, a bulky obstacle arose to block the outcome Title IX was presumed to produce. Grove City College, a Christian liberal arts school in Pennsylvania, sued the federal government, claiming a private institution that refused direct federal and state financial assistance did not have to comply with Title IX's requirements. The Supreme Court of the United States agreed with the college, concluding that penalties for violations of Title IX's antidiscrimination provision applied only to *programs* that received direct federal aid, not to an entire *institution*. The decision outraged women's groups, who concluded that President Ronald Reagan now had a formidable tool to dismantle advances in women's rights. For those promoting sports for women, the Grove City decision seemed to gut their efforts. Sympathetic members of Congress agreed, and in 1987 they proposed an act "to restore the broad scope of coverage and to clarify the application of Title IX." The law, named the Civil Rights Restoration Act, which applied to Title IX and three other civil-rights statutes, would require that any organization or entity—such as a college, medical center, or contractor—that receives federal funds, or indirectly benefits from federal assistance, must abide by laws outlawing discriminatory practices based upon race, religion, color, national origin, age, disability—or gender. As the Senate considered this bill, supporters enlisted Lezlie Leier to make her plea.[3]

Leier's testimony did not decide the issue, because even though Congress passed the measure early in 1988, President Reagan vetoed it. But shortly afterward, a coalition of Democrats and Republicans in both houses of Congress voted to override the veto, and the Civil Rights Restoration Act became the law.[4] This act marked the major turning point in women's college sports; without it, Title IX would have languished. The roads to those laws had been neither smooth nor direct, and satisfying the requirements of gender equity raised conflicts and dilemmas, some of which remained unresolved.

Women's Intercollegiate Athletics before 1972

The background of women's college sports differed importantly from that of men's sports. From the late nineteenth century until the 1970s, women's athletics were lodged in physical education departments and operated under the control of female educators whose philosophy elevated inclusiveness over winning, education over commercialism. Their motto was "a girl for every sport and a sport for every girl."[5] They did not necessarily renounce competition, but, repulsed by the brutality and dishonesty they perceived in male sports, they emphasized health, fair play, and sociability. They believed that women's sportive activity should take place without spectators, both to shield players from lustful men's eyes and to avoid corruption and spectacle. They disavowed athletic scholarships, off-campus travel, ticket sales, and recruiting. And to protect their model and their jobs, female physical educators advocated that women's sports should be coached, administered, and officiated by women only. These principles, called the "education model," were embodied in a platform for women's athletics formulated by the Women's Division of the National Amateur Athletic Federation in 1923.[6]

In contrast, the male model, as it evolved from the 1850s, emphasized high-caliber performance, intense competition, and victory at all costs. Very early, employment of professional coaches and trainers and a quest for championships characterized men's athletics. By the twentieth century, men's teams operated under the aegis of athletic departments independent of physical education and included constituencies within and beyond the institution. To achieve the goal of victory, the men's athletic establishment enlisted alumni and boosters to help underwrite its core of athletes and coaches and an environment that included stadiums, practice areas, locker rooms, and offices. The NCAA, which arose from a meeting to reform the game of football in 1905, regulated and promoted the competitive model. Thus, while women pursued goals of education and inclusiveness; men veered toward professionalization and commercialization.[7]

The most common symbol of women's inclusive model was "play day," an event at which female students from several colleges gathered at one location for racing, ball games, archery, and other physical activities. Competition between schools did not occur; team composition mixed women from different institutions, and the pleasure of participation followed by socialization over refreshments was supposed to replace cutthroat rivalry. When schools did compete against each other, there was no regular scheduling, length of season, or fixed number of contests. In some cases, especially track and field meets, athletes participated on their home campus and results were telegraphed among the various teams.[8]

The inclusive model did not satisfy every female college athlete; many craved the opportunity to test themselves in higher-intensity competition. By the end of the nineteenth century, about one-fifth of American colleges sponsored some type of varsity contests for women, chiefly in basketball, archery, volleyball, and swimming.[9] But the physical education establishment persisted in its philosophy. In 1941, its leaders steadfastly opposed a women's intercollegiate golf championship sponsored by Ohio State University, and as late as the 1950s, physical educators continued to consider campus-based play days and telegraph meets as the appropriate forms of female sportive activity. Not until 1963 did the Division of Girls and Women's Sports (DGWS) within the American Association of Health, Physical Education, and Recreation (AAHPER) approve varsity competition for college women. Even then, the physical educators held fast to their belief that sports should be part of the educational process and that, to protect women from exploitative coaches, there should be no recruitment of, scholarships for, or special treatment given to female athletes.[10]

Nevertheless, in the decade before Congress passed the 1972 Education Amendments, women's intercollegiate competition slowly expanded, and several agencies contested for control. While physical educators in the AAHPER held tightly to their model for women's sports, the NCAA began to advance its own plan of management. Between 1963 and 1968, the NCAA helped sponsor an institute to develop female Olympic athletes, established a committee on women's athletics within the association, brought together male and female athletic representatives to discuss items of mutual interest, and invited women to speak at the association's annual conventions. The NCAA stopped short of wanting to govern women's sports, however. In early 1964, Charles Neinas, NCAA's assistant executive director, reassured a DGWS official that the NCAA would continue to administer only male athletics and intimated that women should feel free to manage their own sports. He wrote in 1966, "A national organization assuming responsibility for women's intercollegiate athletics would not be in conflict with the Association," adding, "We wish the DGWS well in this important endeavor."[11] But Walter Byers, NCAA's shrewd and ambitious executive director, was already casting his net toward the ladies. In 1965, he appointed a committee to explore the feasibility of NCAA supervision of women's sports. When DGWS asked whether this committee represented a shift away from the "hands-off" position that Neinas seemed to have expressed, Byers retorted, "I don't know precisely what you mean by our 'hands off' policy or who told you this was the official position of the Association."[12]

Nervous that the NCAA might try to hijack women's college sports and impose its model of competition, DGWS made a preemptive move in 1966 by creating the Commission on Intercollegiate Athletics for Women (CIAW) to initiate national championships in gymnastics, track and field, swimming, badminton, and volleyball. Unlike the NCAA, CIAW members paid no dues; female physical educators ran it and enforced "common sense" by banning from their tournaments any woman who had accepted an athletic scholarship and forbidding recruitment of athletes. Women were not yet ready to imitate men in the governance of their sports, but a drift toward more formalized intercollegiate competition had begun. At the same time, another offshoot of the AAHPER, the Athletics and Recreation Federation of College Women, was formed, and discussions at its annual conventions revealed greater interest in "athletics" than in "recreation," a sign that major shifts lay ahead.[13]

The NCAA's stance toward women's sports appeared logical to some and conspiratorial to others. In 1969, Neinas and Ernest McCoy, chair of the NCAA's Commission on Women's Athletics, met with DGWS officials Lucille Montgomery and Martha Adams and recommended that DGWS organize a separate women's sports association based on institutional membership like that of the NCAA. The suggestion seemed consistent with Neinas's previous assurance that the NCAA had no designs on women's intercollegiate athletics.[14] Still wary, DGWS leaders moved in 1971 to forestall a male takeover by establishing the Association of Intercollegiate Athletics for Women (AIAW) to supervise championships in women's sports and to replace the CIAW. Formation of the AIAW signified a step toward the male model of competition, but leaders insisted that the AIAW would remain under control of physical educators and not be a duplicate of the NCAA. Rather, they insisted, the AIAW would represent student interests over those of their school. They emphasized institutional accountability rather than centralized enforcement of rules, abjured common academic qualifications for eligibility, renounced recruiting, and forbade athletic scholarships.[15]

Meanwhile, Byers continued to extend his reach. Whether worried over possible legal challenges from female sports groups like the AIAW to the NCAA's male-only dominion or positioning the NCAA for ultimately capturing control of women's sports, in early 1971 Byers wrote the DGWS that "It appears that the NCAA is in a difficult legal position on the basis of its present posture [excluding women's sports] and I suppose it is quite likely that we will proceed to remove each barrier and, in fact, provide competitive opportunities for women as well as men."[16] Byers also convinced the NCAA Council to appoint a committee to review whether the NCAA should begin administering championships in women's college sports, and he asked George Gangwere, NCAA's legal counsel, for an opinion on whether the Association had a legal obligation to provide for female participation in NCAA events. Leaders of women's sports organizations saw Byers's actions as contradicting Neinas's assurance, but they concluded—perhaps naïvely—that by creating the AIAW they ultimately would convince the NCAA to leave them alone.[17]

Gangwere composed an amendment to the NCAA constitution that would establish a separate Women's Division, run by AIAW but under NCAA rules and principles. The women, wedded both to the inclusive model and to self-government, objected. In September 1971, they countered with an offer for AIAW "affiliation" but continued independence. Neinas informed the AIAW that since it was not feasible for women to participate on men's intercollegiate teams, the national legal climate in which women's rights groups were actively pursuing equity for women in all walks of life made it imperative that the NCAA provide competitive opportunities for women in its member institutions. "We hope," he wrote, "that your organization would be the vehicle to fill that need, but if you feel that you cannot make the adjustment necessary to accomplish that end, then I suppose that we will have to look to some other solution."[18]

The threat of "some other solution" inflamed the women, who construed it as a brazen attempt to force them to accept the male model for competitive sports. Rachel Bryant, a consultant to DGWS, promised a "real battle" if the NCAA tried to take over women's sports. Byers retorted that the NCAA had a legal right to regulate *all* intercollegiate athletics and accused Bryant of being "intemperate."[19] By year's end, the NCAA and AIAW had moved far apart. Though it tabled Gangwere's amendment, the NCAA Council voted to continue studying how to deal with women's sports while the DGWS Executive Committee resolved to oppose the NCAA policy of allowing athletic scholarships. At a roundtable during the NCAA convention in January 1972, DGWS chair JoAnne Thorpe argued to the mostly male delegates that AIAW was "better equipped than the various men's organizations to recognize and be sensitive to the needs of women" and warned that the AIAW would "refuse to be dominated by outside groups. It is impossible to legislate allegiance."[20] Speaking for the NCAA, Gangwere bluntly asserted that AIAW lacked ability to offer women "opportunity to compete against each other in intercollegiate athletics" and that only the NCAA had the wherewithal to provide "the same opportunity"—meaning high-caliber competition—to women as it did to men.[21] A duel was about to take place. Meanwhile, the Education Amendments of 1972, with their seemingly innocuous Title IX, was filtering through Congress.

Title IX Arrives

A mere thirty-seven words that bear repeating:

> No person in the United States shall, on the basis of sex, be excluded from participation in, be denied the benefits of, or be subjected to discrimination under any education program or activity receiving Federal financial assistance.

That's it. Title IX. In this instance, brevity has not meant efficiency, because a cascade of lawsuits, speeches, books, articles, and outright squabbling flowed from differing interpretations of terms such as "participation," "discrimination," "program," and "financial assistance," not to mention the entire statement.

Title IX was intended to extend Title VI of the 1964 Civil Rights Act, which prohibited discrimination on the basis of race, color, and national origin in federally assisted programs, by adding sex to the list. Representative Edith Green of Oregon and Senator Birch Bayh of Indiana were responsible for inserting this anti-sex-discrimination clause into the Education Amendments of 1972. Green, once called "the most powerful woman ever to serve in the Congress," was a ten-term Democrat who crusaded for education and women's rights from the time she was first elected in 1954. Daughter of two schoolteachers, and a former teacher herself, Green earned the label "Mrs. Education" for her work toward passage of the National Defense Education Act (1958) as well as the 1972 Education Amendments. Bayh, also a Democrat and offspring of a schoolteacher, was elected senator in 1962 and drafted numerous measures on behalf of women, including the failed Equal Rights Amendment to the Constitution.

Once the Education Amendments became law, clarification and enforcement of Title IX became the responsibility of the federal bureaucracy.[22] The Feds, however, took their time. For the next three years, the Office for Civil Rights mulled over how to interpret those thirty-seven words, aided (and hampered) by ten thousand comments submitted by lobbyists, athletic directors, coaches, parents, teachers, lawyers, and athletes. Could women try out for men's teams? If there were separate men's and women's teams for the same sport, did they require equivalent coaching staffs, locker room facilities, travel allowances? Who knew?

In 1974, the Office for Civil Rights submitted draft regulations to Congress, which formally accepted them on July 21, 1975. The regulations on sports provided for "equal opportunity" as measured across several factors: accommodating athletic interests and abilities of both sexes, provision of equivalent equipment, scheduling of games and practices, travel and per diem allowances, access to coaching and academic tutoring, practice facilities, locker rooms, medical and training facilities, housing and dining facilities, and publicity. Unequal spending was not in itself a violation, but failure by an institution to provide "necessary funds" for a women's team could be considered as unequal opportunity. A final provision gave institutions until 1978 to comply, plenty of time to plan and implement—but also to protest and evade.[23]

Title IX often is identified as the legislation that liberated female athletes from both the discriminatory practices of the male athletic establishment and from deterrents to competition inherent in the female educational model. Unlocking those chains, however, involved finding and using many keys. One key was cut early in 1973, when several Florida female college athletes filed a lawsuit, *Kellmeyer v. NEA*, that sought to undo AIAW prohibitions against athletic scholarships. Before the case went to trial, the AIAW gave in and passed a resolution to allow the awarding of athletic scholarships to women, prompting the district court to dismiss the suit. By abandoning its no-scholarship policy, the AIAW now edged closer toward accepting the male model of competition. Over the next few years, it shifted further, allowing female athletes to compete for prizes, naming All-American athletes, and soliciting television revenues.[24] There must have been some rumbling in the graves of the early leaders of women's athletics.

Once the Office for Civil Rights regulations became official, they, like the Kellmeyer suit, pushed female athletic leaders into an awkward position. If the law and its interpretations placed women's sports on the same footing as men's, was not the door now unlocked for the NCAA to sponsor competition for female teams separate from AIAW control? If that happened, how would colleges afford to finance parallel programs for two types of sports, one managed by AIAW, the other by the NCAA, especially since the nation's economy in the 1970s was wobbling under pressures of soaring inflation and heavy debt? AIAW leaders voiced support for the spirit of Title IX and the Office for Civil Rights regulations but maintained that "equality" meant *sharing* resources and identical per-capita expenditures, a dead-end proposition, because the men had already girded themselves to resist it at all costs. Byers reflected the NCAA attitude when he wrote in his memoir, "To decree that football and women's field hockey immediately deserved the same per capita expenditures was financial lunacy."[25]

Meanwhile, Title IX prompted the NCAA to pursue strategies that moved in opposite directions. One effort involved weakening and ultimately dismembering the law. During the three-year transitional period, 1975–78, the association protested to HEW that the Office for Civil Rights regulations were impossibly vague, because no school could understand whether it was complying with the rules until HEW officials explicitly affirmed that it was in compliance. Several college and university presidents contended that the regulations constituted inappropriate federal interference into institutional prerogatives. Further, congressional allies of the NCAA, and especially of football and men's basketball programs, tried to undercut Title IX by offering legislation to exempt these revenue-producing sports from the law. Their attempts died in committee. Then, at its 1979 convention, NCAA delegates instructed their leaders to resist HEW's interpretation of the Office for Civil Rights regulations, released a month earlier.[26] And in 1980, the NCAA sued HEW, claiming the 1975 regulations exceeded HEW's authority, because they were "arbitrary and capricious," and that they created a sex-based quota system that violated Title IX itself.[27] The challenge, however, died in the courts.[28]

While trying to topple Title IX, the NCAA simultaneously launched an effort to overpower AIAW and absorb women's college sports. Byers contended that the female sports establishment, as represented by AIAW, was thwarting its athletes because it refused to accept "competitive athletics as the proper pursuit for teenage women."[29] To satisfy what Byers believed to be demands by women for true competition, the NCAA would have to assume responsibility. Shortly after Title IX had passed in 1972, the NCAA took steps to cover itself legally by removing the word *male* from its bylaw on championship competitions. Then, in 1974, an NCAA report recommended that the association sponsor championship competition for women just as it did for men, and it proposed pilot programs to begin in 1975. The NCAA's membership balked at the swift and secret way the proposal had been drafted and defeated it at the NCAA convention in January 1975. But members left the door ajar for further discussion.[30]

It did not take long for that opening to widen. In April 1975, the NCAA Council recommended that the association "proceed immediately" to meet the needs of female student athletes, justifying the recommendation with an accusation that women's organizations had neither the resources to manage women's athletics nor the desire to "reach accords" with—meaning submit to—NCAA efforts at alliance. Byers began to push harder to bring women's sports under NCAA control. While the AIAW struggled to ensure two separate sports establishments, Byers argued that his organization faced legal liability of violating Title IX if it did not provide opportunities for women. He sarcastically observed that the NCAA would honor AIAW's control of women's sports only "if the AIAW would indemnify the NCAA" from legal challenges.[31] In response, Dr. Margaret Burke, a physical education professor and former AIAW president, accused Byers and the NCAA of failing to secure women's consent to a takeover and that in "certain circumstances involving men and women, lack of consent is classified as rape."[32]

NCAA membership, less intent than Byers, opted to continue studying sponsorship of women's sports rather than move ahead and schedule championships. But at its 1980 convention, the association succumbed and voted to initiate women's championships in five sports for schools in Divisions II and III. At the same time, the NCAA Governance Committee proposed to allocate four seats to women on the twenty-two-seat Executive Committee and appoint women to other committees. Also, NCAA chief operations officer Tom Hernstadt hired Ruth Berkey, athletic director at Occidental College, to organize the women's championships. Berkey's apparent defection from the AIAW's goal of separatism prompted Donna Lopiano, athletic director for women's sports at the University of Texas and AIAW president, to charge that Berkey "forgot what Title IX did for her and women's sports. Yes, I guess you can say she's a turncoat."[33]

The NCAA's willingness to sponsor women's competition in Division II and III threw down a gauntlet to the AIAW. As it now seemed a foregone conclusion that the NCAA would soon be offering championship competition for women in Division I schools, AIAW found itself in a desperate struggle for its existence. Reflecting on the year ahead, Christine Grant, who succeeded Lopiano as AIAW president, observed in 1980, "This apparently will *not* be our year of the roses."[34]

Those roses never had a chance to grow because a fierce battle over women's sports occurred in Miami Beach at the NCAA's seventy-fifth annual convention in January 1981. There, the NCAA voted on whether it should sponsor championship tournaments for nine women's sports in Division I. A takeover of women's competitions at its most prominent sports schools would weaken if not destroy the AIAW, whose resources, dependent almost exclusively upon membership dues, were dwarfed by those of the NCAA. Not all NCAA interests bought into the venture, however, because it would require the NCAA to finance women's tournaments, something that male sports interests, especially football and basketball coaches, opposed. Consequently, deliberation among Division I members was spirited. The first vote on the measure ended in a 124–124 tie. A second vote narrowly defeated it, 128–127. After a half hour of rancorous debate, a third ballot overturned the second, thereby approving sponsorship for the nine sports and expanding the NCAA Council and Executive Committee to include female members. According to the motion, the NCAA would pay expenses for women's championship tournaments, while women's programs could postpone compliance with NCAA rules on recruiting and financial aid until 1985.[35] The AIAW was doomed. In 1981–82, almost a quarter of its membership dropped out, taking their dues with them, and on June 30, 1982, AIAW ceased all operations but one: a turn to the courts.[36]

On October 9, 1981, the AIAW filed suit in the U.S. District Court for the District of Columbia, claiming that the NCAA violated the Sherman Anti-Trust Act by using its monopoly power in men's sports to annex women's sports and destroy the AIAW. At each step along the lawsuit's path, the AIAW's arguments tumbled. First, a judge denied its request to enjoin the NCAA from offering women's championships until the lawsuit was decided.[37] In June 1982, a court-mediated meeting between plaintiff and defendant failed when each side rejected the other's proposals for settlement. Then, in February 1983, U.S. District Judge Thomas Penfield Jackson rejected all AIAW's claims, ruling that the plaintiff had not proved that the NCAA had plotted to monopolize women's intercollegiate athletics, nor that the NCAA had used "irresistible inducements" to lure away AIAW members.[38] The AIAW's last-ditch effort failed in May 1984 when the U.S. Court of Appeals for the District of Columbia upheld Judge Jackson's decision, affirming that the AIAW's loss of membership resulted simply from a competitive process in which the NCAA "offered a superior product."[39] Now no obstacles blocked full establishment of the competitive model for women's college sports under NCAA aegis. By the early 1990s, the once male-oriented NCAA was conducting 34 championships in women's sports in its three divisions.[40] Then, almost immediately, a new court judgment lifted the weight of Title IX from NCAA management.

The Grove City College Case

In the early 1980s, two contested terms in Title IX's proscription of discrimination moved to center stage: "education program" and "Federal financial assistance." No clear guidelines existed on what a "program" was and what "assistance" encompassed. If, say, a school's engineering department benefited from a federal grant but its English or athletic department received no such aid, did Title IX apply only to the engineering "program"? Or, because the school as a whole benefited from engineering's "federal assistance," did the entire institution thereby fall under Title IX's rules? And, if only a school's disadvantaged students received federal financial assistance, did such aid, which benefited the school only indirectly, require the institution to abide by Title IX?

In 1981, a lawsuit against Temple University addressed these questions. In *Haffer v. Temple University*, eight female undergraduates sued Temple on grounds that its athletic department discriminated against women by failing to spend funds equitably between male and female athletes. They based their claim on the fact that women constituted 42 percent of the school's athletes but women's sports received only 13 percent of the athletic budget. In defense, Temple argued that Title IX applied only to an educational program directly in receipt of federal funds and that its athletic program received no such earmarked monies. The federal district court sided with the women, finding that Title IX's accountability extended beyond educational programs and that activities indirectly benefiting from receipt of federal funds must comply. Thus, because Temple athletics ultimately benefited from federal grants and contracts that enhanced its general budget, Title IX rules applied to the athletic program.[41] Temple appealed the finding but lost.

Just before the court of appeals upheld the Temple decision, another district court reached the same conclusion in a lawsuit involving Grove City College, a small Presbyterian school in Pennsylvania. In 1976, Grove City had refused to sign a Title IX compliance form required by the Office for Civil Rights on grounds that the college deliberately declined all direct federal aid, including grants to professors and educational enhancement funds. The Office for Civil Rights disagreed, claiming that because some Grove City students received financial assistance from Basic Education Opportunity Grants (BEOGs, known popularly as Pell Grants), the school did benefit from federal aid. In response to Grove City's recalcitrance, the Department of Education terminated BEOGs to the college's students. Grove City then sued the federal government, whose chief law enforcement official in 1978 was Attorney General Griffin Bell, to block the cutoff. A district court ruled in the school's favor, but in August 1982 the court of appeals reversed the decision. The case of *Grove City College v. Bell* then went to the U.S. Supreme Court.[42]

Meanwhile, President Ronald Reagan determined to end what he believed were cumbersome government regulations, including certain civil rights laws such as Title IX. Thus even though the federal government was the defendant in the lawsuit, and legally required to enforce the sanction against Grove City College, government lawyers argued for a narrow interpretation of the law. In his brief to the Supreme Court, Reagan's Attorney General William French

Smith contended that because funds from BEOGs were processed by Grove City's financial aid office, only *that office* met Title IX's definition of "program." Consequently, Smith argued, any other office or department except the financial aid office should be exempt from compliance unless it directly received federal funds. The law, claimed Smith, did not mean to equate "institution" with "program." In an attempt to sustain a broader interpretation of Title IX, a number of women's and civil-rights groups submitted briefs in support of the appeals court decision, but they were not allowed to present oral testimony.[43]

In a 6–3 vote, the Supreme Court overturned the appeals court's finding in the *Grove City College* case and, in effect, undercut Title IX. The court agreed that BEOGs fell under Title IX's meaning of "federal financial assistance" and that the penalty rendered because of Grove City's refusal to submit a compliance form was justified. But the justices also accepted the argument that "program" did not mean "institution." According to Justice Byron White, who wrote the majority opinion, "the fact that federal funds eventually reach the College's general operating budget cannot subject Grove City to institution-wide coverage [of Title IX rules]." At Grove City, only the financial aid office had to comply. Athletics were exempted.[44]

In a bristling dissent, Justice William J. Brennan fumed that the Supreme Court's majority, "completely disregards the broad remedial purposes of Title IX that consistently have controlled our prior interpretations of this civil rights statute" because "the Court's narrow definition of 'program or activity' is directly contrary to congressional intent." Reviewing legislative history, Brennan pointed out that enforcement of Title IX was intended to mirror Title VI of the 1964 Civil Rights Act that prohibited racial discrimination. Title VI regulations targeted institutions of higher education in their entirety and, according to Brennan, so should Title IX. He argued,

> According to the Court, the "financial aid program" at Grove City College may not discriminate on the basis of sex because it is covered by Title IX, but the College is not prohibited from discriminating in its admissions, its athletic programs, or even its various academic departments. The Court thus sanctions practices that Congress clearly could not have intended: for example, after today's decision, Grove City College would be free to segregate male and female students in classes run by its mathematics department.

Thus, Brennan concluded, the court's decision "severely weakens the antidiscrimination provisions included in Title IX."[45] Agreeing with Justice Brennan, Margaret Kohn of the National Women's Law Center, grumbled, "Title IX is now like a piece of Swiss cheese."[46]

The Civil Rights Restoration Act

Within weeks of the *Grove City* decision, federal efforts to enforce Title IX ceased. The Office for Civil Rights halted all existing cases and opened no new ones. Moreover, economic pressures across the higher education landscape due to national and global recession caused the elimination of some athletic teams, especially those unable to produce revenue. One athletic director justified cutbacks, declaring, "We're going to drop some women's programs as soon as possible. They don't bring in gate receipts, and the girls don't want to compete anyway."[47] Meanwhile, women's sports leaders fretted over their loss of independence. By 1985, the vast majority of women's college athletic programs had been merged with men's and were run by male athletic directors. Though Title IX had prompted an expansion of women's sports, female coaches suffered because the male coaching establishment took over many newly created women's teams. For example, where in 1973, 90 percent of women's varsity teams at the Division I level were coached by women, in 1984 men held 50 percent of those positions. The new NCAA department devoted to women's sports, headed by Ruth Berkey, had no influence over NCAA rules; it dealt mainly with scheduling. The situation prompted Christine Grant to observe, "We [women] have lost our clout."[48]

But at what seemed the darkest hour, civil-rights advocates, feminists, and congressional allies rallied to restore Title IX's teeth. A bipartisan group in Congress sponsored a bill that would reverse the Grove City decision and apply a collection of civil-rights laws, including Title IX, to all programs that benefited, directly or indirectly, from federal funds. President Reagan's conservative allies in Congress prevented the bill's passage in the 1984 congressional session, but supporters did not give up.[49] Reintroduced in 1987 by Senators Bob Dole, Bob Packwood, and Ted Kennedy, among others, the new "restoration bill" won support from the Senate Committee on Labor and Human Resources—before which Lezlie Leier, the West Texas State volleyball player, testified—by a 12–4 vote. Again, opponents on the political and religious right fought the measure, especially its provisions on gender equality. One foe claimed that if the bill became law, churches would become victims of "militant gays, feminists and others who have no respect for God's laws" and that daycare centers subsidized by the government would be forced to hire transvestites.[50]

Though the Civil Rights Restoration Bill passed the Senate by a 75–14 vote and the House by 315–98 in early 1988, President Reagan, bowing to conservative allies and upholding his vow to reduce federal regulations, vetoed it. In his veto message, the president claimed the bill's provisions "vastly and unjustifiably expanded the power of the Federal Government over the decisions and affairs of private organizations such as churches and synagogues, farms, businesses, and State and local governments."[51] Viewing the bill as a civil-rights measure rather than a regulatory one, House Speaker Jim Wright, a Democrat from Texas, remarked that the president "may want to turn the clock back on civil rights, but the American people do not." Though twenty-one representatives and two senators who originally had voted to pass the Restoration Act switched and voted to sustain Reagan's veto, more than two-thirds of both houses of Congress voted to override the veto in March 1988, propelling the Civil Rights Restoration Act into the law of the land.[52]

By reversing the Grove City College decision, the Civil Rights Restoration Act marked a major turning point in women's college sports because it explicitly intended to "to restore the broad scope of coverage and to clarify the application of Title IX of the Education Amendments of 1972." The act specified that "For the purposes of [Title IX], the term [*sic*] 'program or activity' and 'program' mean all of the operations of . . . a college, university, or other postsecondary institution, or a public system of higher education; . . . any part of which is extended Federal financial assistance."[53] An entire institution was now responsible for assuring gender equity in any and all of its departments, including athletics, and the meaning of "Federal financial assistance," which the courts already had established as including even indirect aid, remained broad in scope.

The Civil Rights Restoration Act was a milestone but not a final destination. Since 1987, the road toward gender equity in college sports has proved to be full of ruts, and the paths taken mostly crossed through the judicial system rather than through legislative bodies. The two most important court decisions occurred in the early 1990s. The case of *Franklin v. Gwinnett County Public Schools* dealt with an issue omitted from Title IX and the Civil Rights Restoration Act: Was a victim of sexual discrimination by a school entitled to monetary damages? The plaintiff, a former high school student, claimed that her school district had insufficiently dealt with the sexual harassment she had suffered from a teacher, even though the Office for Civil Rights had investigated her allegation and confirmed that her rights had been violated. After back-and-forth decisions in district and appeals courts, the case came to the U.S. Supreme Court. In February 1992, the court unanimously affirmed the legality of monetary damages in Title IX lawsuits, implicitly forewarning institutions that they faced costly payouts, not just loss of federal funds, for noncompliance with Title IX.[54] Female athletes who felt aggrieved by noncompliance now could apply stronger pressure.

The other case, *Cohen v. Brown University*, was noteworthy for the Supreme Court's inaction. In 1991, Brown University, as part of a campuswide austerity policy, eliminated four varsity sports, two men's teams and two women's teams. Members of the gymnastics and volleyball teams, the women's programs that were cut, sued, claiming the university's actions violated Title IX by unfairly removing opportunities to compete. They substantiated their argument by showing that only 36.7 percent of the school's athletes were female but were 52 percent of the undergraduate population. If Brown were to lose the case on the basis of these figures, colleges and universities across the country would face difficult challenges if their athletic proportions were similarly skewed toward male participants.

The issue before the court was the policy interpretation of Title IX that the Office for Civil Rights issued in 1979, which established a three-pronged test to determine whether an institution's athletic policy complied with Title IX:

1. Are participation opportunities for women in athletics substantially proportionate to women's enrollment in the undergraduate population?
2. Is there a history and continuing practice of sports program expansion for the underrepresented (female) sex?
3. Is the institution fully and effectively accommodating the athletic interests and abilities of the underrepresented sex?[55]

Brown clearly was not satisfying the first prong, and because it already had expanded the number of female teams in the 1970s after it merged with Pembroke College, its adjacent sister school, it did not have a recent history of adding women's sports. Thus the issue focused on whether the university was accommodating women's interests. Brown took a dual position. It defended its prerogative as a private institution to determine its athletic policy without government interference, and it argued that because women were certifiably less interested in sports than men were, its eighteen female teams and 36.7 participation rate adequately reflected the interests and abilities of its female students. The plaintiffs countered that cutting two women's teams did not accommodate interests and that women would display interest if Brown provided opportunities to compete.

When the federal district court and U.S. Court of Appeals for the First Circuit rejected Brown's argument, the university, with moral support from schools that feared Title IX threatened their big-time men's programs, decided to appeal to the Supreme Court. In April 1997, the court declined to hear the case, thereby upholding the appeals court's decision in favor of the women. Brown then became subject to a court-imposed mandate for compliance with Title IX. According to the settlement, the university was forced to restore the two women's teams, create new ones to meet female interests, and maintain a percentage of female athletes that had to fall within 3.5 percent of the proportion of females in the institution's general undergraduate population. The resolution of *Cohen v. Brown* served notice to other schools that they needed to establish athletic opportunities for women and increase their proportions of female athletes to match the proportions of women in their student bodies.[56]

*   *   *

Though many schools continued to evade Title IX, in part because female athletic interests have been hesitant about investing in lawsuits, women's college sports by the early twenty-first century were much more solidly established than they had been a generation earlier. The Civil Rights Restoration Act sharpened the teeth of Title IX and the case of *Franklin v. Gwinnett County Schools* made schools financially liable for noncompliance. Participation rates seemed to validate the implication from *Cohen v. Brown* that if athletic opportunities were created, women would grab them. Between academic years 1981–82 and 2010–11, the number of female athletes on college varsity teams tripled, from 64,390 to 191,132, and between 1971–72 and 2009–10 the proportion of college athletes who were women swelled from 15.6 percent to 42.9 percent.[57] In 1991, the Office for Civil Rights reversed course. After a decade of retreat from enforcing Title IX, the office included "discrimination on the basis of sex in athletic programs" as a priority issue in equity enforcement.[58] The new landscape prompted Michael Williams, assistant secretary for civil rights in the Department of Education, to comment on Title IX enforcement, "I suspect there is less 'Do we have to?' and more of 'How do we?'"[59] Yet many pathways for women have remained blocked. For example, large gaps still separate men's sports from women's in the allocation of resources, especially in Division I schools, and men still coach a majority of women's teams.[60] Nevertheless, the NCAA has accepted the validity of women's sports and has required female membership on its various boards and committees. Perhaps most important, Title IX, especially as it has evolved since the Civil Rights Restoration Act, has raised the consciousness of parents and educators to the belief that girls and women can be as athletic as boys and men can.

The Roads Not Traveled

What appears as a triumph for women's sports following on Title IX, the Civil Rights Restoration Act, and various court cases also includes irony. By mandating gender equity in matters of funding, opportunities, and competition, the laws and judicial decisions helped transform the women's model of

intercollegiate athletics that emphasized inclusiveness and education into the
NCAA-controlled men's model of victory-above-all, with commercialized
and professionalized competition. The transformation has included greater
visibility of women's sports, higher quality of performance, access of talented
female athletes to expert training, and scholarship opportunities for women
who might otherwise not have been able to attend college. But the process
has had some unintended consequences.

Not long after the AIAW's demise, observers began to uncover evidence
that rules violations had crept into NCAA-sponsored women's competition.
Between 1982 and 1985, the NCAA put Cheyney State in Pennsylvania and
Alcorn State in Mississippi on probation for improper recruiting of female
athletes, and twelve other schools received reprimands for similar offenses.
Though the transgressions tended to be less egregious than those in men's
programs, David Berst, NCAA's enforcement director, told the *New York
Times* in 1985 that rules compliance among women's programs seemed to be
deteriorating.[61] Moreover, as male coaches took control of women's teams,
their attempts to instill physical and mental toughness sometimes crossed
the line between exhortation and abuse, and some female coaches, eager to
please their male administrators and colleagues, adopted similar tactics.[62] A
few female coaches, obsessed with creating "team chemistry" and "a winning atmosphere" intruded into their athletes' personal lives more deeply
than most males would do by insisting that lesbians were not welcome and
intimidating gay team members. Rene Portland, Penn State's women's basketball coach in the 1980s and 1990s, for example, explicitly warned recruits
"I will not have [homosexuality] in my program." After an internal review in
2006, Portland was fined, required to attend diversity training, and warned
of additional sanctions if she engaged in further discriminatory behavior.
She resigned in March 2007.[63]

If they had had their way, female physical educators, though eventually
accepting of a competitive model, might have continued down a different
path than the one that led to the men's model. In its 1963 "Statement of
Policies for Competition in Girls' and Women's Sports," a joint committee
composed of the Division of Girls' and Women's Sports, the National Association for the Physical Education of Women, and a student group recognized
that talented female athletes desired more challenging competition than had
previously existed, but to satisfy such desire the committee asserted that "a
sound, carefully planned, and well-directed program of extramural sports
is recommended."[64] To the physical educators, "a sound, carefully planned,
and well-directed program" meant accepting the competitive model on their
own terms and disavowing scholarships and recruitment, both of which prac-

tices had tainted the men's model, and they reiterated that the emphasis of women's athletics should be full enrichment of the athlete's life. Once athletic scholarships for women became commonplace, attention shifted from those already enrolled to those who could be recruited. As a result, sports for college women migrated from an educational activity to a form of institutional representation and, in some cases, public entertainment.[65]

Furthermore, a clearer path to acceptance of Title IX might have been opened if all parties affected had accepted an alternate view of athletic finances. Once Congress passed Title IX in 1972, men's athletic interests scrambled to protect those varsity programs that attracted the most fan interest, raised the most revenue, and, in their minds, needed the most money to operate. To this end, in May 1974, Senator John Tower, a Republican from Texas, offered an amendment to an education bill that would remove application of Title IX from "an intercollegiate athletic activity to the extent that such activity does or may provide gross receipts or donations to the institution necessary to support that activity."[66] Tower justified the amendment by saying that revenues from football and men's basketball were so crucial to the operations of athletic departments that requiring colleges to add or enhance women's sports would divert funds from major men's sports, thus diminishing their quality, eroding their fan base, and discouraging ticket sales and alumni donations. After energetic opposition from AIAW and various women's groups, a House–Senate Joint Conference Committee dropped the Tower Amendment in favor of an alternative composed by Senator Jacob Javitz, a Republican from New York. The Javitz amendment directed the Secretary of Health, Education, and Welfare to draft regulations for applying Title IX that would "include with respect to intercollegiate athletic activities reasonable provisions considering the nature of particular sports."[67] Exactly what those "reasonable provisions" were never was addressed.

Since 1974, the fear that gender equity in college sports is or will be requiring high-profile men's programs to share income has not been dispelled. To protect those funds, Senator Tower reintroduced his amendment in 1975, but a Senate subcommittee tabled it. Still, the NCAA and big-time sports schools continued to argue that teams that produced money should be allowed to keep all of it. Women, in contrast, contended that intercollegiate athletics belonged to the institution, not to the team, meaning that income should not be hoarded and that certain segments of the athletic enterprise should not be favored.[68] As one female leader, interviewed for an ESPN documentary that aired in 2002, observed, "In a family, you don't serve one child steak while the rest eat hamburg[er]."[69] Over time, women's sports have attained access to more steak, but often the cuts have been less than prime.

Finally, it is worth recognizing that Title IX, now so enshrined as the linchpin for women's sports, might have had more far-reaching effect if the federal government and the courts had induced institutions to satisfy gender equity by applying other laws in addition to Title IX: namely, Titles VI and VII of the Civil Rights Act of 1964 and the Fourteenth Amendment to the Constitution. The wording of Title IX in the Education Amendments of 1972, it must be remembered, did not mention athletics. Its content was adapted from the 1964 Civil Rights Act, specifically Title VI, which prohibits discrimination on grounds of race, color, or national origin in programs and activities receiving federal financial assistance, and Title VII, which prohibits employers from discriminating on the basis of race, color, religion, sex, or national origin. (Sex, specified in Title VII, was omitted from Title VI.) The Fourteenth Amendment contains the equal protection clause, directing that no person may be deprived of "life, liberty, or property, without due process of law."

The potential effects of these laws on women and sports have been explored in a mind-rattling book, *Playing with the Boys: Why Separate Is Not Equal in Sports*, by Eileen McDonagh, a political scientist at Northeastern University, and Laura Pappano, a journalist and blogger. The authors argue that Title IX has restricted rather than advanced women's athletic opportunities because application of the law has "coerced" sex segregation in sports, thereby thwarting some women from realizing their full potential. McDonagh and Pappano claim the nondiscrimination provision of Title VII and the equal protection clause of the Fourteenth Amendment, if appropriately enforced, would truly give women equal rights by enabling talented female athletes to try out for and possibly succeed in certain men's sports. (The authors would retain Title IX enforcement to provide broader opportunities for females in their own separate sports and would not allow men to participate on women's teams because women, as the historically disadvantaged group, are entitled to protected status.) They point out that the Supreme Court has ruled that the equal protection clause prohibits sex discrimination and, although the court has not used the clause in deciding sex discrimination cases involving sports, there have been numerous court decisions that have allowed qualified girls to try out for boys' teams under the Fourteenth Amendment provision.[70]

Since 1972, McDonagh and Pappano claim, men have insulated their teams from women by supporting separate women's programs, and women, too, have pressed for segregation as a way of opening greater opportunities for their gender. To this end, in 1971, even before Congress passed Title IX, George Gangwere, NCAA legal counsel, advised Walter Byers that if the NCAA was to offer equal competitive *opportunities* to women, it should avoid permitting women to compete with or against men. Rather, Gangwere opined, the association must create opportunities for competition "by women among themselves." In other words, women's sports should be separate and (maybe) equal.[71] JoAnne Thorpe, chair of the DGWS, backed this position in a speech before the NCAA in January 1972, declaring that "as a class women cannot compete physically with men" and that "the classification of separate male and female athletics is a reasonable one that should be sustained by the courts."[72]

Consequently, Title IX enshrined segregation. One of Title IX's regulations states that a school "may operate or sponsor separate teams for members of each sex where selection for such teams is based upon competitive skill or the activity involved is a contact sport."[73] To meet the "competitive skill" regulation, schools created parallel men's and women's teams in the same sport, such as basketball and soccer. By defining football as a "contact sport," schools excluded girls and women from that sport but balanced it by establishing teams in field hockey and equestrianism. These efforts found precedent in an implementation regulation of Title VII, which allowed exceptions of bona fide occupational qualifications in certain forms of employment where only one sex could reasonably qualify for the job: a model of women's clothing required a female. Thus, it was assumed—mostly by the male sports establishment—that under Title IX, there were bona fide occupational qualifications, because a woman lacked essential qualities to play football or to play on a men's basketball team.[74]

Title VII provisions, however, do not permit sex discrimination that is based on presumed or average differences between men and women. Bona fide occupational qualifications are rare exceptions; if a woman has necessary qualifications—strength, training, experience—for a job, she cannot be excluded just because she is female. Likewise, say McDonagh and Pappano, there is no evidence that "*attributes of a particular sport* correspond to *attributes of being male or female.*"[75] If a woman meets height, weight, or skill requirements for a particular sport, they claim, federal law allows her to be considered a potential participant, and to exclude women from a contact sport because it may be dangerous is specious because the danger exists for any competitor. Thus, allege McDonagh and Pappano, because the Fourteenth Amendment protects a woman's property—in this case, her athletic skills—and Title VII protects her from gender discrimination—in this case, participation in a sport that provides material reward in the form of a scholarship and other perquisites—these two federal laws should override the coercive segregation of Title IX.[76] Technically, in order for this reasoning to apply to college athletes, those on scholarship or otherwise rewarded for their participation would probably have to be classified as employees. But this change already is becoming a possibility. (See Chapter 8.)

McDonagh and Pappano insist they would not replace women's sports with an open-access model that would slot a few qualified women into men's teams while reducing participation opportunities for the vast majority of female athletes. Rather, they would elevate individual choice: women wishing to play on female-only teams should be allowed to do so, while those who wish to compete on a men's team should not be prevented just because they are female. Civil-rights law, in fact, permits them. Obviously, there are physiological and performance differences between the sexes that will preserve separation in most sports.[77] But, McDonagh and Pappano conclude, sports are not inherently male, and to assume that men always will have athletic ability superior to that of women has deflected sports at the college level from a path that they logically and legally, even naturally, might have taken.[78]

Lezlie Leier, whose testimony in 1987 urged passage of the Civil Rights Restoration Act, became a successful businesswoman in Colorado. Currently, her school, a Division II NCAA member, supports more than 150 female athletes spread over eight teams, and the volleyball team has an assistant coach, a graduate assistant, and a student assistant, as well as a head coach and a trainer. Highly competitive, the team won four consecutive Lone Star League championships between 2007 and 2010. The coaches are involved in recruitment and the school offers athletic scholarships to women.

Leier's congressional appearance came at a critical moment. A generation earlier, female athletes competed within a system supervised by physical educators whose roles were integrated into the educational operations of their schools. But those opportunities also stifled aspirations of talented athletes who sought greater challenges than those available. In 1972, Title IX opened ways to realize those aspirations, but it took government regulations, lawsuits, and acceptance that was sometimes given grudgingly by men to clear away most of the obstacles, enabling schools like West Texas State to boast the kind of women's athletics program it has today. In the minds of many people, Title IX and the power given it by the Civil Rights Restoration Act of 1987 represent one of the truly significant reforms of modern college sports, a genuine change of the playbook. But the history of that reform must also recognize the alternatives that emerged and faded along the way.

6 Scandal, Reorganization, and the Devolution of the Student Athlete

For Bill Clements, money, football, and Southern Methodist University became a driving passion, an ardor so hot that it helped fuel one of the most notorious scandals in the history of college sports. William Perry "Bill" Clements Jr. was a man who wore the mantle of power easily. Tall and square-jawed, Clements favored plaid sport coats and provocative rhetoric. (He once cracked that scuba diving—which was believed to be dangerous for a fetus—might be a good form of birth control.[1]) Born in Dallas, Texas, in 1917, he attended and played football at Southern Methodist University (SMU), and at age thirty, founded SEDCO, a company that became one of the largest offshore oil-drilling corporations in the world. Later, after a stint as U.S. Deputy Secretary of Defense under Presidents Richard Nixon and Gerald Ford, he served as governor of the state of Texas twice, 1979–83 and 1987–91, sandwiched around a term as chairman of the board of governors at SMU.[2] It was amid these last two offices that his cherished university and its football team made headlines in an inglorious way.

During the 1970s, SMU had one of the least successful football teams in the Southwest Conference, racking up only three winning seasons in ten years. A school of nine thousand students, SMU competed against conference rivals most of whom were other Texas universities two to four times as large. Its coaches tried to counter their school's perceived inferiority with athletic successes, which to them meant attracting top-flight athletes. At times, they tried too hard. Between 1974 and 1985, the NCAA placed SMU football on probation five times, mostly for recruiting violations. These infractions occurred at the same time as the Texas oil boom and the transformation of the institution's board of trustees from a body dominated by Methodist bishops to one presided over by a cadre of prominent Dallas businessmen, one of whom was Bill Clements Jr. With tacit, if not active, support from the board of governors and cooperation from head football coach Ron Meyer, SMU boosters began funneling secret payments to players and helped elevate SMU to one of the country's top football teams by 1980. Between 1980 and 1984, the team compiled a record of 45–5–1 and the highest winning percentage of any Division I-A team over those years. During the football ascendancy, contributions poured in, and SMU's endowment surged from $52.5 million to $325 million, making it the twenty-seventh largest in the nation. Annual gifts to the university, worth $11 million in 1976–77, peaked at $29.9 million in 1985–86.[3]

Meanwhile, SMU president L. Donald Shields chose to turn a blind eye to the illicit activity and instead relished the attention and money the football team's prowess was bringing to his university. By 1983, SMU football supporters had created a $400,000 slush fund and were bankrolling football players in violation of NCAA rules. Meyer left in 1984 to coach the NFL's New England Patriots, and his successor, Bobby Collins, along with the athletic director, Bob Hitch, suspected illicit activity but failed to deter the boosters. Meanwhile, the NCAA was sniffing around, eventually compiling a list of eighty alleged infractions that included offers of automobiles and cash to prospective players. Shields seemed powerless to challenge the boosters and Bill Clements besides. When Shields tried to stop the practices, Clements overwhelmed him. At one point, when Shields protested the payments, Clements brushed him aside, ordering him to "go run the university."[4]

As the NCAA expanded its investigation, Clements and Shields deflected the inquiries by promising reform. Referring to one offending booster, Clements testified that he had "had some very heart-to-heart talks with this young man" and that "he was listening to me." Pure bluster. Instead, some players now were being paid to keep them from responding to media and NCAA questions. Nevertheless, the investigation proceeded, and in June 1985, the NCAA struck SMU football with a three-year probation, reduction of scholarships, and bans on television and bowl appearances. The episode was not over. After its chastisement from the NCAA in 1985, SMU continued payouts to players in spite of statements from Clements that the bribery had ended. Soon, however, the cover-up began to crumble. The revelation of persistent violations after 1985 gave the NCAA infractions committee too much evidence to go easy on SMU. In February 1987, the NCAA imposed a "death penalty" that canceled all of SMU's football games for that year and added other harsh penalties. This was the first time an institution had been disciplined so severely.

The SMU affair was one of a long series of scandals that rattled college sports in the 1970s and 1980s. For decades, the college sports establishment had promoted rules of fair play and a level playing field in public, while coaches and boosters surreptitiously sought ways to evade those rules. Now, however, there seemed to be a crisis of ethics, and it stirred up efforts at reform. Those efforts, however, did not lead in the direction that might have been anticipated from the overt events. Though related to the scandals, the major turning points of the era had mixed consequences. Changes in the playbook of college sports between 1973 and 1991 were bounded by two major landmarks: one, seldom heralded but highly significant; the other, much publicized but more symbolic than conclusive. The first, the 1973 NCAA legislation putting Division I athletic grants-in-aid (scholarships) on a one-year renewable basis, highlighted the transformation of the student-athletes into athlete-students, whose commercial value could sometimes prompt others to cheat in order to attract and retain them. The second, the 1991 Knight Foundation report, "Keeping Faith with the Student Athlete," revealed how pervasive the need for ethics reform had become and, in its weak aftereffects, the power the athletic establishment could exert to contain reform and continue the quest for revenue in what had become a high-stakes business.

The One-Year Grant-in-Aid

Before the worst of the scandals erupted, the NCAA, reacting both to fiscal concerns and influence from coaches at big-time schools, set the stage for the era by establishing critical organizational changes. One involved financial aid to athletes; the other divided the structure of college sports into more distinct segments. The reforms did not directly cause the scandals, but they altered the climate in which the obsession with athletic success could better breed dishonesty and academic fraud.

In 1956, after the demise of the Sanity Code, the NCAA formalized the grant-in-aid, a college scholarship that could be awarded for athletic skill without regard to financial need. Athletes still had to meet a school's admission and eligibility standards, but their grant now differed from that offered to other students. To ensure the public that athletes receiving such funds were amateurs, the NCAA used the phrase "in-aid" to mean assistance in the pursuit of education and not a contract for hire. And to protect both aid recipients and athletic departments from tax liabilities and worker compensation claims possibly ensuing from the grants, NCAA Executive Director Walter Byers crafted the term "student athlete" to apply to participants on college varsity teams. Though some schools offered athletic scholarships on a year-to-year renewal basis, many provided four-year packages that allowed aid to continue even if the recipient quit his team.[5] It was not long, however, before coaches found the possibility of a four-year commitment an irksome inconvenience, one that could interfere with their ability to build a winning team and control those players they had so earnestly—and sometimes il-legally—recruited.

The challenges to authority, especially by black athletes, in the 1960s prompted coaches to emphasize that athletes who played under them must perform acceptably on the playing field and unquestionably accept a coach's bidding. In return, athletes would receive the opportunity for a subsidized college education. Early on, however, some coaches and administrators con-cluded that a few athletes were not meeting their part of the bargain—was it a contract?—and were exploiting the system by accepting a scholarship, then deciding not to play. Arizona State's athletic director Clyde Smith complained of the practice, "I think it is morally wrong. Regardless of what anyone says, this is a contract and it is a two-way street."[6] In reaction, the 1967 NCAA convention passed a measure to allow reduction or cancellation of an athletic scholarship if a recipient "fraudulently misrepresents any information on his application, letter of intent, or tender, or . . . engages in serious misconduct warranting substantial disciplinary penalty." "Fraudulent misrepresentation" could include failure to attend practices, and "serious misconduct" could entail refusal to "meet the normal good conduct obligations required of all team members, and defiance of the normal and necessary directions of departmental staff members [meaning coaches]."[7] For the first time, a player who rebelled, did not work hard enough, or quit the team could lose his scholarship. As one coach remarked, "We don't have to put up with trouble-makers any more."[8]

The 1967 rule was not enough. At the same time that athletic departments were dealing with the scholarship issue, higher education and the nation were confronting economic strains. By the 1970s, expenditures on the Vietnam War and domestic programs such as the War on Poverty brought soaring inflation, followed in the early 1980s by a deep recession. Like the federal government, athletic departments, especially big-time programs, had spent lavishly during the 1960s. The lure of television money plus zeal for victory at all costs had pushed schools to expand team rosters and coaching staffs, hike recruiting budgets, increase the number of grants-in-aid, construct lav-ish athletic facilities, and more. Cutbacks now were necessary, and coaches, especially in revenue-producing sports of football and men's basketball, felt pressure to maximize every resource. In 1953, the NCAA had ruled freshmen ineligible for varsity play, and most schools sponsored separate freshman teams. To save costs, the NCAA in 1968 enabled schools to disband these teams by voting to make freshmen eligible for varsity play except in football and basketball, and in 1972 the NCAA okayed freshmen for those teams too. Coaches now could get better value from their rosters, but one sticking point remained. An athlete on scholarship who was underperforming or who sustained an injury that diminished his skills was a liability because he could retain his grant—which the coach considered wasted on dead wood.[9]

Consequently, coaches sought a way to recapture these scholarships for more productive use. In 1967, a measure to limit grants-in-aid to one year rather than four had failed to attract the necessary two-thirds majority from NCAA convention voters. But by 1973, coaches' impulse for control had gained so much momentum that the legislation passed by a show of hands with almost no debate. Now, scholarship athletes could receive aid, but only for one year at a time. If they fulfilled expectations, their grant could be renewed yearly. If they in any way disappointed their coach, their athletically financed education would end. They could transfer to another school but would have to sit out a year before playing again. Byers, who opposed the one-year measure, criticized it as "sports expediency"; its advocates called it cost effectiveness.[10] The one-year scholarship had heightened importance because the 1973 NCAA convention also passed an economy measure reducing the annual number of football scholarships a school could award from 35 to 30 and the total number of football scholarships a school could carry at 120 in any four-year period, making it even more crucial for a coach to make maximum use of every scholarship.

Among schools aspiring for athletic prestige, belt tightening was more rhetorical than actual. As the pursuit of victory heightened the urge to spend on recruiting, salaries, and facilities, the gap between programs with greater and those with lesser assets widened, necessitating reorganization within the NCAA. In 1968, each member institution was asked to identify whether its athletic program belonged in a college or university division. But the expansion in sports at big-time colleges and universities, combined with a quest for revenue from televised football and basketball, caused these schools to seek further separation from other NCAA members. A special NCAA convention in August 1973 realigned schools into three divisions, giving each division authority over membership qualifications, recruitment of athletes, and financial aid. Subsequently, 233 institutions joined Division III (schools offering no athletic scholarships), 194 went into Division II (schools offering scholarships but with fewer teams), and 237 qualified for Division I (high budgets, more teams, and more scholarships).[11] The entire NCAA membership would still meet annually to decide policy on general matters, while each division would determine rules applicable only to itself. The new arrangement was far from ideal, however; it only accentuated the fragmentation of membership that had occurred from debates over television policy, and revenues (see Chapters 3 and 4).

Developments in 1973 both formally separated major athletic programs from lesser ones within the NCAA and isolated college athletes from other students. Establishment of one-year grants-in-aid signaled a momentous turning point because varsity athletes now had single-year contracts; their funding depended on how they performed in their sport, regardless of how they performed in the classroom. (The college might award a scholarship to a student whose athletic grant was not renewed, but there was no guarantee of this happening, especially if the former athlete's academic record was lacking.) But academic success was usually defined by the shorthand of passing grades, and when a school admitted an athlete whose grades fell short of academic standards, there was a simple way to rectify the situation: cheat. The impulse to recruit blue-chip athletes, some of whom lacked the ability to succeed as college students, coupled with the scramble to best any and all opponents—especially in big-time football and men's basketball within the newly constituted NCAA Division I—sparked a burst of scandalous activity that fed newspaper headlines and NCAA investigations.

A System Gone Awry

By 1980, revelations of misconduct of various sorts had left what the *New York Times* called a "stench in college sport." Anyone who thought point-shaving in basketball had ended with the 1951 scandal at City College of New York and other schools was wearing blinders. During the late 1950s and early 1960s, a widespread fixing scheme involving nearly two dozen college teams had resulted in jail time for former Columbia University basketball standout Jack Molinas, the brains behind the conspiracy.[12] Then, in February 1981, Henry Hill, a mob-related criminal already infamous for participating in the Lufthansa heist, the robbery of $6 million in cash and jewels from New York's Kennedy Airport on December 11, 1978, admitted to *Sports Illustrated* that between December 16, 1978, and March 1, 1979, he paid some Boston College basketball players to shave points in several games. Hill, whose colorful and crime-filled career was the subject of the 1990 movie "Goodfellas," had been arrested in 1980 on a charge of drug trafficking and then indicted for the Lufthansa heist, and he bargained for immunity from prosecution in return for details on the basketball swindle. Shortly after Hill told his story to *Sports Illustrated*, a grand jury indicted four gamblers and two members of the BC basketball team. After a four-week trial, the defendants, except one of the BC players, were convicted of conspiracy to commit bribery and received prison sentences, ranging from twenty-eight months for the BC player to twenty years for "Jimmie the Gent" Burke, the mobster who allegedly oversaw the operation.[13]

It was not long before still another point-shaving scandal was uncovered, this one at 150-year-old Tulane University in New Orleans. There, in 1985, three basketball players were arrested for fixing games in violation of Louisiana's law against sports bribery, and two others escaped the charge by testifying under a promise of immunity from prosecution. Also charged were three students, a New Orleans bookie, and another nonstudent. The incident, which allegedly included cash payments by coaches to players, so rattled school president Eamon M. Kelly that he shut down Tulane's men's varsity basketball program. (The faculty wanted him to abolish all athletics, but Kelly compromised by sacrificing just the one team.) Expressing his indignation at the scandal, Kelly told the press, "I think it's critical that we do reaffirm the university's primary mission as an academic institution . . . and to indicate our unwillingness to permit this kind of activity in our intercollegiate programs." The discontinuation was brief, however. Lured by the money sweepstakes that was NCAA basketball competition, Tulane restored its team in 1988.[14]

Game-fixing was one thing; academic fraud elicited just as much outrage. Journalistic investigations in 1980 uncovered instances in which college athletes were receiving credit for courses such as "Safety with Hand Power Tools" and for running wind sprints during practice. Others obtained passing grades in courses they never attended or even knew they were taking. At the University of Southern California, investigators revealed that between 1970 and 1980, 30 academically deficient athletes had been admitted to the school. Most played football, but some members of all twenty-one men's and women's varsity teams had not met USC's standards for entering freshman and transfer students. In 1980, the Pac-10 conference disqualified five of its schools from participating in the 1981 Rose Bowl because of fraudulent academic behavior, including Arizona State, where eight football players had "passed" a summer make-up mathematics course offered by a Montana college without attending a single class. Exposés revealed that at several schools, stand-ins took examinations for athletes, and paid-off tutors fed athletes answers to exam questions.[15]

These revelations, plus the point-shaving scandals at Boston College and Tulane, did not stem the tide of misconduct. One estimate had it that between 1980 and 1989, the NCAA sanctioned half its 106 big-time football programs.[16]

Looking back on the period, Walter Byers wrote, "In 1984 . . . I estimated
. . . that as many as 30 percent of major sports schools were cheating on the
rules—15 percent simply to win, another 15 percent because they felt they
must fight fire with fire."[17] Much of the cheating seemed to take place under
the noses—or with tacit approval from—presidents and deans. For example,
the NCAA found Clemson football boosters to be providing improper cash,
gifts, meals, clothing, and transportation to recruits and parents from the
late 1970s into the early 1980s. As a result, in 1982 the NCAA put the team on
probation for two years, reduced its scholarships from 30 to 20, and banned
it from bowl games and television appearances. Reacting to the penalties,
Clemson president William Atchley admitted, "I think we were very sloppy.
I think we did things very carelessly without thinking what they meant." He
vowed to reform.[18] He failed. In 1985, investigators discovered that Clemson
track coaches had given banned anabolic steroids to their athletes. Atchley
resigned when the school's trustees reversed his firing of the athletic director.[19]

There was more. At the University of Georgia, instructor Jan Kemp complained when school officials intervened to change failing grades for nine
football players in a remedial English class, enabling them to play in the 1982
Sugar Bowl. Demoted in 1982 and fired the next year, Kemp sued the university, and in 1986 a jury awarded her $2.5 million. President Fred Davison
defended the school's practices, insisting that Georgia would not "unilater-
ally disarm" and impose higher academic standards than its sports rivals.
University attorney Hale Almand spoke with unusual candor about how little
an education meant when a winning team was involved, when he admitted,
"We may not be able to make a university student out of him [a hypothetical
athlete], but if we can teach him to read and write, maybe he can work at
the Post Office rather than as a garbage man when he gets through with his
college career."[20]

Other scandals swirled around basketball coach Jerry Tarkanian. During
his tenure at Long Beach State University between 1968 and 1973, Tarkanian
was accused of bending academic standards in his recruiting of junior college
stars. Then, in 1976, while Tarkanian coached at the University of Nevada, Las
Vegas (UNLV), the NCAA charged him with ten major infractions, including
arranging for one member of his team to receive a B for a course he never
took, giving free clothing to another, and arranging for players to receive
free airplane rides courtesy of a booster who was a casino owner. Banned
from coaching, Tarkanian sued the NCAA and won an injunction, getting
his job back. Allegations persisted. In the mid-1980s, a newspaper charged
that UNLV admitted vaunted basketball recruit Lloyd Daniels though he

was functionally illiterate and that Daniels received a car and a rent-free apartment as inducements. The episode ended after Daniels was arrested for buying cocaine from an undercover police officer. UNLV president Robert Maxson tried to accommodate Tarkanian, but eventually the two fell out over team members' association with gambler Richard "Richie the Fixer" Perry, and Tarkanian resigned, effective in 1992.[21]

Special benefits, in violation of NCAA rules, seemed common, if not rampant. One scheme involved friendly automobile dealers furnishing star athletes with cars financed by a "balloon note." The arrangement required little or no payment on a loan for three months, with installments increasing at three-month intervals thereafter. But a dealer could simply restart the note every three months, and the athlete only had to pay a small renewal fee rather than an increasing installment. When regulators caught on to the scheme, boosters shifted tactics, providing purchase funds to an athlete's family member or girlfriend, enabling that person to buy and register the car while the athlete got full use of it.[22]

In the 1980s, public indignation rose over violent criminal behavior among college athletes, especially football players. Nationally ranked teams at the University of Miami were notorious for their outlaw image that included dorm riots and payouts to players for violent plays. More damning were arrests of three football players at the University of Oklahoma in 1989 for gang rape in the football dorm, and a charge against another for shooting a teammate. Between 1986 and 1989, the University of Colorado saw two dozen football players arrested for rape, break-ins, stabbings, and assault. These and other crimes prompted *Sports Illustrated* in 1989 to label college football "an American disgrace."[23] How could the malfeasance be stopped?

Death to SMU, Presidents, and the Test of Power

In the early 1980s, with nationwide scandals unabated and the SMU affair still developing, a group of leaders in higher education proposed establishment of a board of presidents with power over those NCAA regulations dealing with academic and financial matters. The group, led by Harvard's Derek Bok and Georgetown's Father Timothy Healy, was heeding a recommendation from Jack W. Peltason, former chancellor of the University of Illinois at Urbana and president of the American Council on Education (ACE), who, in reaction to the ongoing misconduct, had urged greater presidential involvement in college athletics. The ACE had tried before, in 1952, to enlist presidents to take control of athletic policy but failed when Walter Byers outmaneuvered the reform effort. (See Chapter 1.) At the NCAA convention in January 1984, the

ACE lost the power struggle again. Proposition 35, which would have given presidents influence over issues involving the "academic standards, financial integrity and reputation of member institutions" went down to defeat. Opponents complained the proposition was "undemocratic," placing too much authority in the hands of a small group. Byers, the oligarch who was always protective of his territory, ironically accused Bok and others of trying to be an "elite oligarchy."[24] Instead, the convention approved a weak alternative that had been proposed by the NCAA Governance Review Committee and that created the Presidents Commission with minor prerogatives, but not the veto capability embedded in Proposition 35.[25]

The Presidents Commission did try to rein in the cheating. In summer 1985, with Byers's cooperation, it convened a special NCAA convention to discuss the integrity crisis in college sports. The gathering addressed eight reform proposals, including a provision that each school in Division I, where scandal seemed most prevalent, conduct an athletics self-study every five years and produce an annual academic report. Other recommendations would require outside audits of athletic budgets, tighter control over athletes' eligibility, limits on the number of contests, and restrictions on coaches who committed infractions at one institution then moved to another. Most significantly, the presidents proposed to give the NCAA authority to penalize a school that had committed two or more major rules violations within five years with "prohibition of some or all . . . competition in the sport involved . . . for one or two sports seasons."[26] In other words, repeated misconduct could result in a "death penalty." All eight proposals easily won approval from the members. The death penalty provision passed 427–6. One of those six in opposition was Southern Methodist University.[27]

For the next two years, the Presidents Commission succeeded in prompting the NCAA to pass more reforms, modestly cutting the mounting costs of athletics. At the NCAA's 1987 convention, for example, Division I members agreed to reduce total basketball scholarships from fifteen to thirteen and in football from thirty to twenty-five per year. The illusion of presidential muscle soon faded, however, as coaches of major teams perceived scholarship limits a noxious threat to their ambitions. Indiana's volatile men's basketball coach Bobby Knight spoke for many when he snarled, "You cannot operate a basketball program today with 13 scholarships. . . . Anybody who would propose that or vote for it is an absolute idiot. . . . The Division I people have to get the hell out of the NCAA and form an organization of people who want to play the game and play it right."[28] A special NCAA convention six months later restored the number to fifteen. Knight and friends won the test of power.

While presidents, coaches, and NCAA delegates tussled over financial matters, Bill Clements and the SMU Board of Governors continued their scramble to hide the scandalous behavior inside the school's football program and to dominate SMU president L. Donald Shields. Near the end of the 1986 season, two SMU football players stole the monthly stash that was being used for payments to players and recruits and, when caught, had to be bought off lest they divulge the fund's continued existence. Also in fall 1986, Sherwood Blount, a booster and enemy of President Shields, threatened to divulge the payout scheme. Blount was silenced only by assurances from Clements that if elected as governor he would fire Shields.

Then, shortly after Clements won the election, a local television station and the *Dallas Morning News* released exposés of uninterrupted booster-financed benefits to SMU football players. To distract the NCAA, the Board of Governors forced athletic director Bob Hitch and Coach Bobby Collins to resign, buying out their contracts for $863,000. The board of governors also appointed SMU's NCAA faculty athletics representative Lonnie Kliever, a theology professor who, perhaps appropriately, in light of the role of football at SMU, special-ized in the study of cults, to undertake an internal investigation. The board manipulated Kliever into blaming Hitch and Collins for the payments and shielding Clements and other board members. Eventually, however, Kliever rebelled. In January 1987, he presented the NCAA with a list of violations and implicated the culpable boosters and coaches. He also proposed a package of self-imposed sanctions he hoped the NCAA would accept.

The NCAA infractions committee now had too much evidence to go easy on SMU. The persistence of violations after 1985 qualified the football pro-gram for the newly created death penalty, and the NCAA inflicted it in Febru-ary 1987. It suspended SMU football for the 1987 season, took away all football scholarships through 1988, and prohibited the team from playing home games in 1988. Reeling under such draconian restrictions, SMU canceled its 1988 football season. Clements was forced to acknowledge a role in the scandal, though he denied knowledge of payments made before 1983 and insisted that in 1985 and 1986 his intention had been to "wind down" obligations to football players benefiting from the scheme. A chastened board of gover-nors appointed a committee of Methodist bishops to investigate the episode. The bishops' report recommended reconstituting the board and tightening ties with the Methodist church. The new board then hired A. Kenneth Pye, chancellor of Duke University, as president in place of Shields, who, under pressure from all sides and suffering health problems, had resigned in 1986.[29]

The death penalty, combined with a decline in the oil industry, had dev-astating effects on SMU finances. The year the death penalty was inflicted— which coincided with a downturn in the nation's economy—annual giving dropped to $20.9 million, the lowest in five years.[30] More directly, practically every member of the 1985–86 football team transferred to another school, and SMU lost the $1.5 million in revenues from gate receipts and television appearances that the football team brought in.[31] The penalty had long-term effects as well. Once football resumed at SMU in 1989, the team had only three winning seasons in the next twenty years.

Cheating and recruiting scandals of the 1970 and 1980s reflected the same disconnection of college athletics from academics that was inherent in the one-year scholarship and restructuring of the NCAA. Few coaches and athletic directors considered rules infractions as corrupting the ideals of amateurism; rather, they feared that rivals were gaining competitive advantages by cheating, and so they had to break rules themselves to keep pace. Presidents, viewing athletic success as a means to raise money and grab publicity, were either too naïve, distracted, or mercenary to address the unsavory behavior. When things got too far out of hand, the presidents and the NCAA expressed outrage, proclaimed that educational goals needed to be restored, and called for reforms to set things right. Seldom if ever did they advocate an overhaul of the entire enterprise.[32]

Attempts to Impose Academic Standards

The era's scandals did, however, spark one of the most controversial issues to inflame college sports: establishment of an academic standard for athletic eligibility. Concerned that colleges were admitting athletes with questionable academic qualifications, the NCAA in 1965 devised a complex formula that supposedly predicted whether a high school senior would attain a 1.6, or C minus, grade-point average (GPA; on a 4.0 scale) in college and decreed this measurement as a bottom limit for participation in NCAA-sanctioned sports. The formula combined high school class rank and grade point average with scores on the SAT or ACT standardized tests. Conferences and individual schools were free to establish a higher threshold, but any institution that would not accept the 1.6 minimum would be excluded from NCAA championship competition. About 86 percent of member schools complied.[33]

Establishment of the 1.6 rule marked a major turning point in that it allowed the NCAA to intervene in an institution's autonomy in determining its own academic standards—thereby undermining a school's home rule. Several dissenters opposed the rule, charging that NCAA legislation represented an illegal infringement on admission policies. Others raised the soon-to-be-fervent claim that standardized test scores discriminated against economically disadvantaged students and that the 1.6 standard was racist. Though in the minority, opponents of the rule fueled debate inside the NCAA and in the press. After a contentious eight years, the 1973 convention—the meeting that approved one-year scholarships—replaced the 1.6 formula with a simple 2.0 high school GPA for freshman athletic eligibility in college.[34]

In the 1980s, the American Council on Education entered the campaign to make athletics more academically respectable. Though the ACE lost its attempt to establish broad presidential power over athletics in 1984, it had succeeded in placing an academic reform measure on the NCAA convention's agenda the year before. This legislation, Proposition 48, required an entering freshman athlete in Division I schools to have at least a 700 combined mathematics and verbal score on the SAT (out of a maximum 1600) or a composite score of 15 on the ACT (out of a maximum 25) standardized tests in addition to a 2.0 high school GPA. Prop 48 was introduced to the convention on behalf of the ACE and the NCAA Council by SMU's president, Donald Shields, not yet beleaguered by his school's football scandals.

The new rule triggered immediate uproar. During a raucous debate on the convention floor, representatives from historically black colleges and universities charged that standardized test scores were discriminatory and destructive to efforts to enhance educational opportunities for African Americans. Delaware State University's president Luna Mishoe spoke for many historically black colleges and universities when he asserted that the SAT "is a restraint that penalizes low-income students and does not indicate whether a student can perform college work." Others, such as Grambling State University's president, Joseph Johnson, went further, charging that the legislation was bigoted because no African Americans had participated in Prop 48's creation.[35]

In the end, 52 percent of the NCAA delegates approved Prop 48, and it became a bylaw to go into effect in 1986. (Under NCAA bylaws, the measure needed only a simple majority to pass.) As consolation—not well received—to objectors, the rule included a provision allowing recruits whose qualifications fell below either a high school 2.0 GPA or the 700/15 SAT/ACT score, but not both, to be considered "partial qualifiers," meaning they could receive an athletic scholarship but could not practice or play during their freshman year. Prop 48 salved anxieties of those who worried that schools—usually others than their own—were admitting and exploiting unqualified students just to build winning teams. Also, some African American spokesmen, chiefly sociologist Harry Edwards and professional tennis star Arthur Ashe, took a different stance, asserting that Prop 48 standards were too low and did not send a strong enough message to young blacks that education mattered. But resentment seethed in black administrators and coaches.[36]

Presidents Mishoe and Johnson continued to press the NCAA to modify Prop 48. At the 1986 NCAA convention, both spoke passionately in favor of a new measure, Proposition 14, that would eliminate standardized test scores as criteria for "initial qualifiers." Delegates soundly defeated the measure, 47–289.[37] A year later, Raymond M. Burse, president of the historically black Kentucky State University, joined the drive against test scores when Division II schools debated whether to institute their own Prop 48. Burse, adopting an autonomy stance, argued that a 2.0 GPA in a high school core curriculum was all that was necessary and that he, not the NCAA, should determine how to provide educational opportunity to his institution's students. He too lost the battle; Division II adopted Prop 48 criteria in its own Proposition 64.[38] (Because member schools in Division III did not award athletic scholarships, they remained free to admit athletes according to their own criteria.)

The clash over standards exploded in 1989. The previous year, presidents of the Southeastern Conference had voted to stop awarding scholarships to freshman athletes who had not satisfied all Prop 48 standards, thereby eliminating partial qualifiers from their conference. In January 1989, the NCAA voted narrowly to apply the Southeastern Conference rule to all of Division I. Henceforth, no freshman could receive an athletic scholarship without satisfying both the GPA and the test score requirements of Prop 48. According to its proponents, the new rule, named Prop 42, was necessary because unscrupulous coaches were circumventing Prop 48 by admitting partial qualifiers, then having them take bogus or "gut" courses to become eligible to play. Because many partial qualifiers were African Americans, black coaches bristled over Prop 42. On January 14, Georgetown University's basketball coach, John Thompson, protested by leaving the court before a game against Boston College and announced that he refused to coach again until the NCAA—which he called a "racist organization"—revised its policy. Thompson's radical act provoked a heated response. Frederick Whidden, president of the University of South Alabama, sneered, "I don't give a damn what John Thompson did. He doesn't run this [NCAA] program. If I was the president of Georgetown, it'd be the last time he walked."[39]

After two games, Thompson ended his boycott because the Presidents Commission backtracked and recommended postponing implementation of Prop 42. The next year, the NCAA restored the partial qualifier provision for Division I and decreed that scholarships for partial qualifiers in basketball and football would not be counted against the aid limits legislated for those teams. These moves revealed the power that coaches held over the NCAA and academic reformers. Not only could coaches now recruit and stockpile academically at-risk basketball and football athletes, but also the school, not the athletic department, would have to pay for their first-year scholarships.

The potential for academic fraud returned, as unprepared freshmen could be guided into remedial and other courses that could make them eligible to play as sophomores. William Atchley, who had lost the battle for reform when he was president of Clemson and now was head of the University of the Pacific, was again forced to admit the weakness of presidents in the athletic realm. Opposing the compromises, he confessed, "The coaches seem to have a lot of muscle, and I don't know why that's true, except that the college presidents, and even the . . . rest of the NCAA, don't have the intestinal fortitude to stand up and reaffirm what the membership had voted for [in Prop 42]."[40] Coach Knight, with usual bluster, reacted with an expression of his fraternity's entitlement by scoffing that he doubted that "presidents have ever gotten together and told the chemistry department what the hell to teach or how to lecture. I don't know why they are any more qualified to tell the athletics department what the hell to do."[41] As with the one-year scholarship, coaches' interests prevailed over the welfare of student athletes and the attempted intrusion of presidents.

Still, the crusade for academic reform survived, not just in the Presidents Commission, but now among some members of the U.S. Congress. In the House of Representatives, Tom McMillen, a Maryland Democrat and former Rhodes scholar who had played basketball at the University of Maryland and in the National Basketball Association (NBA)—at 6'11" he holds the distinction of being the tallest person ever to serve in Congress—convinced a congressional subcommittee to begin hearings on "out-of-control" intercollegiate athletics. He also published a book, *Out of Bounds*, which argued that money and unethical conduct were poisoning college sports. McMillen railed especially at the academic degradation in college athletics. "The message is that the rules of academia do not apply to sports stars," he wrote. "Nor do the rules of admission. Nor the rules of class attendance and course requirements. Not even the rules governing test scores and grades."[42] In 1991, McMillen introduced the College Athletics Reform Act, which would redistribute NCAA revenues on a more equitable basis and create a new Board of Presidents that would exercise broad powers over college sports with little opportunity for coaches or the NCAA to reverse their initiatives.[43]

McMillen's bill failed to make it out of committee, but the sharpened attention from Congress roused the NCAA to scurry to avoid federal regulation. (Besides McMillen, New Jersey's Senator Bill Bradley, another All-American basketballer and NBA star, had also threatened federal intervention.) In 1991, the annual NCAA meeting, dubbed a "reform convention," passed legislation directed at cost saving and softening time demands on athletes in Division

I schools. One measure set a weekly limit of 20 hours of supervised practice and playing time that coaches could require of their athletes during a season and 8 hours per week during off-season. The convention also voted to phase out athletic dorms, limit training table meals, reduce coaching staffs (slightly), and cut back on recruiting. The reforms were more cosmetic than substantial. The 20-hour rule did not include conditioning workouts, study of films, and "voluntary" captain's practices, all of which could double weekly athletic time commitments. And the economizing steps had only minimal impact on most athletic budgets.[44] As in the past, the NCAA danced around major changes and mainly tried to ward off intrusion from outside forces by making piecemeal adjustments.

"Keeping Faith with the Student Athlete"

While the NCAA, the ACE, and the presidents struggled with pressures to reform, another group attempted to insinuate itself on behalf of what it believed to be exploited college athletes. The John S. and James L. Knight Foundation originated in 1940 as a small fund that aided needy college students hailing from Ohio communities where Knight newspapers were published. By the end of the 1980s, however, it had evolved into a $400 million operation dedicated to promoting education, the arts, and journalism. According to its mission statement, "We seek to bestir the people into an awareness of their own condition, provide inspiration for their thoughts and rouse them to pursue their true interests."[45] With these intentions, in 1989 the foundation created the Knight Commission on Intercollegiate Athletics, assigning it to investigate current conditions and propose a reform agenda. Under the cochairmanship of William C. Friday, former head of the University of North Carolina system, and Father Theodore M. Hesburgh, president emeritus of the University of Notre Dame, the commission launched its inquiry, guided by a belief that "abuses in athletics had reached proportions threatening the very integrity of higher education, which is one of the principal program interests of the Foundation."[46] Their final report, *Keeping Faith with the Student Athlete: A New Model for Intercollegiate Athletics,* published in 1991 after more than a year of study, reflected the commission's goal "to place the well-being of the student-athlete at the forefront of our concerns."[47] The document outlined a series of reforms and, like the ACE previously, laid responsibility for implementing them at the feet of college and university presidents.

The commission was no enemy of athletics. "The value and successes of college sport should not be overlooked," the report stated. "They are the foundation of our optimism for the future."[48] But the assumed drift of athletics away from educational missions in the nation's largest institutions caused investigators to focus on major schools and conferences. Of sixty-four conference commissioners, faculty athletics representatives, coaches, and student athletes who testified before the commission, all but two had affiliations with NCAA Division I schools. It was in these places, the commission's final report stated, that "the educational context for collegiate athletic competition is pushed aside," leaving "a self-justifying enterprise whose connection with learning is tainted by commercialism and incipient cynicism."[49] The report continued, "It is time to get back to first principles. Intercollegiate athletics exist first and foremost for the student-athletes who participate," and "the reforms we deem essential start with respect for the dignity of the young men and women who compete and the conviction that they occupy a legitimate place as students on our campuses." Moreover, "The root difficulty is not creating a 'level playing field.' It is insuring that those on the field are students as well as athletes."[50]

To achieve its goals, the Knight Commission proposed a comprehensive "one-plus-three" model for change that encompassed practically every aspect of the college sports enterprise. The "one" was elevation of presidential authority over all matters of athletic governance (finance, hiring, administration) on their campuses, over the conferences to which their teams belonged, over NCAA legislation, and over athletic involvement in commercial television.

The "three" consisted of:

1. Academic integrity, meaning the NCAA should strengthen initial eligibility requirements; that the letter of intent to enroll signed by high school athletes take into account the athlete's, not the team's, best interest; that athletic scholarships be offered on a five-year basis to account for time demands on a student athlete; that ongoing eligibility to play depend upon progress toward a degree; and that NCAA certification of a school's athletic program depend upon a school's graduation rates in revenue sports such as football and basketball.
2. Financial integrity, meaning athletic expenditures should be reduced; athletic scholarships cover the full costs of attendance, including personal and miscellaneous expenses; funds raised from independent booster organizations be administered by the institution's financial system, not independently; the NCAA more equitably distribute revenues from basketball television contracts; a coach's outside income, such as from shoe and equipment contracts, be controlled by the institution; coaches receive long-term contracts; and general institutional funds supplement athletic revenues to lessen the responsibility of revenue sports to fund nonrevenue sports.
3. Certification, meaning NCAA accreditation to insure an athletic program's integrity should be applied to all institutions granting athletic aid;

every university undertake annual audits of its athletic program; and the
principles stated in the Knight Commission report guide the certification
process.[51]

In its closing section, "Putting Principles into Action," the report advised
each constituency of its responsibilities. Presidents were warned, "The burden
is on you to insist that athletics reform is a matter of utmost concern to your
institution's *academic* priorities."[52] Chairs of governing boards were told that
without their support for their presidents, "we do not know how reform can
be accomplished."[53] Faculty were admonished, "You cannot remain true to
the tradition you bear by permitting athletes to masquerade as students."[54]
Athletic directors must "transform the athletics culture on your campus . . .
from one in which winning is everything to one in which competition is
grounded in the 'one-plus-three' model."[55] Coaches were urged to emphasize
the value of a college degree and were warned that "if intercollegiate sport will
not police itself, others will."[56] Alumni were told to "insist that [their school's]
athletics program is directed along ethical lines."[57] And student athletes were
encouraged to prepare for the day their playing career was over, and "the
best place to do that is in the classroom, the library and the laboratory."[58]
The report ended with an expression of support for the NCAA, telling critics
that "handcuffing the NCAA is no way to advance athletics reform," but also
counseling the NCAA to accept presidential control and simplify its rules
and procedures.

The Knight reforms, though encompassing in scope, created only a slight
shift, not a full turning point. In 1993, the NCAA did vote to begin certification for all Division I athletics programs, requiring reviews of academic
integrity, fiscal responsibility, and institutional control. Significantly, the process was to be overseen by the NCAA, not by academic accrediting agencies,
and no provision was made to penalize an institution that failed certification.
(The certification process has since been abandoned.) In 1992 the NCAA also
attempted to revise eligibility standards for freshman athletes by replacing
Proposition 48 with Proposition 16. The new rule created a sliding scale
for initial eligibility, allowing a GPA higher than 2.0 in high school core
courses to offset a score below 700 or 15 on standardized tests and a test score
above 700 or 15 to offset a GPA below 2.0. Proposition 16 still riled black
coaches because the standardized test scores continued to be important,
and a threatened boycott of March Madness basketball games by the Black
Coaches Association forced the NCAA to postpone implementation of Prop
16 till 1996, then to overlook SAT or ACT scores completely if a GPA on core
courses was high enough. Black coaches backed down, but protests of racial
discrimination continued.[59]

In recent years, the Knight Commission has focused its efforts on costs and spending in college athletics. Believing that "sustained financial reform is necessary to maintain the health of college sports," the commission began in 2013 to compile an online interactive database that compared athletic spending with academic spending at public Division I institutions. The database, updated annually, is intended to create greater transparency in athletic budgets and to correct the imbalance between the two types of spending.[60] Whether the comparative information has resulted in more restrained athletic spending or in incentives for schools to catch up to or outspend rivals remains to be seen.

Consequences, Expected and Unexpected

By the mid-1990s, the contradictions that characterized college sports had become starker than ever. Several factors bolstered impressions that the NCAA had become a rich and powerful—even imperious—ruling body. Though it had surrendered control of revenues from televised football games, its ever-mushrooming contracts for broadcast of the Division I men's basketball tournament more than compensated for the loss.[61] Also, the Supreme Court had ruled in the Tarkanian lawsuit that the NCAA was not a "state actor" and therefore did not have to abide by due process, as protected by the 14th Amendment, in its investigations and hearings.[62] This prerogative enabled the NCAA to freely conduct intensive, often secret investigations into alleged rule violations that had saturated the 1970s and 1980s. And all athletic programs still depended on the NCAA to organize and fund national championships in many sports.

Starting in the 1970s, restructuring of the NCAA enabled a significant power shift that hobbled the association's authority. Prior to formation of its three divisions, the NCAA had functioned as a democratic association in which each member voted on every issue and bylaw. But inside a separate Division I, major schools and conferences created a platform from which they could use their size and wealth to act more independently. Big-time schools now focused on raising money in earnest—from boosters as well as from television—and spending it—on coaches' salaries, recruiting, and lavish facilities. Moreover, debates over propositions to enforce academic standards proved that special interests, such as advocates for African Americans as well as coaches seeking to recruit blue-chip athletes regardless of their preparation for college, would resist any threats to their causes. And amid all the scandals, while the NCAA clung insistently to the ideal of amateurism, the reality of commercialism and scandal made the ideal an ever-fading dream.[63] Every time the NCAA created a rule to sustain amateurism, ingenious schemers found ways around it.

While the NCAA was reconstituting itself, it also drifted further from its academic mission. Nothing reveals this separation better than the changing structure of NCAA's bureaucracy. In 1953, eleven of sixteen members of the NCAA Council, the NCAA's highest body of management, were faculty representatives and five were athletic directors. By 1987, 70 percent of the NCAA's new Management Council had deep roots in purely athletic affairs: twenty-nine of forty-four-members were athletic directors and two were conference directors.[64] At the same time, coaches increasingly steered or blocked NCAA legislation that might impinge on their interests. For example, in the 1980s, coaches and their allies beat back or modified measures to reduce the number of allowable athletic scholarships and to cut back the maximum number of Division I basketball games, undermining NCAA executive director Dick Schultz's hope for a "new model" that would restore balance between athletics and academics.[65]

By the 1970s, then, there was in place a formidable college sports establishment, dominated by individuals—almost all of them men—who had backgrounds in, and loyalty to, athletic endeavor, and who lacked links to their employer's academic mission other than to do what they could to protect their athletes from ineligibility due to classroom deficiencies. This establishment has overseen events, positive and negative, that have characterized the enterprise ever since. The Knight Commission may not have concluded that college sports were infested with a "stench," as the *New York Times* characterized it, but it did see clearly that the enterprise had gone awry and it earnestly wanted to reconnect the enterprise to its institutional roots. Success was, at best, limited. The quest for money and a win-at-all-costs mentality proved too strong to conquer.

The scandals, the separation of athletics from academics, and the apparent decline in the welfare of student athletes were of a piece. All had been set in motion well before the 1980s, but several episodes—turning points—created a crisis by the end of that decade. The development in Division I and, somewhat, in Divisions II and III as well, of a contractual model—the expectation that a varsity athlete owed loyalty and obedience to a coach above all other elements in the institution—undermined the athlete's status as student and opened the door to fraud and exploitation.

7   The M Connection: Media and Money

In 1970, little-known University of Louisville, originally a small, private institution, merged into the Kentucky state system of higher education and began a journey that brought it fame, an increase in its endowment, more enrollments, more faculty, more research funds, and an expansive building program that included the Papa John's Cardinal Stadium, boasting 42,000 seats painted cardinal red after the university's team color. (Opened in 1998, the stadium now boasts 55,000 seats.) What propelled this ascent? Not Louisville's arts and sciences college; not its medical center, not the city or the state. It was the Entertainment and Sports Programming Network, better known as ESPN.

Louisville's push for sports prominence and media exposure began in earnest when John W. Shumaker, the university's president from 1995 to 2002, forged a bond with ESPN. A Ph.D. in classical Greek studies, Shumaker used a disarming smile and penchant for planning to convince the school's trustees that athletic distinction could enhance the entire university. His first efforts in this direction were to build the stadium and hire Tom Jurich as athletic director. Appointed in 1997, Jurich had been a Kodak All-American and Academic All-American kicker and backup quarterback at Northern Arizona University and had played briefly in the National Football League before finding his calling in athletic administration. Slope-shouldered, beefy, and affable, Jurich acted as foreman for Shumaker's blueprint. The two knew that a sparkly new stadium needed a successful football team to bring about the changes they desired. In 1997, the team had a 1-win, 10-loss record. That would not do. So Jurich brought in a new coach, John L. Smith, who installed an up-tempo, high-scoring offense, just the thing for television.

Meanwhile, ESPN was aggressively seeking to fill its 24-hour all-sports format with college football broadcasts outside the traditional Saturday afternoon time slot. Its programmers already had convinced a few schools to schedule games to be aired on Thursday nights, but now they looked to expand into Tuesday nights as well. At the time, Mike Slive, destined to become one of the most influential leaders in college sports as commissioner of the Southeastern Conference, was commissioner of Conference USA, to which Louisville belonged, and he saw an opportunity to give his member schools greater national visibility. In 2001, Slive signed an eight-year agreement with ESPN to televise ten midweek football games per year. Although some conference members balked at scheduling games on a school night, Jurich had no qualms. In 2001, ESPN and its sister, ESPN2, telecast five Louisville football games, and six in 2002, including four on Tuesday and Thursday. The partnership worked for both Louisville and ESPN. Coach Smith's high-octane style drew viewers to ESPN's week-night telecasts and national attention to the university. Direct benefits to Louisville included television revenue, a revived men's basketball program energized by Coach Rick Pitino, plus a donor- and corporation-funded $252 million building program that by 2012 had erected a football practice facility, baseball stadium, soccer stadium, golf center, rowing center, and natatorium. Between 2001 and 2015, the University of Louisville switched conferences twice, first to the Big East and, starting in 2015, the Atlantic Coast Conference, the latter of which promised to reward the school with $16 million a year from its television agreement with ESPN. By 2014, the Louisville football team had played in bowl games thirteen of the previous sixteen years, and the men's and women's basketball teams had attained high rankings in many of those years. The athletic department's budget ballooned from $14 million in 1997 to $77 million in 2012. Whether related to athletic success or not, Louisville experienced other improvements: research funding doubled, test scores of applicants rose, and new president James R. Ramsey raised $140 million for academic, research, and building purposes.[1]

The University of Louisville story illustrates the power that media—chiefly television, but print, radio, and Internet as well—have come to exert over college sports, almost always with eager cooperation from the institutions involved. As Mark Shapiro, former head of programming and production at ESPN, has testified, "Louisville came to us and said, 'We'll play anyone, anywhere, anytime.'" For athletic administrators, the results have been gratifying. Tom Jurich told the *New York Times* in 2014, "If it wasn't for ESPN, we would be a fraction of what we are today."[2]

No single event marks the major turning point, but between 1995 and 2001, media and money intertwined with college sports to create one of America's most powerful entertainment entities. In spite of the swollen amounts of dollars to be earned from the NCAA television basketball contract; the burgeoning number of football bowl games; the dizzying number of games broadcast on local, regional, national, and conference TV sports networks; and the gifts, modest and gargantuan, from donors, that entertainment business operates in a manner that would frighten a corporate CFO: They almost always lose money and act as a financial drain on the institutions whose names are attached to the teams involved. In 2013–14, of the 340 or so college athletics programs in Division I where most opportunities for income lie, fewer than two dozen had incomes that exceeded expenses. Of course, at many schools, especially those in the NCAA's Divisions II and III, sports function as an extracurricular activity without expectations of breaking even financially.

There is reason to conclude that athletic budgets everywhere are whirling out of control, and, when compared to stringencies placed on academic budgets, are creating an athletic-academic divide that troubles observers inside and outside the academy. Those who oversee college sports, from coaches to athletic directors to presidents, harbor a three-pronged motivation that prevents them from reversing the tide: (1) They want more money so they can spend more. (2) They need more money because their competition is getting more. (3) They are caught in a spiral where they need money because they think it will enable them to win, and they need to win because they think success on the field is going to bring more money. Media exposure is one means to these ends. The big money that now flows into athletic departments from television provokes resentment from the academic side, but those in athletics who bask in the limelight of an adored sport exude an attitude that is simultaneously cynical and realistic. As fabled Alabama football coach Paul "Bear" Bryant once quipped, "It's kind of hard to rally 'round a math class."[3]

On the Air, Anywhere, Anytime

Fans have always been eager to rally 'round their football team, especially if the guys were invited to a bowl game, and today bowls have become television phenomena in the extreme. They were not always so. The Rose Bowl, granddaddy of them all, was first played in 1902 to help finance the Pasadena, California, Rose Parade and has continued uninterrupted since 1916. The Orange (1933), Sugar (1935), Cotton (1937), Gator (1946), and Fiesta (1968) bowls all were launched to promote tourism at their cities' homes: Miami,

New Orleans, Dallas, Jacksonville, and Phoenix, respectively. Between the 1930s and the present, dozens of other bowl games have been conceived for the same purpose; some failed early—such as Fresno's Raisin Bowl and Tampa's Cigar Bowl—while others survived, sometimes feebly.

Beginning in the 1970s, television rights fees replaced ticket sales as principal sources of bowl game revenue, and currently, the networks that broadcast the games exercise considerable control over when those events take place. No longer strictly a New Year's Day attraction, bowl games—by 2014 there were thirty-eight, including Bitcoin St. Petersburg (formerly Beef O'Brady) Bowl and the Famous Idaho Potato Bowl—entice (or exhaust) TV viewers from mid-December through early January. Unsurprisingly, ESPN owns eleven of these extravaganzas. Though sometimes half or more of the stadium seats are empty, what matters most to the schools involved is the presumed prestige of appearing on a televised bowl game. (One wonders whether someone who has played in the Beef O'Brady Bowl will want to brag about it to his grandchildren forty years later.) Major bowls are spread across several days to attract prime-time television audiences. The BCS National Championship Game, begun in 1998 to determine the best football team in Division I, once culminated the bowl season; it now is replaced by a four-team playoff that lasts well into the new year.[4] ESPN anted up $5.64 *billion* to televise the event, plus six associated bowl games, each year between 2014 and 2025.[5]

No doubt: football is, and has been, the big money-earner. Total revenues from football at schools that earned the most money from this sport rose 150 percent between 2000 and 2011, an annualized increase of 9 percent.[6] Dollar amounts are staggering. In 2011–12, football at national champion University of Alabama earned $82 million, against $37 million in expenses, and University of Texas football produced $104 million, against expenses of $25 million. Yet these two are exceptional: Alabama not only earned more but also spent more than any football school to achieve its number 1 ranking, and Texas earns millions from its Longhorn television network as well as from licensing of its logo on merchandise. All top-25 football programs profited in 2011–12, but 51 others—43 percent of those in the then-Football Bowl Subdivision—lost money.[7] Profits from football are used to fund non-revenue sports, including women's teams, but also, football itself is a very costly sport, with large rosters, high-salaried head coaches, multiple assistant coaches, travel and equipment expenses, and medical services. Though a football team often costs more than it earns, administrators are willing to see it as a loss leader, the merchandising ploy to use a money loser to attract attention.

Football is not the only college sport to embrace the television cameras; basketball entered the same courtship. Though schools traditionally have scheduled most basketball games on weekends, weeknight games are not uncommon because a basketball season includes nearly three times as many contests as football. This situation matches ESPN's needs perfectly, giving the network multiple opportunities for broadcasts throughout the week. Cheaper to produce than football games, basketball telecasts fit neatly into two-hour time slots. Consequently, ESPN worked out relatively inexpensive deals with major conferences in the late 1970s and began airing games during weekday evenings, giving the Big Ten and Big East a regular time block on Monday nights. Happy for the national exposure, the schools involved readily surrendered to the network's scheduling. Broadcasts enabled viewers across the country to see teams they ordinarily would not be able to watch, giving coaches new means of recruiting high school stars who now could view a team on TV and be bedazzled by an opportunity to play for that school before a future national audience.[8] One contrast illustrates how television coverage of basketball exploded. On the first Saturday in February 1983, Chicago-area fans could view four college basketball games on two local networks. On the first Saturday in February 2009, Chicagoans had their pick of thirty-seven college basketball games, broadcast across eighteen national, cable, and regional networks.[9]

Most college basketball games lack the large viewership common to football, except for one time of the year: the March Madness of the NCAA Division I Men's Basketball Tournament. Unlike Division I football, where, until recently, multiple bowl games left a murky path to the number-one ranking because there was no definitive way to identify the champion, the basketball tournament determines an undisputed national champion in an elimination tournament, ending in an exciting climax of Final Four competition. By the 1980s, the NCAA and CBS realized the boon the tournament could generate, and they negotiated ever-mounting dollar amounts for broadcast rights. In 1995, the beginning of the new media-and-money era, CBS agreed to its first megasports deal when it signed to pay the NCAA $1.725 billion to telecast basketball games, including March Madness, for the 1995–2002 period, and upped its commitment to $6 billion for 2000–2013. Then, in 2010, the NCAA worked out a new deal, this one with CBS and Turner Broadcasting, that pays $10.8 billion over fourteen years.[10] Basketball contracts provide the NCAA with 95 percent of its annual revenues, most of which it distributes to member schools (see below), and since 1979, when the duel between Indiana State's Larry Bird and Indiana State's "Magic" Johnson promised to light up the tournament—a promise it did not deliver; it was a dull game—television viewership of the final tournament games has usually equaled or surpassed that of the highest-rated bowl games. In 2013, some 15.7 million TV sets tuned to the March Madness final won by Louisville over Michigan.[11] Currently, ESPN has an additional contract with the NCAA for $55 million to televise the Division I women's basketball tournament, the Baseball College World Series, and twenty other college championships through 2016.

In recent years, the proliferation of on-air sports media has been extraordinary. The Disney Corporation owns numerous networks that broadcast college sports—ABC, ESPN, ESPN2, ESPNU—and profits handsomely, especially from ESPN, which in 2014 charged $5.54 monthly to each of its 100 million cable subscribers. But ESPN is not alone. Fox Sports Network, a division of Fox Broadcasting Company, entered the market in 2007 and currently holds broadcast rights to Big Ten and Pac 12 football games, plus Pac 12 and Big East basketball games. Both CBS and NBC also have launched separate sports programming networks, which air college basketball (CBS) and men's ice hockey (NBC). The newest and potentially most lucrative arrangements have been made by each of the power conferences in Division I—Pac 12, Big Ten (actually 12), Big 12 (actually 10), Southeastern Conference, and Atlantic Coast Conference—with the television industry. These conferences sport their own networks that broadcast "nonrevenue" as well as revenue sports programming. The Southeastern Conference, for example, has joined with ESPN to create a network to air events from all twenty-one sports that conference schools sponsor, including forty-five football games, one hundred men's basketball games, sixty women's basketball games, and seventy-five baseball games per year. SEC network also presents original content and analysis programs. On the air all day every day, the SEC network annually provides 8,700 hours of its own conference sports. Annual revenues to the conference, generated by fees of around $1.40 per month that the network charges to cable television subscribers, are estimated to reach $500–600 million, or more than $35 million for each conference school.[12] This money does not include $55 million that CBS pays the Southeastern Conference each year to air premier conference football games. Thus, for the major schools, TV exposure has become standard. For example, on an ordinary weekend in 2013 when all sixteen Pac 12 football teams were playing each other, four of the eight games were on the Pac 12 network, two were on ESPN2, one was on Fox Sports 1, and one—the premier game between Stanford and USC—was on ABC. Division II and III schools also are benefiting from on-air and on-screen exposure, though their shares are crumbs.

Media and money clearly drove the conference realignment frenzy that occurred between 2009 and 2013, at least among the big-time schools. The "power" conferences, having created their own television networks, looked to broaden their viewer markets and reap rewards from sponsoring postseason basketball and football playoffs, postseason games to name conference champions. Consequently, in 2009, the Big Ten, already having added Penn State as an eleventh member, accepted Nebraska, and in 2010, the Pac 12 added Colorado and Utah. In 2014, Maryland and Rutgers also joined the Big Ten. In 2011, Texas A&M and Missouri bolted the Big 12 for the Southeastern Conference, and in 2012, the Atlantic Coast Conference grew to fifteen. Meanwhile, the Big East, chiefly a basketball conference, underwent turbulent change, marked by the departures for other conferences by West Virginia, Pittsburgh, Syracuse, Notre Dame, Louisville, and Rutgers. The remaining Big East schools—DePaul, Georgetown, Marquette, Providence, St. Johns, Seton Hall, and Villanova—were joined by Creighton, Butler, and Xavier. A new American Athletic Conference now contains fourteen football-playing schools, some of which had been members of the Big East. These additions and subtractions have been costly. Fees for both entry to a conference and exit from one range as high as $50 million, yet most have been willing to pay the price in order to reap anticipated windfalls from TV deals down the road. Stringency in the national economy seemed to make no difference; schools moved around virtually oblivious to the financial crisis of 2008–13. Second-tier conferences also shuffled membership to more easily schedule football championships and gain access to television money, but they, and many lesser conferences, also realigned for cost-saving reasons, mainly to make intraconference travel less expensive.[13]

Until 1984, the NCAA controlled football on television—and other sports as well, except basketball. Then, as noted in Chapter 4, the Supreme Court released schools and conferences to make their own broadcast deals. In his passionate dissent to that decision, Justice Byron "Whizzer" White, the former college halfback, issued an ominous warning that the Court was allowing the successful litigants to subjugate the NCAA's educational goals "to the purely competitive commercialism of [an] 'every school for itself' approach to television contract bargaining." If alive today, White could look at the college sports scene, shake his head, and mutter, "I told you so."[14]

Money Madness

The American public has generally reckoned college sports in terms of big-time football and men's basketball, a reasonable view, since these are the sports that dominate television broadcasts and other media attention. These sports also are where the money is, and that money has transformed the landscape in significant ways. But not necessarily in the way the public has assumed.

Opportunities for lucrative dollar amounts from athletics, at least at major schools, seem to be everywhere: television contracts, ticket sales, alumni and booster donations, distributions from the NCAA, sales of apparel sporting the school logo. Yet the vast majority of college sports programs lose money, often millions of dollars. In 2012, for example, just 23 out of 340 Division I athletic programs ended the year in the black, and the average deficit among the rest was more than $7 million. What accounts for such shortfalls? The simple answer—indeed, the only answer—is that though athletic departments spend more, often much more, than they make, they seldom have to worry about their excess because their home institutions tolerate the deficits and often make up for them. In the 1970s, the NCAA required that athletic budgets be self-sustaining, but most sports programs skirted this rule by relying on subsidies from their school's operating budgets. In 2012, for example, Rutgers, a state university, propped up its athletic department with $28 million in aid, or 44 percent of its $64 million athletic budget. Between 2005 and 2012, the Rutgers athletic department spent more than $100 million more than it raised. Also in 2012, five of the eleven athletic programs with annual budgets of $30–40 million received half or more of their operating funds from their parent schools.[15] Even the wealthiest athletic departments needed institutional subsidies. At the University of Alabama in 2012, an athletic budget of $125 million included $5.25 million from the school, even though sports generated an $11 million surplus. Auburn University's $109 million athletic budget contained $4.3 million from the school in spite of a $5.4 million surplus.[16]

Subsidies, however, are not always sufficient to plug budgetary gaps. By fall 2013, the University of Colorado's athletic department carried an accumulated debt to the university of almost $30 million, in spite of an annual institutional contribution of $5.5 million. In almost all instances, deficits were covered from student fees, as well as from state support.[17] Like the subsidies, student fees can be substantial. In 2010, at Longwood University in Farmville, Virginia, $2,022 out of the $9,855 charged to each student for tuition and fees supported the school's Division I athletic program.[18] Thus, nonathletes and taxpayers foot the bill for athletic profligacy.

Athletic spending is not only high but also expanding rapidly. According to a study undertaken by the NCAA for the years 2004–2012, median expenditures at the 120 Football Bowl Subdivision (formerly Division I-A—big-time athletics) schools rose by 94 percent—from $29 million to $56.3 million in constant dollars—and outlays for sports at other Division I schools, including those without football programs, climbed by almost as much.[19] Spending per student-athlete compared to spending per ordinary college student reveals an extraordinary gulf. The American Institutes for Research's Delta Cost Project discovered that between 2005 and 2010, average spending per athlete in Football Bowl Subdivision schools rose from $61,000 to more than $92,000 (a 51 percent increase), while per capita spending for all other students rose from $11,000 to $14,000 per student (a 27 percent increase). At the highest-spending athletic schools, the difference in 2010 was even wider: $150,000 per athlete versus $16,500 per nonathlete.[20] To be sure, a football or ice hockey squad is more expensive than an English class or a debating club, but lavish spending on sports can be hard to justify when classrooms are crumbling, faculties are being reduced, and research resources are scarce.

The Delta Cost Project found that across Division I, distributions of athletic expenditures are remarkably similar. Just over a third of budgets in 2010 went to salaries and benefits (rising by about 10 percent annually), about 15–20 percent to facilities and equipment, a little over a tenth to game expenses and travel, and 12–15 percent for "other expenses" such as fundraising and marketing. The remaining amounts, where the largest variations occurred, involved funds spent on scholarships (rising at about 8 percent annually). Football Bowl Subdivision schools devoted significantly less of their total budgets to scholarships than did other football schools and schools without a football team—around 14 percent as opposed to about 25 percent; mostly, the percentages were skewed because Football Bowl Subdivision schools spend more of their budgets on travel and marketing than do other Division I schools.[21]

The compensation category draws the most attention from journalists, economists, and the public because in it reside the earnings of celebrity coaches. Supposedly driven by market forces, salaries of coaches in revenue-producing sports, chiefly football and men's basketball, have soared, rising 55 percent between 2006 and 2011 alone.[22] According to figures compiled by the *USA Today* sports staff, in 2014, seventy-two Football Bowl Subdivision football coaches received base (institutional) salaries of more than $1 million, fifty-one received $2 million or more. The University of Alabama's Nick Saban topped the list with a total salary of $7,160,187.[23] Among Division I basketball coaches in 2014, thirty-five pocketed over $1 million and twenty-one of them received more than $2 million. The leader in this category was Duke University's Mike Krzyzewski, with an annual take of $9,682,032. The rarefied height of coaches' salaries often exists far above the messy surface of institutional predicaments. When John Calipari jumped from the University of Memphis to become head basketball coach at the University of Kentucky in 2009, he received an eight-year contract for $31.5 million, at a time when the state of Kentucky faced large deficits and reduced the university's total budget by 2 percent. And while Duke University in 2013 continued to struggle to recover from the 2009–11 financial crisis, it still gave Coach Krzyzewski a 35 percent raise.[24] In almost every case, football and basketball coaches were the highest-paid employees at their institution and, in state schools, the highest-paid public employees.

For many coaches, salary is just a start. A football or men's basketball coach can also benefit from a shower of bonuses for conventional and unconventional accomplishments. South Carolina's football coach Steve Spurrier can pull in up to $650,000 on top of his $3.3 million salary by winning nine or more games in a season. Louisville wanted to keep its football coach Charlie Strong, hired in 2010, so badly that it promised to pay him a bonus for every year he remained as coach until 2018. (He left for the University of Texas and a much larger salary in 2014 anyway.) Mike Leach, at Washington State, gets $25,000 each time his team beats football rival University of Washington. Some basketball coaches profit handsomely from contracts that promise to outfit their team with shoes and apparel from a certain company. Nike paid Arizona's men's coach Lute Olsen $500,000 in 2007, and premier women's coaches Geno Auriema at the University of Connecticut and Pat Summitt, formerly at the University of Tennessee, also garnered large payouts from shoe companies.[25] Coaches get to keep all this income even though they act in the name of their school in requiring their team to wear the shoes.[26] Only rarely does a coach receive credit for a team's academic accomplishments, but P. J. Fleck, Western Michigan's football coach, can bolster his $392,500 pay with a bonus for each player selected first- or second-team academic all-conference and first-team academic All-American. He also gets extra pay based on the team's grade point average.[27] On top of the bonuses, celebrity coaches might receive other perks, such as an automobile, travel in private jets, country-club membership, life insurance policy, and low-interest loans.

A football team that rarely compiles a winning record still can find extra income by becoming a sacrificial lamb. That is, a powerhouse football squad eager for a pushover victory to pad its record and give its players a respite from high-intensity competition may invite a supposedly weak team to its campus to suffer a drubbing but go home with extra cash. For example, in 2012, the little-regarded football team from Towson University traveled to Baton Rouge to play undefeated Louisiana State University, ranked number three in the nation. The Towson footballers lost 38–22 and pocketed $510,000 for showing up, a sum Louisiana State could easily afford because it sold out its 90,000-seat stadium regardless of the opponent. That same year, Idaho State was paid $600,000 to be slaughtered by Nebraska 73–7. To the sacrificial lambs, the games were less important than the marketing boost from playing a powerhouse. As Towson's athletic director commented after the Louisiana State game, "I think what it means for the university is a branding opportunity. It's another national television appearance. It's another chance for people to get to know who we are."[28] Nowhere in his statement did he mention whether being crushed physically and psychologically was worth $510,000 to the players.

The Arms Race

The urge for victory and the prestige accompanying it drive the hiring and compensating of high-profile coaches, plus the lavish expenditures on recruiting, facilities, and marketing. Because victory is the result of competition, spending is highly competitive as well. The outcome is the arms race, the continuing assumption that unless a team or school competes—keeps up with or surpasses rivals by building more and spending more—it will lose games, athletes, coaches, and respect; in other words, its brand will suffer. The arms race is usually funded by a combination of loans and donations. State schools, for example, often finance stadium construction and upgrades from bond issues, whose principal and interest payments are borne by the school, not usually by the athletic department. Just as frequently, wealthy benefactors bankroll projects, often with help from the federal tax code. Most schools that have an expensive varsity sports program are subsidized by some kind of booster club or foundation. Often, money from these organizations is substantial. In 2011, for example, Ohio State collected $38.7 million from boosters. These donors love their school team—usually football, basketball, or ice hockey—and are willing to pay to express their affection, for example, by forking over several thousand dollars in rights fees to purchase season tickets for basketball or football. That is, they pay a premium just so they can buy a prime ticket. In some circles, this might be considered a bribe; in college sports, it is a privilege.[29] In addition, donors can purchase special treatment such as priority parking and access to posh stadium clubs. Schools employ other creative ways to extract donor funds. In 2010, an athletic gift of $5,000 to the University of Arkansas would enable the donor's photograph to be printed in the Razorback football program. That same year, a contribution of $50,000 would enable a patron to travel with Stanford's football team.[30]

Boosters receive tax benefits for their largesse because the Internal Revenue Service treats these gifts as charitable, in the same category as donations to a library, church, or homeless shelter. Fans who pay fees for season tickets may write off 80 percent of the cost, and other athletic donations get full exemption. Thus, a Stanford donor who normally pays a 35 percent tax rate would have gotten a $17,500 tax deduction for a ride with the football team.[31] In consequence, ordinary citizens, including those with no interest in college sports or allegiance to a particular school, underwrite teams because of the tax breaks for donations made to support athletics. Bloomberg Financial estimates that the annual loss to the federal government as a result of such breaks approaches $1 billion.[32]

Sometimes donors come through in grandiose fashion. In 2005, for example, energy magnate and financier T. Boone Pickens gave his alma mater, Oklahoma State University, $165 million for athletics, chiefly to bring Oklahoma State sports to a competitive level with those of rival University of Oklahoma. His largesse refurbished the football stadium—renamed after the man himself—and built a village of facilities for the track, baseball, tennis, and women's soccer and equestrian teams. (Pickens also has lavished the academic side; Oklahoma State boasts a T. Boone Pickens School of Geology.)[33] More recently, University of Oregon alum Phil Knight, founder of Nike, funded a $68 million "Football Performance Center" at that school, a practice and relaxation facility only for athletes, replete with Nepalese rugs, Italian and Brazilian hardwood couches, leather chairs, barber shop, and locker room accessible by biometric thumbprint. (Knight also gave $27 million to the University of Oregon library that bears his name.) Not to be outdone, the University of Alabama has used funds from wealthy donors to renovate its football building to include marble floors, two huge therapy pools, a lounge surrounded by flat-screen televisions, a weight room the size of a small supermarket, and, yes, a waterfall.[34] Palaces such as these occupy the top tier of their kind, but country-club facilities for athletes have arisen at most big-time schools and even some lesser ones. The ongoing race to reward and attract athletes has few winners, but the fear of losing out loosens all reservations about the process. Critics claim colleges and universities are selling their souls to donors for the uncertain possibility of a winning team, but coaches and administrators are unabashed about the process. "We are the University of Nike," said Jeff Hawkins, senior associate athletic director of football administration and operations at the University of Oregon. "We embrace it. We tell that to our recruits."[35]

A principal goal of arms race combatants is to get a team into a bowl game or basketball championship, where, supposedly, publicity and ever more dollars await. Every team that makes it into these events garners media coverage, but the financial consequences are not so dependable. In 2014, each participant in the four major bowls earned $17 million, and the two teams in what was then the national football championship game each received $18 million. A team qualifying for the new four-team Division I football playoff reaps $35 million or more. Meanwhile, teams in minor bowls earned considerably less. The per-team payout for participating in the 2014 Famous Idaho Potato Bowl, for example, was $325,000.[36] These sums, whatever their size, are deceptive. Most conferences require a bowl participant to share its income with all conference schools, after covering travel and other expenses. Those expenses can be sizable. First, bowl sponsors usually expect a participating school to purchase a certain number of tickets—10,000 or more for a major bowl. If the school fails to resell all its tickets, which frequently happens, it must absorb the cost. Second, travel, lodging, and meal charges for athletes, coaches, trainers and other staff, cheerleaders, and band, usually for multiple nights, can reach hundreds of thousands of dollars. A conference might subsidize some expenses, but not everything. Because of a combination of payout sharing and costs of participation, between 2005 and 2011, 50 percent of schools that played in major bowl games lost money doing so, and percentages ran higher among competitors in minor bowls. Deficits ranged from tens of thousands to $2 million.[37] In this regard, then, schools not successful enough to participate in a bowl game may come out better; they share in the payout but do not have to shoulder the costs.

Returns from playing in the Division I men's 68-team basketball tournament are safer, though tournament teams still must share income among conference members. Roster sizes are relatively small (usually around 16 compared to more than 100 for football), and so participation expenses are far less than for football. Also, the surging income from the tournament's television contract ensures heavy rewards for competitors. For payout purposes, the NCAA, which controls the money and takes its own cut from tournament income, counts each tournament game played as a unit, and each bracket that a team reaches counts as a unit, so a team reaching the title game would have played in six brackets and earned six units (excluding the extra "play-in" games). Units accumulate on a six-year rolling basis, so the more years a team participates in the tournament and the more brackets it plays in, the more payout units it collects. In 2012, a unit was worth more than $245,000; just by keeping that unit for six years and not winning another tournament game, a school could reap more than $1.5 million (based on slight yearly increases in unit values). Though a school shares tournament income with its conference members, the more teams from a conference that compete in the tournament and the farther teams go in the brackets, the greater the earnings. Recently, each of the five power conferences regularly has placed five or more teams in the tournament, and many of those teams have advanced to the top Sweet Sixteen or Final Four, creating very large pools of cash allocations. One study estimated that in a six-year span, Big Ten schools could divide between $30 and $40 million from tournament participation. The same study projected that between 2014 and 2019 the perennial tournament team from Duke will have earned a minimum of $17 million and, with potential victories, much more.[38] No wonder there is an arms race.

Risks and Rewards

In this climate of obsession, how realistic are expectations that entering the arms race, winning championships, and seeking every opportunity for donations and branding will yield windfall benefits to a school as well as to its athletic program? Is there a connection, for example, between victory, television exposure, and increases in a school's popularity as measured by undergraduate enrollment and applications? On November 23, 1984, Boston College quarterback Doug Flutie threw a miraculous hail Mary pass for a last-second touchdown that beat heavily favored University of Miami in full view of millions of television viewers. The game's finish has been celebrated as one of the most dramatic in college football history. (What is not remembered is that CBS paid off Rutgers $80,000 to change the date of its game with Boston College so the network could televise the anticipated match between two highly publicized teams.) In the following three years, undergraduate applications to BC rose 30 percent. During the mid-'80s also, similar spikes in applications occurred at Georgetown, whose men's basketball team became a national power, and at Northwestern, after its football team reversed a long string of losing seasons and won a bid to the Rose Bowl.[39]

Athletic success does seem to create a Flutie effect, at least in the short term. A study by Harvard economist Douglas Chung concluded that when a school's football team rises from mediocre to excellent, its undergraduate applications increase on average by 18.7 percent. Cynics claim that the Flutie effect attracts college-bound youths more interested in the hoopla, parties, and free-flowing alcohol that accompany football games than in academic achievement.[40] But Chung's data indicate that the expanded pool includes applicants with high SAT scores as well as those with below-average academic qualifications. Schools do not invest in football or basketball to attract applicants, Chung observes, but a successful team has great appeal to a sports-crazed youth culture saturated in ESPN programming.[41] The relationship between a winning team and college applications is just that: a relationship, not necessarily cause and effect. One study concluded that college applicants valued jobs, internships, clubs, and intramural sports as more important to them than varsity sports.[42] And there is no evidence that the Flutie effect has made much of an appearance at Division II and III schools. Moreover, studies have not measured long-term patterns to show whether application numbers level off with continued athletic success or decline if a football or basketball team falls upon hard times. Still, the belief remains strong that, if other factors such as academic reputation and costs of enrolling are approximately equal, football or basketball prowess begets media exposure which begets applications.

What about the consequences of booster donations? Is there a "Pickens effect?" There is strong belief that it exists. Louisiana's former senator, Russell Long, a Louisiana State University alumnus and football fan, once likened athletic contributions to "fertilizer for a farmer," musing, "They increase the yield."[43] No doubt; big money makes a difference. In the years following Pickens's gift, Oklahoma State's football team, once a doormat in the Big 12 Conference, became a bowl-regular power. Moreover, regular donations to the school ballooned—$327 million in the four years before Pickens's munificence; $1.2 billion, including the Pickens money, in the four years afterward. Also, applications rose steadily, and several new academic buildings were financed.[44]

Largesse such as that from Pickens may produce desirable results, but when viewed from the other direction, the one presuming that athletic success incites alumni/ae and booster generosity, the picture is blurred at best. Economists have concluded that over the past forty years there has been no positive relationship between victory on the playing field and alumni/ae generosity. Not only is the extent of alumni/ae giving variable in relation to athletic success, but also there is no spillover effect in which athletic success increases donations to an institution's academic side. The only exception seems to be some positive response to a football team's appearance in a major bowl game and negative reaction to bad publicity from scandal and NCAA sanctions.[45] Also, the donors who usually respond most positively to winning teams are subway alumni, boosters who never attended their favorite college but are emotionally attached to its football or basketball teams and who contribute money exclusively for athletics.[46]

Counterintutively, the more the general public attaches itself to college sports, the less students become involved. Attendance at football and basketball games continues to rise—aided by huge investments in stadiums—but student sections are showing increasing numbers of vacant seats. According to a 2014 analysis by the *Wall Street Journal* of attendance records from some 50 public colleges with high-profile football teams, student attendance has declined by 7.1 percent since 2009. At the University of Florida, it fell by 22 percent between 2009 and 2013, and the drop was 11 percent between 2011 and 2013 at the University of Michigan. Meanwhile, enrollment at four-year colleges has increased markedly, up by 3.2 million between 2006 and 2011, though there have been slight decreases recently, as a result of ongoing problems in the U.S. economy and a reduction in size of the college-age birth cohort.[47] Reasons cited for the declining presence of students at games are soaring ticket prices, disappointing win-loss records, and the ease of watching a game on television—or on a tablet, computer, or smart phone—rather than in person.[48]

Some big-time football schools are trying to lure students back to the stadium by adding amenities such as broader food and beverage choices (a few have even started serving alcohol), more giveaways, and enhanced sound systems. The objective, however, is to keep current students interested so they become committed and generous alumni/ae. As Dan Rascher, sports management professor at the University of San Francisco, observed, "You're trying to turn those current students into former students who are still fans decades later. You want students, when they become alumni, to have that attachment and come back for the games, and that's what's concerning athletic departments."[49] Regardless of facts, the belief remains strong that sports opens the doorway to loyalty and contributions.

On December 1 2014, one school gave up on that faith, when the University of Alabama–Birmingham (UAB), a Division I school in the heart of a crazed college-football region, announced that it was shutting down its football program, along with two minor sports. University president Ray Watts, a Birmingham resident and alumnus of the school, made the decision after a comprehensive strategic planning study concluded there would be other ways to achieve financial growth and athletic success. UAB had been subsidizing $20 million of the athletic department's $30 million budget, and a consulting group had estimated that an additional $49 million would be needed over the succeeding five years on top of the $20 million per year plus $22 million to upgrade football facilities—all to keep the football team competitive with its Conference USA rivals. As Watts concluded in his announcement about the shutdown, "Investments in football were unlikely to produce a sustainable return relative to the required investments."[50] UAB rethought its priorities. Would others follow its lead? The results are not yet in, but the rising and staggering costs associated with the media and money madness can produce casualties as well as winners.[51]

Back in 1951, Lloyd Jordan, Harvard University's football coach and president of the American Football Coaches Association, candidly remarked, "We must recognize that colleges are in the entertainment business." That statement harbored a truth more prophetic than Jordan could have comprehended. Today, intercollegiate athletics is one of America's biggest entertainment industries as well as the centralizing activity and front door of practically every college and university campus. And though athletic budgets generally represent no more than 5 percent of an institution's overall finances, the multimillion-dollar dimensions of college sports make the enterprise a voracious seeker and expender.

The seeking and expending does not occur on a level playing field. Large financial gaps exist, even within the same conference, that box lower-income competitors into a dilemma: either spend more, and jeopardize financial stability, to compete with rivals, or hold the budgetary line and risk perpetual losing records, especially in high-exposure sports that give a school its reputation. In the mid-1970s, Stephen Horn, president of Long Beach State University, shook up big-time athletic schools by advocating that revenues from televised college football be shared more equitably by all colleges and universities that sponsored the sport. His colleagues quickly shot down the proposal, but others periodically have revived it. In 1989, Judd Heathcote, men's basketball coach at Michigan State, offered a plan for distributing only $6 million of March Madness television income to participating teams and sending equal shares of the remaining $20 million to each school in Division I.[52] Again, no success. In 2012, Jeffrey Orleans, former executive director of the Ivy League, similarly suggested distributing March Madness money equitably across all 340-plus Division I institutions to provide less-wealthy institutions with financial stability and generate more competitive rivalries. Like earlier proposals, this one sparked immediate resistance. John Lombardi, president of Louisiana State University, mused that he could never convince his trustees to altruistically share income with schools that were "losing their shirts" on athletics. Moreover, he somewhat disingenuously pointed out, the federal government does not allocate research grants equally. Those moneys, he said, like television money, are distributed unevenly "in terms of concentration and superstar competition."[53] Lombardi's stance attests that athletic lucre, once in the pocket, will probably not ever be extracted.

The business aspects of the college sports enterprise have become so complex that many athletic directors and conference executives no longer have roots in the "jock culture" of coaching and playing; rather, they come to their jobs with degrees and experience in business and law—and they are almost all white and male.[54] They engage in a commercialized dance of public relations called branding. This situation is not new. College sports have been integrated into American commercial culture since a railroad company sponsored the first intercollegiate rowing race between Yale and Harvard in 1852. But at present, the language of marketing, which makes a team, its nickname, and its insignia a brand, signifies ways that institutions make athletics their principal means of advertising themselves in the same ways that McDonalds and Toyota advertise themselves.

The process turns young men and women into "product," whose athletic skills are valued assets. As one administrator who assists college athletes bluntly confessed, "My job is to protect The Entertainment Product. . . . It is who and what these kids are. You can hate that, you can hate the system. But at the end of the day, it's who they are. They're the raw material in a multibillion-dollar sports and entertainment business."[55] To be sure, the main components of the entertainment business are football and men's basketball players, but when it can be beneficial to the larger enterprise, the entertainment product can just as easily be swimmers, lacrosse players, or wrestlers. These late-adolescent athletes are stars, more renowned than practically all other college students, and subjects, along with their coaches, of interviews and articles, most of which are idolizing. It is the blend of celebrity with business under the media spotlight that sharply separates athletics from academics in today's higher education.

8 What's to Become of College Sports?

Courageous, talented, shrewd, compassionate, tenacious—all these qualities and more have been ascribed to Ed O'Bannon. A 6'8" former standout for UCLA's basketball team in the early 1990s, O'Bannon after his brief professional career was behind him, threatened to upend the NCAA and all of college sports. In 2009, O'Bannon filed a lawsuit against the NCAA, the sports video game company Electronic Arts, and the Collegiate Licensing Company. He did so on behalf of current and former Division I football and men's basketball players, claiming the defendants' use of players' images for commercial purposes violated antitrust law and property rights guaranteed by the Fourteenth Amendment. At stake were hundreds of millions of dollars generated by television contracts, video games, trading cards, and other products for which college athletes' names, photographs, and uniform numbers were used without compensation. The most serious implication of O'Bannon's lawsuit was its threat to the NCAA's amateur code because the suit claimed that athletes who generate huge revenues should be able to license their names and likenesses just as professional athletes do.[1] The O'Bannon case, however, was just one of several shocks to rock the enterprise in the early twenty-first century.

Not long after O'Bannon filed his claim, an alarming scandal exploded inside one of the nation's most hallowed football programs. In 2011, long-time Penn State assistant football coach Jerry Sandusky was charged with sexually assaulting at least eight boys on or near university property over a period of 15 years. University officials, including the athletic director, president, and revered head coach Joe Paterno, were accused of covering up the crimes. In 2012, a criminal court convicted Sandusky on 45 counts of sexual abuse, and the judge sentenced him to prison for a term of 30 to 60 years. An investigation carried out by former FBI director Louis B. Freeh accused Penn State leaders of "total disregard for the safety and welfare of Sandusky's child victims," and subsequently, the NCAA, citing lack of institutional control, imposed severe penalties on Penn State, including loss of ten football scholarships per class from the 2013–14 academic year through 2016–17, a four-year ban on postseason football competition, and a $60 million fine.[2] In addition, the NCAA wiped out all Penn State football victories between 1998–2011, dropping Paterno from being one of the winningest coaches in college football history to one of the most shamed. Fired by the university in November 2011, Paterno died of cancer two months later, insisting to the end that he had not known the extent of Sandusky's crimes.

Another omen arose in January 2013, when Northwestern University quarterback Kain Colter and some teammates petitioned the National Labor Relations Board (NLRB) to become certified as a labor union. Backed by lawyers from the newly formed National College Players Association, their goal was to obtain better conditions for college football players directly and all college athletes generally. Specifically, they sought higher scholarship dollar amounts; guarantees of scholarship retention for injured athletes; tighter safety regulations, especially to minimize brain trauma; better medical coverage; elimination of restrictions on athletes who transfer schools; and the ability to benefit financially from commercial opportunities. Colter, a native of Englewood, Colorado, who graduated in 2014 with a degree in psychology and was drafted by the Minnesota Vikings, believed a union would give athletes a long-needed seat at the table. "The current model," he claimed, "resembles a dictatorship with the NCAA putting rules and regulations on students without their input." The NCAA, though not directly a party to the case, responded tersely, asserting, "This union-backed attempt to turn student-athletes into employees undermines the purpose of college: an education. Student-athletes are not employees, and their participation in college sports is voluntary. We stand for all student-athletes, not just those the unions want to professionalize."[3] Two months later, the director of the Chicago NLRB ruled that the Northwestern athletes could be considered employees with the right to organize and bargain collectively. The university appealed to the national NLRB, and as of early 2015 both the players and the university were awaiting the ruling from the full NLRB in Washington, D.C. The possibility of a right for scholarship athletes to unionize has thrown college sports into a frenzy of uncertainty over the whole future of the enterprise.

And at its January 2015 NCAA convention held across the Potomac from Washington, D.C., delegates from Division I schools ratified what is perhaps the most consequential turning point of all of these. From that point on, the five power conferences—ACC, Big Ten, Big 12, Pac 12, and the Southeastern Conference, plus Notre Dame, consisting of the sixty-five schools that sponsor big-time football and men's basketball—may operate with autonomy, meaning that their governance structure allows them, among other things, to raise scholarship amounts to the "full cost" of college attendance (a few thousand dollars above current awards), offer multiyear scholarships, provide more extensive insurance coverage against career-ending injuries, and pay travel expenses for family members to attend competitions.[4] Though the conferences argued that such financial compensations were necessary because NCAA rules banned athletes from earning extra cash from jobs to pay for expenses such as travel to and from school, the effort marked another challenge to amateurism. And when some conference and college officials spoke of secession from the NCAA if their autonomy were not recognized, their threat highlighted the growing lopsidedness of college sports favoring the haves over the have-nots.

These episodes illuminate controversial issues swirling around college sports: whether athletes who produce huge material benefits for their schools deserve to organize and be paid for their efforts, which often come at risk to their health and safety; whether a jock culture is so obsessed with victory at all costs, national rankings, and television exposure that it neglects core values of virtue and justice; and whether the lure of money has seduced some of the nation's most prestigious universities into resembling professional sports franchises. The issues emerge, however, from a larger debate over the role of athletics in higher education. With all the perceived problems, how should college sports be reformed, if at all? To what extent has obsession with sports undermined academic missions? Has the time come for Congress, the courts, or both to intervene to prevent events from spinning further out of control? Should schools and conferences with the biggest incomes and biggest budgets be allowed to spend their dollars without NCAA restraints? Has the NCAA become too autocratic in enforcing its rules? Or is the NCAA too weak and inconsistent, and should it be replaced by a new governing body? Given potential liabilities for long-term consequences from concussions and other injuries, will future college sports even exist in the same way they do today? These questions and more have roots in the past, and they combined to create what arguably is the most uncertain state of affairs since the modern era of college sports began with the regularization of athletic scholarships and creation of the student-athlete in the 1950s.

Pay for Play

According to the NCAA, amateurism

> "is a bedrock principle of college athletics. Maintaining amateurism is crucial to preserving an academic environment in which acquiring a quality education is the first priority. In the collegiate model of sports, the young men and women competing on the field or court are students first, athletes second."[5]

For years, critics of big-time college sports have labeled this statement hypocrisy. They claim that coaches, athletic departments, and colleges and universities reap millions of dollars from football and men's basketball while athletes responsible for earning the money, often at great risk to their physical and mental well-being, are exploited and underrewarded. True, say commentators, a college scholarship makes for some compensation, but not enough, considering the hours that athletes labor and the aid's shortfall in covering the full expenses of a college education. *New York Times* columnist Joe Nocera has written, "The N.C.A.A.'s often-stated contention that it is protecting the players from 'excessive commercialism' is ludicrous; the only thing it's protecting is everyone else's revenue stream."[6] Some even equate athletes' situation with bondage. Civil-rights author Taylor Branch accused "corporations and universities (of) enriching themselves on the backs of uncompensated young men, whose status as 'student-athletes' deprives them of the right to due process guaranteed by the Constitution."[7] Applied chiefly to revenue sports of football and men's basketball, claims like these attract wide attention and get applied, simplistically, to all college sports.

NCAA president Mark Emmert, former president of the University of Washington, has adamantly voiced opposition to paying college athletes, resting his argument on several bases, some shakier than others. First, he has claimed, schools cannot afford compensation because the vast majority lose money on athletics. (See Chapter 7.) This reasoning is somewhat spurious because what athletic departments can afford depends on how they decide to spend their money; adjusting expenditures for some things can always release funds for others. Moreover, the autonomy model now in place for the five power conferences does include enhanced scholarship stipends of several thousand dollars each that, somehow, conference member schools will have to afford. Second, Emmert has argued that scholarship athletes already receive "enormous benefit from going to college." That reward, he said, includes not just financial aid, but also "the best coaching staff, the best facilities, the best trainers, the best educational environment anybody can get anywhere in the world."[8] Though hyperbolic, he may have a point. Dollar values of scholarships range between $30,000 and $60,000 annually. But opponents of pay for play estimate the real value to an athlete in revenue sports to be $120,000–$140,000 annually, if the calculation of total benefits includes access to multimillion-dollar facilities with state-of-the-art workout rooms, supervised by strength and conditioning experts and replete with saunas and whirlpools; lounges stocked with posh furniture, televisions and snack bars; deluxe academic centers with free tutors, books, and computers; high-quality medical treatment; free game tickets; and free shoes and everyday apparel furnished by companies that have deals with teams to sport their logo.[9] (I omit unsanctioned extra benefits, such as low-interest auto loans, reduced rents, and outright cash payments that some extra-privileged athletes allegedly receive.) None of these advantages are available to such an extent to ordinary undergraduates.

Still, supporters of unionization believe athletes should be able to bargain for their benefits. The idea of a union for college athletes is not new. In 1981, sociologist Allen Sack and former professional and college football standout Kermit Alexander created the Center for Athletes Rights and Education (CARE), with the goal of giving athletes at big-time sports schools bargaining rights and protecting them from exploitation. Among the organization's objectives were multiyear scholarships, due process in disputes with coaches; and a share of revenues generated by their athletic endeavors. At the time, the NLRB declined to certify CARE as a bargaining agent, but the NCAA remained nervous that either the NLRB would change its mind or that CARE had raised ideas that might lead to problems later on. The NCAA was right to worry.[10]

The move by Northwestern athletes to unionize raised a dilemma that had haunted college sports from 1950s onward: Should athletes who receive scholarships and other benefits as a condition for playing a sport be considered employees? The NCAA has always forestalled a "yes" by insisting that academic values always prevail over athletics, and therefore participants should be known as student-athletes, not as athletes who happen to be students. Defining college athletes as employees entitled to collective bargaining poses knotty problems for schools and coaches. For one, if football and men's basketball players can bargain for employee prerogatives, what about men and women who work just as hard at soccer, hockey, swimming, and other sports? Should they not be able to unionize and be paid also? Just because an employer—even if defined as a team—loses money, those who work for it are still employees and are qualified for benefits. Moreover, if certified as a union, athletes would, under federal labor law, have liberty to strike, at least at private institutions not subject to state law. (In the wake of the Northwestern suit, several state legislatures considered laws to prohibit athletes at publicly supported schools from unionizing.) Those injured on the job would be entitled to paid medical leave, extended medical care, and worker compensation. Conceivably, colleges and universities could be required to establish pensions for retired athletes, and just as athlete laborers achieved free agency in professional sports, a union could do the same for collegians, enabling them to shift without penalty to another school with more attractive compensation. Much of this speculation may border on fantasy, but it seems unlikely that the NCAA and its members can cling to a bygone fiction of amateurism. The reality is that the culture of college sports more often than not requires athletes to prioritize their sport over their studies, a culture to which most athletes willingly subscribe.

Student First, Athlete Second?

Late in spring 2005, an investigation at Auburn University, whose football team went undefeated and ranked second nationally in 2004, revealed that a lone sociology professor had been offering an astonishing number of independent directed reading courses, many of them to football players and other athletes. In addition to his full-time course load and service as interim department chair, the professor had supervised 120 such courses in fall 2004 and 152 in spring 2005. The courses required minimal reading—at most, one book—one brief paper, and no class attendance. Some 81 percent of football players who enrolled in these courses received A's. As one player who had taken two such courses testified, "I didn't do nothing illegal or anything like that. . . . It was definitely real work."[11] (The course content was sociology, not grammar.) Once exposed, the professor reduced the number of directed reading courses he offered and gave out fewer high grades.[12]

In 2012, a reporter for the Raleigh, North Carolina, *News and Observer* uncovered an arrangement whereby tutors in the athletic department at the University of North Carolina (UNC), one of the nation's top-ranking public universities, had been funneling athletes into paper courses taught by the chair of the Department of African and Afro-American Studies. Like those at Auburn, these classes required little work or attendance and awarded high grades. Mary Willingham, a learning specialist and former tutor-turned-whistle-blower, recounted that hundreds of UNC athletes, including some members of the 2009 national championship men's basketball team, took as many as twelve such classes over four years in order to remain academically eligible to play. One paper course was a summer class for football players that the professor never taught. He eventually was indicted on charges of receiving state property—the $12,000 he was paid for the course—under false pretenses. In another course, an athlete received an A-minus for submitting just one assignment: a 146-word paragraph that created a fictionalized conversation between Rosa Parks and the Montgomery bus driver who ordered her to yield her seat to a white rider.[13]

Early in 2014, UNC hired Kenneth L. Wainstein, formerly of the U.S. Department of Justice, to investigate the academic irregularities. Eight months later, Wainstein issued his report. He found that the paper-class ruse had been in existence for eighteen years and involved a conservative estimate of 3,100 students, including athletes in a wide range of sports, not just revenue sports. Wainstein also revealed that an assistant to the African and Afro-American Studies history professor had devised the scheme out of sympathy for athletes and other students who were not "the best and the brightest." Whistle-blower Mary Willingham, had informed Wainstein of others involved, including a former women's basketball academic adviser and five athletic academic counselors. The university reacted to the exposé by abolishing paper classes and removing responsibility for the tutoring program from the athletic department. At first, the NCAA briefly investigated the circumstances and concluded that no rules violation had occurred. But after the Wainstein report appeared, the NCAA reopened its investigation.[14]

Scandals like these are not new; academic fraud to admit athletes to college and keep them eligible has been common since the dawn of college sports. Many believe the Auburn and UNC episodes reveal only the most glaring tips of a deep iceberg of duplicity that continues unabated. (Scandal occurs at even the most vaunted schools. Between 2001 and 2011, Stanford allegedly kept a list of easy A classes available only to athletes; at Harvard, varsity athletes were said to account for more than half the 125 students implicated in a 2012 cheating scandal.[15]) But today, stakes are so lofty—millions to be gained from bowl games, national championships, donors—that temptations to make athletes' academic lives easy so they can focus on their sport are too great to resist.

Moreover, an additional issue has entered the process in an ironic way. In an effort to promote educational attainment and improve poor graduation rates among Division I athletes, the NCAA in 2004 introduced a new means of gauging academic progress: the Academic Performance Rate (APR). A composite measurement of term-by-term performance by a team's scholarship athletes, the APR is derived from a formula based on retention (staying in school), grades, and progress toward a degree. A perfect score of 1000 indicates that all a team's members on athletic scholarship are staying in school, have earned grades that keep them academically eligible, and are moving expeditiously toward completion of a major. A team with a score below 930 (roughly a 50 percent graduation rate) must raise its score above 930 within a reasonable period or face loss of scholarships and practice time; if its score falls below 900, harsher penalties kick in, such as a ban from postseason competition. For example, the University of Connecticut (UConn) men's basketball team lost two scholarships for the 2011–12 season and a postseason ban for the 2012–13 season because of a sub-900 APR.[16]

APR regulations have had some salutary effects. Scores have risen since the measure was introduced, as have graduation rates. The problem is that academic eligibility depends upon course grades and grades depend on who gives them. Complicit professors can have considerable influence. After the scandalous practice at Auburn was revealed, the football team's APR plunged from fourth place to near the bottom among big-time football programs. UNC's APR scores in football and men's basketball were well within acceptable levels during the years that athletes earned high grades in paper courses and dropped after the fraud ended. Meanwhile, aided by a program to help athletes become more successful students, the APR for UConn's men's basketball team rose markedly during the team's exclusion from postseason play and reached a perfect 1000, enabling the ban to be lifted for 2013–14—the year the team captured the national championship.[17] Coaches, most directly affected by penalties, complain that the APR is unfair because low scores result when team members change majors, transfer, or are dismissed for nonacademic reasons, an impact felt especially hard by small-roster teams such as basketball. A more serious complaint comes from schools that have trouble satisfying APR standards because they lack resources to help athletes who are struggling academically. According to NCAA records, 19 percent of all limited-resource school teams failed to reach the 930 threshold in 2012–13, in contrast with just 3 percent of teams from the five power conferences. A 2008 report found that the athletic department at the University of Oklahoma spent $2.9 million on academic assistance, almost $6,000 per athlete and far more than any low-revenue school could afford.[18] The APR figures also reflect a racial component, as half the 36 teams receiving postseason bans for the 2014–15 season were from historically black colleges and universities.[19]

More than anything, the APR is a measure of how successfully a coach and athletic department with means to do so keep athletes eligible. The APR established an incentive for athletic programs to take education seriously, but it also has tempted coaches to protect their interests by steering athletes into easy majors that require less study time, ensure continuing academic eligibility, and facilitate staying in school. As Walter Byers cynically wrote in 1990, "Believe me, there is a course, a grade, and a degree out there for everyone."[20] Also, an athletic scholarship and a lax academic program delude high school and college athletes, especially in basketball and football, and more especially African Americans, who see college only as a stepping-stone to a career in professional sports and end up unprepared and without the skills necessary to succeed in the real world.[21] Although academic accountability does reinforce a basic principle of the NCAA, guiding students and promoting educational experiences that serve each individual's best interests are institutional responsibilities and ought not be forfeited to an athletic association.[22]

Critics charge that fraud and low school performance occur because colleges and universities are admitting athletes unqualified for academic rigor. Mary Willingham, the tutor who exposed academic fraud at UNC, alleged that 60 percent of athletes admitted to the school read between fourth- and eighth-grade levels. Between 8 and 10 percent read below a third-grade level.[23] (In this regard, athletes do not differ much from other college freshmen, whose reading level, on average, is at the seventh grade.[24]) As with sham courses, this pattern is not new. A study of thirty selective colleges and universities in Divisions I and III, published in 2001, found SAT scores for high-profile athletes (football, men's basketball, men's ice hockey) in a 1989 cohort averaged 150 to 250 points lower than scores for students at large.[25]

Some marquee athletes are "special admits," applicants with special talents allowed to enroll even though their academic credentials fall well below those of other matriculants. At large universities, this category—sometimes labeled at risk—can comprise 40 to 80 applicants, and half or more can be athletes. A 2013 study at the University of California–Berkeley, for example, found that several athletes who averaged an unusually low score of 370 out of a possible 800 in each SAT subject—mathematics, reading, and writing—were invited to enroll.[26] (Most of these low-qualifying athletes had high school grades that enabled them to meet NCAA eligibility standards, but, as with college grades, high school grades can be, and are, manipulated—a whole other story.) Special admits often do not perform well once admitted. A survey conducted by the *Baltimore Sun*, using open records from Atlantic Coast Conference schools, discovered that special-admit athletes graduated at a lower rate and dropped out at a higher rate than other athletes. The *Sun* found, for example, that in 2005 the Universities of Maryland and North Carolina State each admitted twenty-three at-risk athletes; only twelve of those (56 percent) at Maryland and eight (35 percent) of those at North Carolina State eventually graduated, a frequency well below graduation rates of other athletes.[27]

Some college sports advocates excuse academic underperformance by saying demands of their sport leave athletes less time and energy to devote to studies than other students have. NCAA rules limit official athletic activities—coach-supervised practices and games—to twenty hours per week in season (maximum four hours per day) and eight hours off-season, but the regulation has little meaning because it excludes time spent on conditioning, meetings, film viewing, unofficial captain's practices, rehabilitation from injury, and more. According to a 2010 NCAA survey, Division I football players devoted an average of 43.3 hours per week to their sport from August through November, plus 15–20 hours per week in spring and summer. Division I baseball and basketball players spent almost the same amount of time at their sport. (Athletes in other sports devoted about ten hours less per week.) A Division I basketball team involved in travel and practice for conference playoffs and March Madness competition could miss one-fourth of the spring semester. In Division II (scholarships but fewer sports) and Division III (no scholarships) schools, where varsity sports supposedly are more voluntary and less prominent, athletes still put in considerable time. Division II football and male and female basketball players devoted 37.5 hours per week in season. In Division III, football took up 33.1 hours per week; basketball entailed 30.8 hours for men, 29.8 for women.[28] Equally important, there no longer is any off-season for rest and other activities.

Are these time commitments unique? Observers who decry the hours student-athletes devote to their passion simultaneously applaud—or at least accept—a college musician or journalist who devotes four or more hours a day at her or his activity. Though there may be no coach to require the time commitment, a cellist or editor wants and needs those hours to become successful. Who is to say that a college athlete is more tired or distracted to perform well in class than the musician or journalist?

The difference may be reflected in what has been termed the athletic–academic divide. Since the onset of NCAA-sanctioned athletic scholarships in the 1950s, since the growing independence of athletic departments from the institutions that house them, and since the mushrooming of athletic income and expenditures, the trend, especially in big-budget Division I schools, has been toward development of an isolated—and insulated—athletic culture. NCAA officials argue, with probable accuracy, that the majority of athletes are serious students and act responsibly, but too many enter college with overly weak qualifications and are shepherded through the academic system in a manner often unavailable to other students. They also have tended to live, eat, and socialize together (as have other students who share mutual interest); dress alike in team apparel; take the same (sometimes easy) courses; benefit from their own tutors; luxuriate in their own training and study facilities; and, especially among those in high-profile sports, be celebrated by their peers and the public at large. This separation can create a feeling that, somehow, athletics is beyond the reach of the institution. These factors have operated most strongly among male athletes, but they have begun to define female athletes as well.[29] This divide has long been a concern of the NCAA; yet that same organization has been responsible for intensifying it.

Wherefore the NCAA?

On the first page of its bible, the *NCAA Manual*, the NCAA states that its mission is "to maintain intercollegiate athletics as an integral part of the educational program and the athlete as an integral part of the student body, and by so doing, retain a clear line of demarcation between intercollegiate athletics and professional sports."[30] As previous chapters have indicated, that demarcation line has been breached: by television, money, the courts, and the association's own members. How much is the NCAA a victim of these forces, these turning points in the history of college sports, and how much has it contributed to its own predicament? The NCAA is very good at congratulating itself, often with good reason. Few would disagree that the association provides valuable service in organizing national championships for a range of varsity sports that includes not only football and basketball but also rifle shooting and bowling. It has tried to elevate its image and recognize new social realities by creating special programs and offices for women and minorities, dispersing funds for academic enrichment, and initiating efforts to help members deal more effectively with issues of health and safety. But it also can be seen as two-faced, upholding an ideal of amateurism with one hand and striving for every dollar with the other.

It has long been fashionable to blame the NCAA for everything deemed wrong in college sports. Its size is an asset and a liability. From its early days operating out of a Chicago hotel room, the NCAA has become a huge, wealthy sports operation. It does not operate like professional leagues such as the NFL or NBA, but it often is expected to do so. It is an affiliation of 1,300 institutions of higher education and nearly a half million student-athletes in three divisions, each with widely diverse members who hold widely diverse opinions on how their own athletic interests should be protected. It also is a bureaucratic mass of departments, cabinets, boards, committees, subcommittees, working groups, and more, with a headquarters campus in Indianapolis, a lobbying office in Washington, D.C., and programs too numerous to count. The NCAA operates under bylaws, promulgates rules, and punishes violators, but it is not a court of law, has no subpoena power, and settles appeals to its own decisions. It cannot control how much money an athletic department may make or how much a school may pay its coaches.

It is sometimes secretive, sometimes inconsistent in its treatment of rules infractions. Its unwieldy manual lists precise regulations for every sport; efforts to simplify it have generally run up against special interests of coaches who want to make sure no competitor can evade a regulation—it recently did regularize the categories of violations and range of penalties. When things go wrong, there is a hue and cry for the NCAA to do something. But the NCAA must tread a narrow path between enforcing necessary restrictions and infringing on prerogatives of its member institutions.

Though the NCAA can and does flex its muscle in a number of ways, its power is limited both by its own membership and by external forces, chiefly the courts. Over the years, it has suffered major defeats at the hand of both entities. In 1951, for example, the Sinful Seven member schools refused to accept the rule limiting athletic scholarships to economic need and academic merit. (See Chapter 1.) In 1984, the Supreme Court of the United States dealt the NCAA a setback by deciding, under antitrust law, that the association could not control televised college football. (See Chapter 4.) Other defeats have occurred at a frequency often overlooked by the public, but it could be argued that the NCAA currently faces unprecedented challenges on three fronts: its most powerful members, the judicial system, and, possibly, the U.S. Congress.

Internal rifts have long riven the NCAA, but the most serious crack began to open in 1976, when major football schools formed the College Football Association (CFA) and threatened to secede unless released from NCAA control of the television football policy and granted prerogatives to govern their own affairs. The CFA plaintiffs, chiefly the University of Oklahoma, won a Supreme Court decision in 1984, and though the CFA dissolved, the major schools gradually expanded their autonomy, especially in the 1990s, when new governance provisions enabled them to occupy more seats on the NCAA's highest policymaking bodies. Formation of the Bowl Championship Series in 1997 gave major schools power over the premier bowl games and selection of the national Division I football champion. The same schools, distilled to five power conferences of 64 schools, plus independent football contender Notre Dame, also seized influence over who could participate in the Division I football championship playoff.

Still unsatisfied, power conference members in 2014 pushed for even more independence. Representing the highest-revenue athletic programs, these conferences, some of whose commissioners threatened secession if they did not get their way, pressured the NCAA to allow their schools to supplement athletic scholarships to cover the "true cost" of education (mostly extra spending money) and to establish rules pertinent to their interests without having to win sufficient votes from less affluent Division I schools.[31] Officials from schools outside the five power conferences saw this as a raw power play. In May 2014, Bob Kustra, president of Boise State University, wrote an E-mail to media outlets, calling the effort by the five power conferences "subterfuge for fueling the arms race." "The NCAA," he warned, "cannot fall prey to phony arguments about student welfare when the real goal of some of these so-called reformers is to create a plutocracy that serves no useful purpose in American higher education."[32] Kustra, whose school's athletic budget was $37 million, as compared with the University of Alabama's $124 million, spoke for other presidents who found their budgets similarly dwarfed and would not be able to afford add-ons to scholarship aid, when he concluded that the reforms were intended only to provide big-time schools with competitive advantages and leave less flush competitors in the dust. Kustra failed to mention that he had just signed a deal with Albertson's grocery chain for $12.5 million a year naming rights to the Boise State football stadium, and that he had cajoled the Mountain West Conference into giving Boise State a favorable television deal. Still, the gulf between high- and low-resource schools prompted his accusations—he wanted to compete with the Big Boys.[33]

Objections notwithstanding, at the 2015 NCAA convention, the five power conferences achieved their goals when Division I created a new governance structure that gave those conferences weighted voting strength over general legislative matters and allowed them to operate with near-financial autonomy. Beginning in academic year 2015–16, day-to-day legislation, such as rules governing on-field play and scheduling, would be handled by a forty-member Division I Council, consisting of representatives from all thirty-four Division I conferences plus two each of student-athletes, faculty athletics representatives, and university presidents. Voting on the council, however, is heavily weighted in favor of the five power conferences. In addition, the five power conferences members—and any other Division I school that thinks it can afford it—may fund scholarships an amount up to the full cost of attendance, plus guaranteed multiyear scholarships, offer lifetime financial aid to former athletes wishing to return to school to complete a degree, provide long-term health care and insurance, enable athletes to meet with an agent under loosened restrictions, and cover expenses for an athlete's family to attend postseason games. Wealthy athletic programs may now spend without answering to less wealthy programs, and they can use their voting strength to advance their self-interest. Mike Slive, commissioner of the Southeastern Conference, had threatened in summer 2014 that if the five power conferences did not get their way within Division

I, they might form a separate Division IV or perhaps even break away from the NCAA altogether. After the 2015 convention his threat faded away, but a major turning point had been passed.

The NCAA survived this internal upheaval by yielding to the five power conferences, but litigation has continued to threaten the economic structure on which the NCAA and all of college sports stand. As in 1984, the NCAA has been confronting antitrust accusations. In 2008, four former student-athletes filed suit, alleging that the NCAA rule restricting a scholarship to the cost of tuition, books, housing, and meals was an unlawful restraint of trade because the NCAA was earning billions of dollars from broadcast and licensing deals and not fairly compensating the athletes who produced the income. The NCAA headed off a court battle by agreeing to create a $10 million fund to reimburse educational expenses for the class of plaintiffs—football players and male basketball players in 11 Division I conferences who competed between 2002 and 2007.[34]

In March 2014, a more serious challenge arose from a consolidation of antitrust lawsuits against the NCAA and entered in federal court. The cases, chiefly *Alston v. NCAA* and *Jenkins v. NCAA,* accused the NCAA and the five power conferences with unlawfully capping the value of an athletic scholarship by restricting it to tuition, room, board, books, and incidentals. The plaintiffs sought an injunction against the NCAA's limits on scholarships, plus damages. The plaintiffs' attorney, Jeffrey Kessler, a high-profile sports attorney from New York City, argued that no cap was legal and that the NCAA and its members were acting as an illegal cartel by fixing prices of what athletes could receive. Kessler asserted, "We're looking to change the system." He wanted a fairer portion of the millions made by the defendants to go to the athletes, "many of whom never graduate or . . . have a pro career but along the way contribute to the revenue pie of college sports."[35] As of the beginning of 2015, the NCAA had succeeded in delaying the case, and the new Division I governance structure, which enables schools in the Power Conferences to increase scholarship amounts to cover full costs of an education, may have headed off the lawsuits' challenge.

The Kessler suit was just one segment of antitrust accusations against the NCAA. The most notable was the O'Bannon case that went to trial on June 9, 2014. A month earlier, the plaintiffs—the case had been certified as a class-action suit in 2013—dropped their claim for individual damages, seeking only an injunction that would allow Division I football and basketball players the right to sell the use of their images and services in an open market. In a related case, in 2009, Sam Keller, former quarterback for Arizona State and Nebraska, sued to be compensated for use of his image in video games and advertisements. On the eve of the trial in the O'Bannon suit, Electronic Arts

Sports, a video game maker, settled the Keller case by awarding $20 million to be distributed among football and basketball players who appeared in games between 2003 and 2013. Those athletes still in college received a waiver to obtain their portion of the settlement without violating NCAA amateurism rules. The deal left the NCAA alone as the target of litigation, and the case remained unresolved at the beginning of 2015.[36]

Still another legal attack was launched against the NCAA's amateurism rules in October 2014, this time on behalf of *all* Division I male and female student-athletes, not just those in major men's sports. The plaintiff, Samantha Sackos, a women's soccer player at the University of Houston, claimed that student-athletes met the criteria of temporary employees under the wage-and-hour provisions of the federal Fair Labor Standards Act and that therefore they were entitled to receive at least minimum hourly wage for their participation in varsity sports. In other words, athletes should receive at least minimum hourly wages just as do the work-study participants who sell programs or usher at athletic events. According to the complaint, "By comparison to student participants in work study part-time employment programs, student athletes perform longer, more rigorous hours . . . are subject to stricter, more exacting supervision by full-time staff . . . and confer many, *if not more*, tangible and intangible benefits on" Division I schools. In response, the NCAA's chief attorney, Donald Remy, stated that "NCAA regulated sports are extracurricular activities in the same manner as 'dramatics, student publications, glee clubs, bands, choirs, debating teams, radio stations, intramural and interscholastic athletics . . . conducted primarily for the benefit of the participants as part of educational opportunities' and, thus exempt from FLSA requirements."[37] At no time in its history had the NCAA faced such intense challenges in the courts.

In the background to the lawsuits, another threat lurked. How could colleges and their athletic departments justify multimillion-dollar revenues from television contracts, corporate sponsorships, memorabilia sales, and more as education-related income, such as from tuition? Should not sports-related moneys be subject to the "unrelated business income tax" (UBIT) because they did not further an institution's tax-exempt educational functions? Back in summer 1977, the Internal Revenue Service had made a preliminary decision to tax income that major colleges earned from broadcast rights to their football games. These moneys, claimed the IRS, were subject to the UBIT. The IRS contention, had it been made final, would have cost affected schools millions and undermined their aspiring athletic programs. That possibility impelled a furious letter-writing campaign to the Treasury Department by education administrators, athletic interests, and allied legislators opposing such a decision. At that time, the lobbying paid off. The IRS abandoned its claim and reverted to longstanding assumptions that sports were an integral part of college education, that college athletes were true amateurs, and that television income should remain untaxed. It is true that, even if the IRS had stood by its original belief, the UBIT would have existed only as a paper tiger because most schools claim deficits in their athletic budgets and therefore have no net income to tax.[38] Still, according to some analysts, a current Congress, if it so wished, could attach conditions to exemptions from UBIT. It might, for example, mandate that revenues from big-time sports be used to subsidize other "charitable outputs," such as increasing opportunities in nonrevenue sports or for women. Or, it could even set caps on coaches' salaries. Thus, the UBIT represents a plausible way for the federal government to check runaway spending and perceived corruption in intercollegiate athletics.[39]

One issue has loomed over others and may pose more damaging consequences. Late in 2013, a panel of judges combined nearly a dozen class-action suits filed in federal court against the NCAA alleging that it had ignored the serious issue of concussions for decades. Just as the National Football League has been forced to establish a huge payout to former players suffering long-term effects from concussions and other brain injuries, the NCAA faces the possibility of paying dearly for not adopting a formal concussion policy until 2010. The attorney who represents two former football players, a former soccer player, and a former hockey player central to one of the suits has stated, "Continuing to turn a blind eye and continuing to essentially pretend that the concussion issue isn't as severe as it is, those are the things we say make the NCAA negligent." The NCAA entered into mediation to head off the suit, and in July 2014 offered a $70 million fund to test, but not treat, thousands of current and former athletes for brain trauma and put aside $5 million for research. Also, NCAA member schools would be required to institute tighter policies on concussion management. Attorneys for the plaintiffs were not completely satisfied with these provisions, because to be compensated for medical treatment of a brain injury, a former athlete would have to sue his or her institution and prove negligence.[40] At the time of this writing, the parties involved were awaiting the judge's final approval of the proposed settlement. Ironically, colleges and universities—institutions dedicated to improving young minds—may in the future be held liable for destroying those minds, and the enterprise of intercollegiate sports may have to undergo changes unforeseen in all lawsuits and NCAA reforms.

Targeting intercollegiate athletics for criticism is endemic in American culture. Take, for example, the following invective: "College athletics, under the spur of commercialism, has become a monstrous cancer, which is rapidly eating out the moral and intellectual life of our educational institutions."

Is this a rant from one of today's many critics of runaway television coverage of college sports? Against coaches' multimillion-dollar salaries? Against manipulation of varsity athletes by tawdry sports agents? No, the statement comes from muckraker Upton Sinclair in his 1922 attack on American higher education, *The Goose-Step*.[41] Similar diatribes can be found in every era since Sinclair wrote his, and current critics are no less acerbic, filling books and articles with adjectives like "corrupt," "greedy," "exploitive," and "hypocritical."

A case can be made that challenges to intercollegiate athletes today surpass all those of the past sixty-five years. A parallel case also can be made that nothing will change, at least not radically. Dismal conclusions come easily: The athletic arms race will continue unabated, fueled by ever-increasing booster donations. Athletic budgets and expenditures will continue to grow at a faster rate than those for the rest of higher education. Athletes in revenue sports at big-time colleges and universities may win some monetary benefits beyond their scholarship provisions, but they will remain "amateurs," at least in the sense that they will not be compensated with six- and seven-figure contracts. Televised college sports have not reached a saturation point. The academic–athletic divide will not be bridged. Athletes will still cluster in easy courses, coaches' salaries will continue to soar, and the NCAA will fend off antitrust litigation with the aid of politicians who harbor loyalties to teams of their state schools and alma maters.

Calls for changing the system ring loudly across the airwaves and flash from publications. Disparate proposals have been advanced: define athletes as employees and pay them accordingly; define athletes as interns and pay them accordingly; remove the masquerade that athletes are students and have the NBA and NFL sponsor college basketball and football as minor leagues; eliminate extra benefit rules that prohibit athletes from receiving outside money and gifts from a corporation or boosters (as one former athlete has observed, "If you went to Oregon, Nike would pay you, but who cares?"[42]); stop the runaway arms race (no one knows how without interfering in institutional prerogatives to spend money, pay coaches, and admit students according to their own standards); distribute the huge sums earned by the NCAA and its most elite members more equitably across divisions and conferences; create a new governing body for college sports; and many more equally ambitious schemes.

Any realistic changes in all probability would have to be piecemeal, but reform to some of the most gnawing issues can be achieved.

- One reform would be for every school to follow the lead of the NCAA and five power conferences, who are taking steps toward easing the burdens of student-athletes, especially in areas of medical care and protecting an athlete's scholarship from being taken away so as to allow for four or five years of funded education.

- A more difficult, but not impossible, reform would entail a return to pre-1970s conditions, when freshmen could receive athletic scholarships but were ineligible for varsity play so they could adjust to college life. This adjustment would eliminate the egregious "one-and-done" practice, wherein first-year basketball players can be enrolled in college for only one year before entering the NBA draft and dropping out of school. Though this practice involves only about fifty or sixty individuals per year and is fostered by the NBA, not the NCAA, critics point to it as a major hypocrisy of college sports.[43]

- More radically, the NCAA could still confine an athletic scholarship to tuition, room and board, and incidental expenses but drastically expand, or remove, limits on an athlete's outside income—that is, revising extra benefit rules that sit at the heart of so many time-consuming and often petty NCAA investigations. By this reform, the IRS becomes the watchdog because such benefits are taxable, and donors—the main source of benefits—would be considered employers, subject to all federal and state regulations.

- The gap between athletics and academics might be filled and the need for an undemanding academic program lessened if more varsity athletes could be funneled into legitimate and useful majors. About 375 American colleges and universities offer undergraduate degrees in sports management. More schools could do the same with programs that, if tailored in an appropriate way, could genuinely assist athletes who wished to pursue a career in a field most familiar to them and who may have only a brief or nonexistent career as a playing professional.

One avenue for more comprehensive reform already has been charted by a seemingly unlikely source. Walter Byers, who was so influential in defining college sports and the NCAA from the 1950s into the 1980s, turned away in 1995 from what he had wrought, writing in his memoir that his "visionary efforts had come to naught," chiefly because reform efforts "never reformed much of anything." He especially blamed the same culprits who are identified today: the feudal lords of the power conferences, whose obsession with money prevented them from making necessary changes to the system. Each member of this oligopoly, he charged, exercised its muscle to ensure that no rival achieved an advantage, whether in recruiting or in competition. The result: student-athletes lost their freedom.[44]

As a remedy, Byers proposed that Congress pass a College Athletes Bill of Rights (CABR). This plan would end the NCAA's one-year limit and cap on scholarship amounts and award athletic scholarships according to the same formula as that used for nonathlete students—basing scholarships on need, as the Sanity Code of 1949 intended. But also, the CABR would repeal the NCAA provision that prevents an athlete from holding a job during the school year and allow the jobholder to receive whatever an employer wants to pay, regardless of whether the remuneration is commensurate with the job being done. The wages would be subject to taxes, and the quality of work would be the concern only of the employer. Third, Byers would permit athletes to transfer schools freely without having to sit out a year of competition before becoming eligible to play. Finally, the CABR would enable athletes to consult agents in determining decisions about which school to attend and require colleges and universities to provide worker compensation for their injured athletes. As a complement, Byers proposed a "Competitive Opportunity Plan" that would lessen the domination of the biggest and wealthiest programs by imposing roster limits to prevent high-income schools from stockpiling the best athletes, and he would temporarily allow weaker programs to offer more paid campus visits to prospective athletes and to exceed regular limits on numbers of scholarships.[45]

Is any kind of serious transformation possible? During the past sixty-five years comprehensive reform of college sports has failed in the only country in the world where extensive, high-quality athletic competition is an integral part of institutions of higher learning. Sports organizations such as the NCAA and the conferences have not mustered the will, and nonsports agencies, such as the American Council on Education and the Knight Foundation, lack the power to change the culture of commercialism and victory at all costs. The federal government and the courts have the force, but it remains to be seen whether they really care to get involved.

In spite of attacks over the years, from Upton Sinclair to current journalists and academics, the trends of college athletics have been survival and growth over control and destruction. Though much of the playbook has changed, some of its vital chapters have stayed the same. Whether it was the confrontation of the Sinful Seven, the revolt of the black athlete, the rise of the CFA and its Supreme Court victory, the challenges posed by Title IX, the persistence of scandal, or antitrust litigation, sports has remained the activity most identified with college student life and the strongest link between an institution and the public. And in the end, though it sometimes is easy to assume differently, the great majority of college athletes are genuine college students and should be treated as such. Rather than simply paying them for what they do on the field of play, the school that admits them—not the NCAA, not the government, not the media—should shoulder the responsibility for stimulating and feeding their intellectual curiosity and developing them into productive members of society.

Notes

Introduction

1. Michael Oriard, "NCAA Academic Reform: History, Context, and Challenges," *Journal of Intercollegiate Sport* 5 (June 2012), p. 7.

2. Ibid.; Richard O. Davies, *Sports in American Life: A History.* 2nd ed. (Malden, Mass.: Wiley-Blackwell, 2012), pp. 131–32.

3. Joseph N. Crowley, *In the Arena: The NCAA's First Century* (Indianapolis: NCAA, 2006), pp. 67–70.

Chapter 1. Abolishing the Sanity Code and Launching the Modern College Sports Establishment

1. Robert J. Brugger, with Cynthia Horsbaugh Requardt, Robert J. Cotton Jr., and Mary Ellen Hayward, *Maryland: A Middle Temperament, 1634–1980* (Baltimore, MD: Johns Hopkins University Press, 1996), p. 565.

2. Ted Patterson, *Football in Baltimore: History and Memorabilia* (Baltimore, MD: Johns Hopkins University Press, 2000), p. 41; David Ungrady, *Tales from the Maryland Terrapins* (Champaign, IL: Sports Publishing, 2003), pp. 18–20, 24.

3. "What Price Football?" *Time,* January 23, 1950. http://content.time.com/time/magazine/article/0,9171,858594,00.html

4. Joseph N. Crowley, *In the Arena: the NCAA's First Century* (Indianapolis: NCAA, 2006), p. 69.

5. Walter Byers, with Charles Hammer, *Unsportsmanlike Conduct: Exploiting College Athletics* (Ann Arbor: University of Michigan Press, 1995), p. 68; John Watterson, *College Football: History, Spectacle, Controversy* (Baltimore, MD: Johns Hopkins University Press, 2000), p. 215. See also Allen L. Sack and Ellen J. Staurowsky, *College Athletes for Hire: The Evolution and Legacy of the NCAA's Amateur Myth* (Westport, CT: Praeger, 1998), p. 46; Ronald A. Smith, *Pay for Play: A History of Big-Time College Athletic Reform* (Urbana: University of Illinois Press, 2011), p. 99.

6. Crowley, *In the Arena*, pp. 68–69.

7. "NCAA Presidents See Need for Flexible Code," *Chicago Tribune*, April 8, 1950, p. A5.

8. Sack and Staurowsky, *College Athletes for Hire*, p. 45.

9. *Yearbook of the NCAA*, 1950–51 (Chicago: Rogers Park Press, 1951), p. 198.

10. Byers, *Unsportsmanlike Conduct*, pp. 41–43; Watterson, *College Football*, p. 276.

11. *Yearbook of the NCAA*, 1950–51, p. 200.

12. *Yearbook of the NCAA*, 1950–51.

13. "NCAA Abolishes Sanity Code," *Chicago Tribune*, January 13, 1951, p. B1.

14. Mark F. Bernstein, *Football: The Ivy League Origins of an American Obsession* (Philadelphia: University of Pennsylvania Press, 2001), p. 180; Bernard Gwertzman, "Ivy League: Formalizing the Fact," http://www.thecrimson.com/article/1956/10/13/ivy-league-formalizing-the-fact-pthe/.

15. In 2000–2001, the Patriot League, which consists of eight northeastern schools in Division I, attempted to apply a modified Ivy League model, requiring that athletic scholarships be based on "merit," but the policy did not survive the pressures for supremacy. In 2010, the league formally restored scholarships not based on need.

16. "Education: Basketball v. Learning," *Time*, December 17, 1951, p. 56.

17. Crowley, *In the Arena*, p. 84. Walter Byers, hired as NCAA executive director late in 1951, admitted in his memoir that had Kentucky decided to contest the penalty, it probably would have succeeded in garnering enough support from other schools to "carry the day." See Byers, *Unsportsmanlike Conduct*, p. 59.

18. Joe Goldstein, "Explosion: 1951 Scandals Threaten College Hoops," *ESPN Classic*, November 19, 2003, http://espn.go.com/classic/s/basketball_scandals_explosion.html

19. Charles Grutzner, "Athletic Problems Handicap Schools," *New York Times*, March 20, 1951.

20. Crowley, *In the Arena*, p. 70. See also Murray Sperber, *Onward to Victory: The Crises That Shaped College Sports* (New York: Henry Holt, 1998), pp. 358–59.

21. Beth J. Shapiro, "John Hannah and the Growth of Big-Time Intercollegiate Athletics at Michigan State University," *Journal of Sport History* 10 (Winter 1983), pp. 30–33; Watterson, *College Football*, p. 230; Sperber, *Onward*, pp. 363–64. Ironically, in 1964 the Big Ten conference placed Hannah's Michigan State on probation for improprieties involving its athletic department and the Spartan Foundation, and MSU also became the object of one of the NCAA's first rule infraction cases. See Sperber, *Onward*, p. 380.

22. Quoted in Crowley, *In the Arena*, p. 66.

23. Watterson, *College Football*, p. 231.

24. Watterson, *College Football*, pp. 232–33; Smith, *Pay for Play*, pp. 118–19; Crowley, *In the Arena*, p. 96.

25. Manning M. Patillo Jr., "The North Central Association and Intercollegiate Athletic Reform," *Bulletin of the American Association of University Professors*, vol. 38, no. 2 (Summer 1952), 209–19.

26. Don Yaeger, *Undue Process: The NCAA's Injustice to All* (Champaign, IL: Sagamore, 1991), p. 8.

27. Jack McCallum, "The Kingdom of the Solitary Man," *SI.com* (October 6, 1986) http://sportsillustrated.cnn.com/vault/article/magazine/MAG1065309/3/index.htm.

28. Ibid.; Crowley, *In the Arena*, pp. 101–2.

29. Keith Dunnavant, *The Fifty-Year Seduction: How Television Manipulated College Football, from the Birth of the Modern NCAA to the Creation of the BCS* (New York: St. Martin's Press, 2004), p. 19.

30. Yaeger, pp. 13–15; Dunnavant, *Fifty-Year Seduction*, p. 23.

31. Quotation from Watterson, *College Football*, pp. 235–37. See also Crowley, *In the Arena*, p. 84; Smith, *Pay for Play*, pp. 127–28; Sperber, *Onward*, p. 373.

32. Watterson, *College Football*, pp. 273–76; Smith, *Pay for Play, Pay for Play*, p. 128. The state of Oklahoma and its flagship institution, the University of Oklahoma, had a national notoriety for football enthusiasm, resulting from a comment made in 1950 to the state legislature by university president George L. Cross, who half-seriously asserted, "I would like to build a university of which the football team could be proud." See Kitty Pittman, *"George Lynn Cross (1905–1998)," Encyclopedia of Oklahoma History and Culture, http:// www.okhistory.org/publications /enc/entry.php?entry=CR017 12/9/10.*

33. Quoted in Sperber, *Onward*, p. 320.

34. *NCAA Yearbook*, 1956–57 (Kansas City: White, Lowell Press, 1957), p. 4; Sack and Staurowsky, *College Athletes for Hire*, p. 47.

35. Byers, *Unsportsmanlike Conduct*, p. 68.

36. *University of Denver v. Nemeth*, 127 Colo. . 387, April 20, 1953; Christopher W. Haden, "Foul! The Exploitation of the Student-Athlete: Student-Athletes Deserve Compensation for Their Play in the College Athletic Arena," *Journal of Law and Education* 10 (October 2001), pp 291–92.

37. Byers, *Unsportsmanlike Conduct*, pp. 70–71.

38. Byers, *Unsportsmanlike Conduct*, pp. 65, 72; Watterson, *College Football*, p. 285; Sack and Staurowsky, *College Athletes for Hire*, p. 47; Dunnavant, *Fifty-Year Seduction*, p. 36.

39. Sack and Staurowsky, *College Athletes for Hire*, p. 47.

40. Byers, *Unsportsmanlike Conduct*, p. 69.

41. Byers, *Unsportsmanlike Conduct*, p. 71.

42. Quotation from Byers, *Unsportsmanlike Conduct*, p. 72. See also Crowley, *In the Arena*, p. 218; Dunnavant, *Fifty-Year Seduction* p. 36; Brian Porto, *A New Season: Using Title IX to Reform College Sports* (Westport, CT: Praeger, 2003), p. 179. By 1956, the NCAA compliance committee was flexing its newfound muscle, handing out penalties to schools for violating the association's growing list of rules. At the NCAA convention in Los Angeles that year, the committee announced eight penalties, mostly for violations in which high school athletes were contacted in unauthorized ways. More significant, the University of Oklahoma was given a two-year probation for paying the medical expenses of family members of its athletes, and for fringe benefits of clothing and other gifts provided to athletes by university patrons. See *NCAA Yearbook*, 1955–56 (Kansas City, MO: Brown, White, Lowell Press, 1956).

43. Byers, *Unsportsmanlike Conduct*, p. 73.

44. Ibid.

45. Porto, *New Season*, p. 179.

46. Sack and Staurowsky, *College Athletes for Hire*, p. 80. See *Van Horn v. Industrial Accident Commission*, 33 Cal. Rpr. 169 (1963).

47. Sack and Staurowsky, *College Athletes for Hire*, pp. 81–82.

48. *Rensing v. Indiana St. Univ. Bd. of Trustees,* 44 N.E. 2d 1170 (1983); Sack and Staurowsky, *College Athletes for Hire,* p. 85.

49. Sack and Staurowsky, *College Athletes for Hire,* pp. 131–32.

50. Crowley, *In the Arena,* p. 93.

51. Sack and Staurowsky, *College Athletes for Hire,* p. 133.

52. Quoted in Sack and Staurowsky, *College Athletes for Hire,* p. 134.

53. Crowley, *In the Arena,* pp. 93–94.

54. Though not exclusively, much of the rebellious behavior involved contention between coaches and African American team members over individual, and often race-related, display such as facial hair and expressions of political protest against racism and the Vietnam War. See chapter 2.

55. Michael Oriard, *Bowled Over: Big-Time College Football from the Sixties to the BCS Era* (Chapel Hill: University of North Carolina Press, 2009), p. 136; Sack and Staurowsky, *College Athletes for Hire,* p. 83.

56. Oriard, *Bowled Over,* pp. 130, 140.

57. Dave Meggyesy, *Out of Their League* (New York: Paperback Library, 1971), p. 40.

58. Byers, *Unsportsmanlike Conduct,* pp. 338–39.

59. Ibid., p. 340.

Chapter 2. Integrating the Team

1. *Chicago Tribune,* March 16, 1963, sec. 3, p. 1.

2. *Jackson Daily News,* March 6, 1963, p. 10.

3. Russell J. Henderson, "The 1963 Mississippi State University Basketball Controversy and the Repeal of the Unwritten Law: 'Something More Than the Game Will Be Lost.'" *Journal of Southern History,* Vol. 63, No. 4 (November 1997), pp. 827–54.

4. Ibid. MSU remained all white for another two years, but in 1965, Richard Holmes became the first African American student admitted to MSU.

5. Amherst College, the first white school to integrate its football team, was an exception, suiting up African Americans William Henry Lewis and William Tecumseh Sherman Jackson in 1889. Northwestern also had two, Joe Lattimore and Alton Washington, in 1900.

6. Eliot quoted in Joseph N. Crowley, *In the Arena: The NCAA's First Century* (Indianapolis: NCAA, 2006), p. 185.

7. Samuel G. Freedman, *Breaking the Line: The Season in Black College Football That Transformed the Sport and Changed the Course of Civil Rights* (New York: Simon & Schuster, 2013), pp. 155–56; Crowley, *In the Arena,* pp. 185–86. Florida A&M served as continual host of every Orange Blossom Classic between 1933 and the final game in 1978, giving it the prerogative to play in every game. The Rattlers compiled a record of 26-19.

8. Freedman, *Breaking the Line,* p. 213.

9. Rita Liberti, "'We Were Ladies, We Just Played Like Boys': African-American Womanhood and Competitive Basketball at Bennett College, 1928–1942," in Patrick B. Miller and David K. Wiggins, *Sport and the Color Line: Black Athletes and Race Relations in Twentieth-Century America* (New York: Routledge, 2004), pp. 83–99.

10. John Sayle Watterson, *College Football: History, Spectacle, Controversy* (Baltimore, MD: Johns Hopkins University Press, 2000), pp. 299–302.

11. Watterson, *College Football*, pp. 312–14.

12. Mark F. Bernstein, *Football: The Ivy League Origins of an American Obsession* (Philadelphia: University of Pennsylvania Press, 2001), pp. 53, 228.

13. *McLaurin v. Oklahoma State Regents*, 33 U.S. 637 (1950).

14. Ronald A. Smith, *Pay for Play: A History of Big-Time College Athletic Reform* (Urbana: University of Illinois Press, 2011), pp. 116–17; Crowley, *In the Arena*, pp. 187–88.

15. http://www.legacy.com/obituaries/oklahoman/obituary.aspx?pid=3306668 #fbLoggedOut.

16. Watterson, *College Football*, p. 316.

17. Watterson, *College Football*, p. 318; Crowley, *In the Arena*, p. 188.

18. http://www.rollbamaroll.com/2010/9/7/1593198/alabama-vs-penn-state-a-historical.

19. Quoted in Michael Oriard, *Bowled Over: Big-Time College Football from the Sixties to the BCS Era* (Chapel Hill: University of North Carolina Press, 2009), p. 60.

20. Bryant biographer Keith Dunnavant credits Bryant with shrewdly manipulating circumstances and using the USC game to overcome Wallace's segregationist influence in Alabama. Others, however, fault Bryant for failing to move more quickly and use his stature in Alabama to "do the right thing." Quotation from Oriard, *Bowled Over*, p. 62. See Oriard, *Bowled Over*, pp. 61–63; Keith Dunnavant, *Coach: the Life of Paul "Bear" Bryant* (New York: Simon & Schuster, 1966), pp. 249–66; Allen Barra, *The Last Coach: A Life of "Bear" Bryant* (New York: W.W. Norton, 1996), p. xxv.

21. Alexander Wolff and Armen Keteyian, *Raw Recruits: The High Stakes Game Colleges Play to Get Their Basketball Stars—and What It Costs to Win* (New York: Pocket Books, 1991), p. 102; http://espn.go.com/classic/biography/s/Rupp_Adolph.html. Wolff and Keteyian allege, without direct proof, that Rupp's racism explains his refusal to recruit Connie Hawkins.

22. This was Riley's unsubstantiated recollection. See http://espn.go.com/classic/s/013101_texas_western_fitzpatrick.html.

23. http://cards6.wordpress.com/2011/03/14/texas-western-vs-kentucky-the-ncaa-game-of-the-ages-1966/.

24. Frank Fitzpatrick, "Texas Western's 1966 Title Left Lasting Legacy," http://espn.go.com/classic/s/013101_texas_western_fitzpatrick.html.

25. Wallace's story, including his experiences as a lonely but resolute African American struggling with his relationship to white society and the civil-rights movement, is presented in Andrew Maraniss, *Strong Inside: Perry Wallace and the Collision of Race and Sports in the South* (Nashville, TN: Vanderbilt University Press, 2014).

26. Glenn Logan, "The Integration of UK Basketball in the 1960s," http://www.aseaofblue.com/2008/7/31/583522/the-integration-of-uk-bask.

27. Bomani Jones, "Progress Yes; But HCBUs Paid a Price for It," http://sports.espn.go.com/espn/blackhistory2007/news/story?id=2780876.

28. Jack Olsen, "The Black Athlete: A Shameful Story," *Sports Illustrated*, July 1, 8, 15, 22, 29, 1968.

29. John Underwood, "Shave Off That Thing!" *Sports Illustrated*, September 9, 1969, p. 23.

30. "Halfback Shaves, Returns," *Corvallis Spokesman-Review*, April 12, 1969 https://news.google.com/newspapers?nid=1314&dat=19690412&id=HbZWAAAAIBAJ&sjid

=gukDAAAAIBAJ&pg=5091,4088166&hl=en; Underwood, "Shave Off That Thing!";
Oriard, *Bowled Over*, pp. 92–95.

31. Watterson, *College Football*, p. 321.

32. Oriard, *Bowled Over*, pp. 102–11; Watterson, *College Football*, pp. 322–24.

33. Robert McG. Thomas Jr., "Ben Schwartzwalder Dies at 83; Revitalized Football at
Syracuse," *New York Times*, April 29, 1993; Watterson, *College Football*, p. 325.

34. Underwood, "Shave Off That Thing!"p. 24.

Chapter 3. Television and College Sports as Mass Entertainment

1. Jerry Wizig, "It's Been Twenty Years Since They Played the Game of the Century,"
Houston Chronicle, January 20, 1988; Robyn Norwood, "Game of the Century," *Los Angeles
Times*, January 20, 1998.

2. Ibid.

3. Ronald A. Smith, *Play by Play: Radio, Television, and Big-Time College Sport* (Baltimore, MD: Johns Hopkins University Press, 2001), p. 184.

4. "Fordham Checks Waynesburg, 34–7," *New York Times*, October 1, 1939, p. 89; Smith,
Play by Play, p. 51.

5. Orrin E. Dunlap Jr., "Television Forward Passes Football to the Home," *New York
Times*, October 15, 1939, p. 150.

6. Keith Dunnavant, *The Fifty-Year Seduction: How Television Manipulated College
Football from the Birth of the Modern NCAA to the Creation of the BCS* (New York: St.
Martin's Press, 2004), p. 5.

7. Ibid.

8. James T. Patterson, *Grand Expectations: The United States, 1945–1974* (New York:
Oxford University Press, 1996), p. 348.

9. http://www.high-techproductions.com/historyoftelevision.htm.

10. Brian L. Porto, *A New Season: Using Title IX to Reform College Sports* (Westport,
CT: Praeger, 2003), p. 33; Joseph N. Crowley, *In the Arena: The NCAA's First Century*
(Indianapolis: NCAA, 2005), p. 85. As noted in Chapter 1, at this time the NCAA was
a weak, advisory association that lacked real power to impose policies and regulations
beyond codification of on-field and contest rules.

11. *Yearbook of the NCAA*, 1950–51 (Chicago: Rogers Park Press, 1951), p. 201.

12. Ibid., p. 205.

13. Andrew Zimbalist, *Unpaid Professionals: Commercialism and Conflict in Big-Time
College Sports* (Princeton, NJ: Princeton University Press, 1999), pp. 93–94; Porto, *New
Season*, p. 34; Crowley, *In the Arena*, p. 85; Murray Sperber, *Onward to Victory: The Crises
That Shaped College Sports* (New York: Henry Holt, 1998), p. 387; John Sayle Watterson,
College Football: History Spectacle, Controversy (Baltimore, MD: Johns Hopkins University
Press, 2000), pp. 270–71.

14. Figures derived from Smith, *Play by Play*, p. 73.

15. Smith, *Play by Play*, pp. 56–57; Crowley, *In the Arena*, p. 85.

16. Sperber, *Onward to Victory*, pp. 387–88.

17. *New York Times*, January 16, 1951, p. 48.

18. Smith, *Play by Play*, pp. 65–66. Mark F. Bernstein, *Football: The Ivy League Origins
of an American Obsession* (Philadelphia: University of Pennsylvania Press, 2001), p. 199.

Smith uncovered the unusual plan for a superconference among Cavanaugh's papers in the Notre Dame archives.

19. *Yearbook of the NCAA,* 1950–51, p. 201.

20. Smith, *Play by Play,* pp. 69–71; Bernstein, *Football,* p. 199.

21. Walter Byers, with Charles Hammer, *Unsportsmanlike Conduct: Exploiting College Athletics* (Ann Arbor: University of Michigan Press, 1995), p. 84. Gallery subsequently negotiated NBC's first contract to televise the Rose Bowl for $200,000.

22. Sperber, *Onward to Victory,* pp. 400–402; Crowley, *In the Arena,* p. 86; Watterson, *College Football,* p. 270; Zimbalist, *Unpaid Professionals,* p. 94.

23. Dunnavant, *Fifty-Year Seduction,* p. 28.

24. Crowley, *In the Arena,* p. 87.

25. Sperber, *Onward to Victory,* pp. 395–96; Dunnavant, *Fifty-Year Seduction,* pp. 31–32.

26. *Yearbook of the NCAA,* 1952–53 (Kansas City: Brown, White, Lowell Press, 1953), pp. 230–32.

27. Ibid., pp. 87–90.

28. Sperber, *Onward to Victory,* p. 405; Watterson, *College Football,* p. 271.

29. Smith, *Play by Play,* p. 93; Zimbalist, *Unpaid Professionals,* p. 95.

30. Crowley, *In the Arena,* p. 87.

31. Byers, *Unsportsmanlike Conduct,* p. 94. See also Zimbalist, *Unpaid Professionals,* Table 5.1, p. 95; Smith, *Play by Play,* pp. 111–12; Dunnavant, *Fifty-Year Seduction,* pp. 55–58; 83.

32. Dunnavant, *Fifty-Year Seduction,* pp. 60–63.

33. Dunnavant, *Fifty-Year Seduction,* pp. 81–82; Watterson, *College Football,* p. 301. Though it was dubbed the Game of the Century, the contest itself proved to be less than expected. With just over a minute left to play, Notre Dame coach Ara Parseghian chose to let his team run out the clock to preserve a 10–10 tie rather than try to move the ball downfield for a potential winning field goal. Resenting the lack of resolution, fans and journalists alike castigated Parseghian for his cautiousness, but his decision allowed his team to retain its number one ranking at season's end.

34. Smith, *Play by Play,* p. 109.

35. Smith, *Play by Play,* p. 144.

36. "Dick Bailey: Television Executive, 80," *New York Times,* November 1, 1991.

37. Ibid., p. 182.

38. Byers, *Unsportsmanlike Conduct,* pp. 259, 269; Crowley, *In the Arena,* p. 101.

39. "Television Factbook (1979)," quoted in Stanley M. Besen and Robert W. Crandall, "The Deregulation of Cable Television," *Law and Contemporary Problems* 41 (Winter 1981), pp. 79–80; Smith, *Play by Play,* p. 134.

40. See, for example, *Carter Mountain Transmission Corporation v. FCC,* 35 F. 2nd 359 (1963); FCC, *First Cable Television Report and Order* (1965); and FCC, *Second Cable Television Report and Order* (1966).

41. Smith, *Play by Play,* pp. 136–37.

42. *Home Box Office, Inc., v. F.C.C.,* 567 F. 2nd 9 (1977); *Home Box Office, Inc., v. F.C.C.,* 587 F. 2nd 1248 (1978); *F.C.C. v. Midwest Video Corp.,* 440 U.S. 689 (1979).

43. Museum of Broadcast Communications, "United States Cable Television," http://www.museum.tv/eotvsection.php?entrycode=unitedstates; Smith, *Play by Play,* pp. 138–39.

44. Funding Universe, "ESPN, Inc.—Company History," http://www.fundinguniverse.com/company-histories/ESPN-Inc-company-History.html.

45. Byers, *Unsportsmanlike Conduct,* p. 253.

46. *Los Angeles Times,* February 11, 2011; California State University–Long Beach, "Remembering President Steve Horn," cf.papubs.csulb.edu/cms/?contentid=205.

47. Watterson, *College Football,* p. 304. Horn quoted in Smith, *Play by Play,* p. 147.

48. Crowley, *In the Arena,* p. 88.

49. Watterson, *College Football,* pp. 303–4.

50. Ibid., pp. 334–35.

51. Long Beach State had been engaged in multiple scandals involving cash benefits to athletes, free lodging and jobs for athletes' parents, fraudulent test scores, and improper recruiting practices. According to Byers, the infractions were "among the most serious [the NCAA] had ever considered." Byers, *Unsportsmanlike Conduct,* p. 197. Most had occurred before Horn became president and many were related to head basketball coach Jerry Tarkanian, whom Horn fired and who had a subsequent controversy-filled college-coaching career at the University of Nevada–Las Vegas and Fresno State University, ultimately resulting in a highly charged lawsuit by Tarkanian against the NCAA and a Supreme Court decision upholding the NCAA's right to discipline members but also requiring greater rights of due process to those accused of a rule violation. See Byers, *Unsportsmanlike Conduct,* pp. 197–99, and *NCAA v. Tarkanian,* 488 U.S. 179 (1988).

52. Canham quoted in Watterson, *College Football,* p. 335.

53. Smith, *Play by Play,* p. 149.

54. Ibid.

55. Dunnavant, *Fifty-Year Seduction,* p. 123.

56. Watterson, *College Football,* pp. 335–36; Smith, *Play by Play,* p. 150.

57. Norwood, "Game of the Century."

58. Gordon S. White Jr., "TV Ruling Creates Confusion: Ivy League Makes Deal," *New York Times,* June 29, 1984. The Ivy League made an agreement with the Public Broadcasting Service to televise nine Ivy games in the Northeast in fall 1984 after being shut out of the schedule of major network games as a result of efforts by the major football powers to dominate national telecasts of their games. See Chapter 4.

59. James J. Duderstadt, *Intercollegiate Athletics and the American University* (Ann Arbor: University of Michigan Press, 2003), p. 73; Smith, *Play by Play,* pp. 2–3. 73.

60. Dunnavant, *Fifty-Year Seduction,* pp. 66–68, 84–87.

61. Byers, *Unsportsmanlike Conduct,* p.79; Dunnavant, *Fifty-Year Seduction,* pp. 64–65.

62. "The World's Richest Sports League," www.schmoop.com /nfl-history/economy/ html.

63. Hart quoted in Smith, *Play by Play,* p. 2.

Chapter 4. "Earthquake": Board of Regents v. NCAA

1. In this era, football players played on both offense and defense.

2. Dennis J. Hutchinson, *The Man Who Once Was Whizzer White: A Portrait of Justice Byron R. White* (New York: Free Press, 1993), chapters 3, 4, and 7.

3. *NCAA v. Board of Regents,* 468 U.S. 85 (1984) 122.

4. Keith Dunnavant, *The Fifty-Year Seduction: How Television Manipulated College Football, from the Birth of the Modern NCAA to the Creation of the BCS* (New York: St.

Martin's Press, 2004), pp. 120–24, Joseph N. Crowley, *In the Arena: The NCAA's First Century* (Indianapolis: NCAA, 2006), p. 89; John Sayle Watterson, *College Football: History, Spectacle, Controversy* (Baltimore: Johns Hopkins University Press, 2000), pp. 336–37; Ronald A. Smith, *Play by Play: Radio, Television, and Big-Time College Sport* (Baltimore, MD: Johns Hopkins University Press, 2001), p. 150; Michael Oriard, *Bowled Over: Big-Time College Football from the Sixties to the BCS Era* (Chapel Hill, NC: University of North Carolina Press, 2009), p. 157.

5. Father Joyce quoted in Dunnavant, *Fifty-Year Seduction*, p. 121.

6. Joyce had special reason to resent Byers and the NCAA. As a penalty for rule violations, the NCAA banned Michigan State from playing on television between 1976 and 1979, thereby removing the possibility of a telecast of the annual Michigan State–Notre Dame football game and thus preventing Notre Dame from a lucrative television appearance. See Walter Byers, with Charles Hammer, *Unsportsmanlike Conduct: Exploiting College Athletics* (Ann Arbor: University of Michigan Press, 1995), p. 254.

7. Watterson, *College Football*, p. 336; Smith, *Play by Play*, p. 150; Dunnavant, *Fifty-Year Seduction*, p. 122; Oriard, *Bowled Over*, p. 157.

8. Paterno quoted in Dunnavant, *Fifty-Year Seduction*, p. 123.

9. Watterson, *College Football*, p. 339; Gordon S. White Jr., "Byers Urges N.C.A.A. to Reorganize," *New York Times*, January 13, 1977; White, "N.C.A.A. Realigns Football," *New York Times*, January 13, 1978; "NCAA Rejects, Then OKs 'Super' Football Division," *Chicago Tribune*, January 13, 1978.

10. Gordon S. White Jr., "N.C.A.A. to Maintain Division I-A Makeup," *New York Times*, January 7, 1979; Smith, *Play by Play*, p. 151.

11. "NCAA rejects reforms, cutbacks in Division I," *Chicago Tribune*, January 13, 1977; Gordon S. White Jr., "N.C.A.A. Retains Full Athletic Scholarships," *New York Times*, January 12, 1977.

12. Gordon S. White Jr., "N.C.A.A. Title Basketball Sold to CBS for $48 Million," *New York Times*, March 5, 1981; White, "N.C.A.A. List Large, Not Select," *New York Times*, March 10, 1981; Alexander Wolff and Armen Keteyian, *Raw Recruits: The High Stakes Game Colleges Play to Get Their Basketball Stars—and What It Costs to Win* (New York: Pocket Books, 1991), pp. 21–22.

13. Byers, *Unsportsmanlike Conduct*, p. 264.

14. Gordon S. White Jr., "Attorney to Cite N.C.A.A. 'Untouchables,'" *New York Times* February 4, 1978; White, "N.C.A.A. Accused of Bribery to Uncover Rules Violations," *New York Times* February 28, 1978; Crowley, pp. 164–65.

15. Gordon S. White Jr., "N.C.A.A. Policies Criticized," March 1, 1978. Both Michigan State and Mississippi State had been given two-year probations for what the two schools believed were petty rule infringements. At Michigan State, an athlete who had missed a bus home for Thanksgiving had been given a ride a short distance by a coach. The Mississippi State case involved a football player who had bought two pair of pants and two shirts at a discount not available to all students. See White, "N.C.A.A. Policy Labeled Inconsistent on Penalties," *New York Times*, March 15, 1978; and White, "N.C.A.A. Gets Warning on Penalizing Mississippi State," *New York Times*, March 15, 1978.

16. Gordon S. White Jr., "House Urged to Get More N.C.A.A. Facts," *New York Times* January 11, 1979.

17. Lawsuits against the NCAA had rarely occurred because it was assumed that the NCAA, registered as a nonprofit organization, could not be subject to antitrust law. But in a 1975 case, *Goldfarb v. Virginia State Bar*, the Supreme Court determined that a not-for-profit association—in this case, the Virginia State Bar—was not necessarily exempt from the restraints of trade proscribed by the Sherman Anti-Trust Act, thereby opening up the possibility that the NCAA might be vulnerable. See, *Goldfarb v. Virginia State Bar*, 421 U.S. 773 (1975); Smith, *Play by Play*, pp. 154–55.

18. Watterson, *College Football*, p. 345.

19. *Hennessey v. National Collegiate Athletic Association*, 564 F. 2nd 1136 (Dec. 16, 1977); Smith *Play by Play*, p. 153. In one somewhat obscure passage in its decision, the Appeals Court noted that the NCAA had recommended that a coach's contract "include the assignment of faculty rank, benefits of tenure and retirement and such other rights and privileges as are enjoyed by other members of the contracting institution's faculty." If an institution truly wanted to retain its coaches, wrote the judges, it should provide them with such benefits and tenure; yet the University of Alabama had not done so for the two plaintiffs in the case and therefore could not protect them from the NCAA provision.

20. Neinas was later appointed interim commissioner of the Big Ten in 2011.

21. Byers, *Unsportsmanlike Conduct*, pp. 255–57; Smith, *Play by Play*, p. 151.

22. Watterson, *College Football*, p. 340; Smith, *Play by Play*, p. 156.

23. Quoted in Watterson, *College Football*, p. 346.

24. Frank and Davison quoted in Dunnavant, *Fifty-Year Seduction*, p. 137.

25. "2-Network Football in N.C.A.A.'s Plans," *New York Times*, April 3, 1981; Gordon S. White Jr., "College Football Goes to 2 Networks," *New York Times*, July 31, 1981; Smith, *Play by Play*, pp. 155–57; Byers, pp. 264, 268, 276–77; Crowley, p. 90; Dunnavant, *Fifty-Year Seduction*, pp. 139–40.

26. Smith, *Play by Play*, p. 159.

27. Gordon S. White Jr., "College Football Outlook Lies in TV Talks," *New York Times*, June 21, 1981.

28. Gordon S. White Jr., "Big Colleges Defy N.C.A.A. over TV," *New York Times*, August 9, 1981; Dunnavant, *Fifty-Year Seduction*, pp. 142–43.

29. Gordon S. White Jr., "In Peace Bid, N.C.A.A. May Allow Schools More TV Control," *New York Times*, September 3, 1981; White, "N.C.A.A. Calls Convention on TV Policy," *New York Times*, September 9, 1981; Dunnavant, *Fifty-Year Seduction*, p. 146.

30. Gordon S. White Jr., "Compromise Expected in N.C.A.A. Rift on TV," *New York Times*, December 4, 1981.

31. Atchley quoted in Dunnavant, *Fifty-Year Seduction*, p. 151.

32. Gordon S. White Jr., "N.C.A.A. Puts Off Vote on TV Dispute," *New York Times*, September 24, 1981; White, "Compromise Expected in N.C.A.A. Rift on TV," *New York Times*, December 4, 1981; White, "College TV Showdown Near," *New York Times*, December 13, 1981; White, "N.C.A.A. Prevails in TV Fight," *New York Times*, December 15, 1981; Smith, *Play by Play*, pp. 161–62; Byers, pp. 276–77.

33. Gordon S. White Jr., "N.C.A.A. Tightens Grip on TV Football," *New York Times*, January 13, 1982; Dunnavant, *Fifty-Year Seduction*, p. 152.

34. Pepperdine University, "Past Pepperdine Presidents: William Banowsky," http://www.pepperdine.edu/president/past-presidents/banowsky.htm (accessed 3/15/2012); Charlotte Gay, "Associated with Success," *Sooner Magazine* (Spring 2004) http://www

oufoundation.org/sm/spring2004/story.asp?ID=108 (accessed March 15, 2012; Crowley, p. 122. Banowsky later had a checkered career in business. In 1989, he was charged with insider stock trading and paid a $750,000 fine to the Securities and Exchange Commission.

35. Smith, *Play by Play*, pp. 163–64.

36. District court decision summarized in *NCAA v. Board of Regents of the University of Oklahoma*, 468 U.S. 85 (1984); Byers, p. 278.

37. District Court decision summarized in *NCAA v. Board of Regents of the University of Oklahoma*, 468 U.S. 85 (1984).

38. Burciaga quoted in Gordon S. White Jr., "N.C.A.A. Telecast Rights on Football Struck Down," *New York Times*, September 16, 1982.

39. "N.C.A.A. Rebuffed on TV Contracts," *New York Times*, May 13, 1983; "TV Football Ruling Stirs Legal Debate," *New York Times*, May 14, 1983.

40. "N.C.A.A. Wins Delay on Football TV Issue," *New York Times*, July 19, 1983.

41. See Smith, *Play by Play*, p. 165.

42. Oriard, *Bowled Over*, p. 158.

43. *NCAA v. Board of Regents of the University of Oklahoma*, 468 U.S. 85 (1984); Linda Greenhouse, "High Court Ends N.C.A.A. Control of TV Football," *New York Times*, June 28, 1984.

44. *NCAA v. Board of Regents of the University of Oklahoma*, 468 U.S. 85 (1984).

45. Ibid.

46. Gordon S. White Jr., "Ruling Adds Options for Colleges and Television," *New York Times*, June 28, 1984; "N.C.A.A. Submits Modified TV Plan," *New York Times*, July 5, 1984; Gordon S. White Jr., "Major Football Colleges Await Signals for a New TV Plan," *New York Times*, July 8, 1984.

47. Gordon S. White Jr., "Major Football Colleges Await Signals for a New TV Plan," *New York Times*, July 8, 1984; White, "N.C.A.A. TV Plan Is Rejected," *New York Times*, July 11, 1984; Smith, *Play by Play*, p. 169.

48. Smith, *Play by Play*, pp. 171–72. The Sports Broadcasting Act permitted major professional sports leagues to negotiate television packages with a network or networks. The law permitted the blackout of a televised game in the home territory of a team whose game was not sold out.

49. "Big 10, Pacific 10 Reject C.F.A.," *New York Times*, July 12, 1984; "C.F.A. Agrees on Plan," *New York Times*, July 13, 1984; Skip Mysienski, "Big 10, Pac-10 Sign With CBS," *Chicago Tribune*, July 20, 1984; Smith, *Play by Play*, pp. 170–71.

50. Dunnavant, *Fifty-Year Seduction*, pp. 170–74.

51. Gordon S. White Jr., "Colleges May Find TV's Golden Egg Is Tarnished," *New York Times*, August 26, 1984; "College Football TV Suit," *New York Times*, August 18, 1984; Dunnavant, *Fifty-Year Seduction*, p. 179.

52. Skip Mysienski, "Federal Judge Interferes with CFA's Air Game," *Chicago Tribune*, September 11, 1984; Dunnavant, *Fifty-Year Seduction*, pp. 175–76.

53. Byers, pp. 288–90; Watterson, *College Football*, p. 350.

54. Quotation, originally attributed to Walter Cronkite, in Joel G. Macey, "The 1997 Restructuring of the NCAA: A Transactions Cost Explanation," in John Fizel and Rodney Fort, eds., *Economics of College Sports* (Westport, CT: Praeger, 2004), p. 24. See also Watterson, *College Football*, p. 350; Oriard, *Bowled Over*, pp. 180–81; Dunnavant, *Fifty-Year Seduction*, p. 219.

55. Smith, *Play by Play*, pp. 171–75, 184–85, 189–90; Byers, pp. 259, 269; Crowley, p. 87; Wolff and Keteyian, *Raw Recruits*, p. 31.

56. Dunnavant, *Fifty-Year Seduction,* pp. 172–73 and 180–81.

57. Gordon S. White Jr., "N.C.A.A. TV Plan Is Rejected," *New York Times,* July 11, 1984; "Taking Away the N.C.A.A.'s Ball," *Time,* July 9, 1984, p. 77.

58. Smith, *Play by Play*, pp. 175–76; Dunnavant, *Fifty-Year Seduction,* pp, 223, 241; Oriard, *Bowled Over,* p. 193.

59. Dunnevant, pp. 31–32; Rick Telander, *The One Hundred Yard Lie: The Corruption of College Football and What We Can Do to Stop It* (Urbana: University of Illinois Press, 1990), p. 31.

60. Switzer quoted in Byers, p. 277.

61. Smith, *Play by Play*, pp. 151–52.

62. *NCAA v. Board of Regents of the University of Oklahoma,* 468 U.S. 85 (1984).

63. Public Law 87–331 (75 Stat. 732), September 30, 1961.

64. Smith, *Play by Play*, p. 141.

65. *NCAA v. Board of Regents of the University of Oklahoma,* 468 U.S. 85 (1984).

Chapter 5. *The Civil Rights Restoration Act and Enforcement of Title IX*

1. *Hearings before the Comm. on Labor and Human Resources on S. 557* 100th Cong., 1st sess., April 1, 1987, (1987), pp. 490–91.

2. See Welch Suggs, *A Place on the Team: The Triumph and Tragedy of Title IX* (Princeton, NJ: Princeton University Press, 2005), pp. 81–85

3. Suggs, *A Place on the Team, pp. 90–91.*

4. Suggs, *A Place on the Team,* p. 92.

5. Suggs, *A Place on the Team,* p. 3.

6. Allen L. Sack and Ellen J. Staurowsky, *College Athletes for Hire: The Evolution and Legacy of the NCAA's Amateur Myth* (Westport, CT: Praeger, 1998), p. 67.

7. Joseph N. Crowley, *In the Arena: The NCAA's First Century* (Indianapolis: NCAA, 2005), p. 189; Sack and Staurowsky, *College Athletes for Hire,* p. 65.

8. Crowley, *In the Arena,* p. 190.

9. Susan Cahn, *Coming On Strong: Gender and Sexuality in Twentieth-Century Women's Sport* (Cambridge, MA: Harvard University Press, 1994), pp. 85–86.

10. Crowley, *In the Arena,* p. 190.

11. Charles Neinas to Richard Larkin, quoted in Sack and Staurowsky, *College Athletes for Hire,* p. 119.

12. Walter Byers to Katherine Ley, quoted in Sack and Staurowsky, *College Athletes for Hire,* p. 120.

13. Mary Jo Festle, *Playing Nice: Politics and Apologies in Women's Sports* (New York: Columbia University Press, 1996), pp. 98–101; Ying Wushanley, *Playing Nice and Losing: The Struggle for Control of Women's Intercollegiate Athletics, 1960–2000* (Syracuse, NY: Syracuse University Press, 2004), pp. 43–44. There were other overlapping women's organizations as well. I have chosen, for example, not to add to the confusion by discussing the short-lived National Joint Committee on Extramural Sports for College Women (NJCESCW), which competed with the DGSW but yielded to it in 1965.

14. Neinas, quoted in Sack and Staurowsky, *College Athletes for Hire*, p. 119.

15. Sack and Staurowsky, *College Athletes for Hire*, pp. 112–15; Wushanley, *Playing Nice and Losing*, pp. 47–48; Festle, *Playing Nice*, pp. 109–10; Crowley, *In the Arena*, p. 191.

16. Walter Byers to Elizabeth Hoyt, February 2, 1971, AIAW Papers, box 37, quoted in Wushanley, *Playing Nice and Losing*, p. 49.

17. Wushanley, *Playing Nice and Losing*, pp. 49–50; Festle, *Playing Nice*, p. 119. Crowley (*In the Arena*, p. 192) asserts that the NCAA began discussions in the early 1960s with women's sports leaders about how to administer competition in women's sports and that in 1964 the NCAA Executive Committee agreed that the association would prohibit female student athletes from competing in NCAA championships so that women's groups could retain control over their own sports. But he notes also that as early as 1967 the NCAA investigated the feasibility of supervising women's college sports while at the same time assuring women's sports groups that the NCAA was interested in only studying such feasibility.

18. Charles Neinas to Lucille Magnusson, September 23, 1971, AIAW Papers, box 37, quoted in Wushanley, *Playing Nice and Losing*, p. 55.

19. Walter Byers to Rachel Bryant, October 12, 1971, AIAW Papers, box 37, quoted in Wushanley, *Playing Nice and Losing*, p. 56; Festle, *Playing Nice*, p. 120.

20. *Proceedings of the 66th Annual Conventions of the NCAA* (Overland Park, KS: NCAA, 1972), p. 80.

21. Ibid., p. 84; Wushanley, *Playing Nice and Losing*, p. 59.

22. Festle, *Playing Nice*, pp. 111–13; Wushanley, *Playing Nice and Losing*, p. 76; Linda Jean Carpenter and R. Vivian Acosta, *Title IX* (Champagne, IL: Human Kinetics, 2005), p. 3.

23. Carpenter and Acosta, *Title IX*, pp. 8–11; Suggs, *Place on the Team*, pp. 71, 210–11.

24. Wushanley, *Playing Nice and Losing*, pp. 63–74; Sack and Staurowsky, *College Athletes for Hire*, pp. 117–18; Eileen McDonagh and Laura Pappano, *Playing with the Boys: Why Separate Is Not Equal in Sports* (New York: Oxford University Press, 2008), p. 128; Ronald A. Smith, *Pay for Play: A History of Big-Time College Athletic Reform* (Urbana, IL: University of Illinois Press, 2011), pp. 145–46.

25. Walter Byers, with Charles Hammer, *Unsportsmanlike Conduct: Exploiting College Athletics* (Ann Arbor: University of Michigan Press, 1995), p. 243; Wushanley, *Playing Nice and Losing*, pp. 84–87.

26. Festle, *Playing Nice*, pp. 168, 187–88; Sack and Staurowsky, *College Athletes for Hire*, p. 121.

27. *NCAA v. Califano*, 622 R. Supp. 2d 1382 (10th Cir. 1980).

28. Suggs, *Place on the Team*, p. 77; Crowley, *In the Arena*, p. 195.

29. Byers, *Unsportsmanlike Conduct*, p. 243.

30. Wushanley, *Playing Nice and Losing*, pp. 91–94; Festle, *Playing Nice*, p. 177.

31. Quoted in Wushanley, *Playing Nice and Losing*, p. 102.

32. Quoted in Festle, *Playing Nice*, p. 200.

33. Festle, *Playing Nice*, p. 201; Wushanley, *Playing Nice and Losing*, pp. 133–34; Byers, *Unsportsmanlike Conduct*, p. 247. Lopiano quoted in Gordon S. White, "N.C.A.A. Women Criticized," *New York Times*, January 13, 1981, p. C10.

34. Quoted in Wushanley, *Playing Nice and Losing*, p. 136.

35. *New York Times*, January 14, 1981, p. A19; Crowley, *In the Arena*, pp. 193–94.

36. Wushanley, *Playing Nice and Losing*, pp. 139–41; Festle, *Playing Nice*, pp. 209–14; Smith, *Pay for Play*, pp. 147–49.

37. Crowley, *In the Arena*, p. 157.

38. 558 F. Supp. 487 (D.D.C. 1983)

39. *735 F. 2d 577, Association for Intercollegiate Athletics for Women v. National Collegiate Athletic Association*, 236 U.S. App. D.C. 311, 1984–1 Trade Cases 66,007; Wushanley, *Playing Nice and Losing*, pp. 146–49.

40. Byers, *Unsportsmanlike Conduct*, p. 247.

41. Haffer v. Temple University, 524 F. Supp. 531 (E.D.Pa.1981); Carpenter and Acosta, *Title IX*, pp. 126–28; Brian L. Porto, *A New Season: Using Title IX to Reform College Sports* (Westport, CT: Praeger, 2003), p. 151.

42. *Grove City College v. Bell*, 687 F. 2d 684 (1982).

43. *Grove City College v. Bell*, 465 U.S. 555 (1984); Suggs, *Place on the Team*, pp. 88–89; Festle, *Playing Nice*, p. 219.

44. *Grove City College v. Bell*, 465 U.S. 555 (1984); Carpenter and Acosta, *Title IX*, pp. 120–21.

45. *Grove City College v. Bell*, 465 U.S. 555 (1984).

46. Quoted in Festle, *Playing Nice*, p. 220.

47. Quoted in C. Tong, "The Reawakening Discrimination against Women in Sports," *Christian Science Monitor*, (January 23, 1986), p. 13; Suggs, *Place on the Team*, p. 90.

48. Peter Alfano, "Signs of Problems amid the Progress," *New York Times*, December 15, 1985, p. A1.

49. Suggs, *Place on the Team*, pp. 90–91.

50. *St. Petersburg (Florida) Times*, March 20, 1988, p. D2.

51. Veto message quoted in Suggs, *Place on the Team*, p. 92.

52. "Reagan Vetoes Civil Rights Restoration Act," *Washington Post*, March 17, 1988, p. A1; Nicholas Laham, *The Reagan Presidency and the Politics of Race: In Support of Color-Blind Justice and Limited Government* (Westport, CT: Praeger, 1998), pp. 188–92.

53. Civil Rights Restoration Act of 1987, 100 P.L. 259; 102 Stat. 28; 1988.

54. *Franklin v. Gwinnett County Public Schools*, 503 U.S. 60 (1992).

55. Suggs, *Place on the Team*, pp. 232–35.

56. Suggs, *Place on the Team*, pp. 109–24; Carpenter and Acosta, *Title IX*, pp. 143–44.

57. Amy Wilson, "The Status of Women in Intercollegiate Athletics as Title IX Turns 40," an NCAA publication, 2012, p. 6; *NCAA News*, December 10, 2010.

58. "Title IX: A 20-Year Search for Equity," *New York Times*, June 21, 1992, p. A1.

59. Ibid.

60. Wilson, pp. 12–14.

61. Alfano, "Signs of Problems," p. A1.

62. Murray Sperber, *College Sports, Inc.: The Athletic Department vs. the University* (New York: Henry Holt, 1990), p. 329.

63. Quotation from Jody Diperna, "Personal Foul: Rene Portland," *Pittsburgh City Paper* March 9, 2006. See also "Training Rules," a documentary film produced and directed by Dee Mosbacher and Fawn Yacker a WomanVision Film, released in 2010.

64. *Journal of Health, Physical Education, and Recreation* (September 1963), quoted in Festle, *Playing Nice*, p. 82.

65. Suggs, *Place on the Team*, p. 61.

66. *Congressional Record*, Senate Proceedings, 93rd Congress, 2nd sess., May 20, 1974, vol. 120, part 15, p. 322.

67. S. Rep. No. 93–1026, at 139 (1974).

68. Festle, *Playing Nice*, pp. 168, 177

69. Arlene Gorton, "Cohen v. Brown," ESPN broadcast, August 6, 2002.

70. Eileen McDonagh and Laura Pappano, *Playing With the Boys*, pp. 124–25. The authors identify the Supreme Court case of *Reed v. Reed*, 404 U.S. 71 (1971), as the landmark decision applying the equal protection clause to issues of sex discrimination. Because the Kellmeyer case is discussed briefly in the text, I think the passage referring to it in the footnote can be deleted.

71. George Gangwere to Walter Byers, June 17, 1971, AIAW Papers, box 37, quoted in Wushanley, *Playing Nice and Losing*, p. 50.

72. *Proceedings of the 66th Annual Convention of the National Collegiate Athletic Association* (1972), p. 80, quoted in Wushanley, *Playing Nice and Losing*, p. 57.

73. Quoted in McDonagh and Pappano, *Playing with the Boys*, p. 29.

74. Ibid., pp. 220–21.

75. Ibid., p. 221. Italics are theirs.

76. Ibid., pp 123–24.

77. Definitions of "sex" recently have confounded institutions and the NCAA as cases have arisen involving the team on which a transgender athlete may play, if any.

78. McDonagh and Pappano, *Playing with the Boys*, pp. 237–38.

Chapter 6. Scandal, Reorganization, and the Devolution of the Student Athlete

1. James C. McKinley Jr., "Bill Clements Dies at 94; Set Texas on G.O.P. Path," *New York Times*, May 30, 2011.

2. Ibid.

3. John Sayle Watterson, *College Football: History, Spectacle, Controversy* (Baltimore, MD: Johns Hopkins University Press, 2000), pp. 364–72.

4. Carolyn Barta, *Bill Clements: Texian to His Toenails* (New York: Eakins Press, 1996); *The Bishops' Committee Report on SMU—Report to Board of Trustees of Southern Methodist University from the Special Committee of Bishops of the South Central Jurisdiction of the United Methodist Church, Friday, June 19, 1987* (Dallas, TX: United Methodist Church, 1987).

5. Joseph N. Crowley, *In the Arena: The NCAA's First Century* (Indianapolis: National Collegiate Athletic Association, 2006), pp. 91–92; Michael Oriard, *Bowled Over: Big-Time Football from the Sixties to the BCS Era* (Chapel Hill: University of North Carolina Press, 2009), pp. 129–30; Allen L. Sack and Ellen J. Staurowsky, *College Athletes for Hire: The Evolution and Legacy of the NCAA's Amateur Myth* (Westport, CT: Praeger, 1998), pp. 47–48.

6. Smith quoted in Sach and Staurowsky, *College Athletes for Hire*, p. 83.

7. Ibid.

8. Oriard, *Bowled Over*, pp. 130–36.

9. Crowley, *In the Arena*, pp. 92–93.

10. Sack and Staurowsky, *College Athletes for Hire*, p. 84; Crowley, *In the Arena*, p. 92; Ronald A. Smith, *Pay for Play: A History of Big-Time College Athletic Reform* (Urbana: University of Illinois Press, 2011), p. 132.

11. Crowley, *In the Arena*, pp. 88–89.

12. Charley Rosen, *The Wizard of Odds: How Jack Molinas Almost Destroyed the Game of Basketball* (New York: Seven Stories Press, 2002).

13. David Porter, *Fixed: How Goodfellas Bought Boston College Basketball* (Boulder, CO: Taylor, 2000). Whether the Boston College scandal would have gone undetected if not for Hill's testimony is open to question, but the incidence of point shaving continued, as evidenced by publicized scandals at Tulane in 1985, Arizona State in 1997, and Northwestern in 1998. Because it is relatively easy to carry out, however, there are many observers who believe occurrences of point shaving are, and have been, more common than what has been revealed.

14. Francis Frank Marcus, "8 Indicted in Tulane Scandal; School to Give Up Basketball," *New York Times* (April 5, 1985), http://www.nytimes.com/1985/04/05/sports/8-indicted-in-tulane-scandal-school-to-give-up-basketball.html.

15. "The Stench in College Sport," *New York Times*, June 28, 1980, p. 20; Gordon S. White Jr., "Preferred Admission Reported at U.S.C.," *New York Times*, October 15, 1980, p. B7.

16. John Sayle Watterson, *College Football: History, Spectacle, Controversy* (Baltimore, MD: Johns Hopkins University Press, 2000), pp. 353–54.

17. Walter Byers, with Charles Hammer, *Unsportsmanlike Conduct: Exploding College Athletics* (Ann Arbor: University of Michigan Press, 1995), p. 11.

18. Byers, *Unsportsmanlike Conduct*, p. 354, http://www.shakinthesouthland.com/2008/10/clemsons-ncaa-infractions-and-truth.html.

19. Bill Brubaker, "A Pipeline Full of Drugs," *Sports Illustrated*, January 21, 1985 http://www.si.com/vault/1985/01/21/546258/a-pipeline-full-of-drugs; Watterson, *College Football*, p. 354.

20. Byers, *Unsportsmanlike Conduct*, pp. 186–90; Watterson, *College Football*, pp. 354–55; "Brief Setback for College Gladiators," *New York Times*, February 19, 1986. http://www.nytimes.com/1986/02/19/opinion/brief-setback-for-college-gladiators.html.

21. http://www.1st100.com/part3/tarkanian.html. Tarkanian returned to coaching in 1995 at Fresno State University, where he remained until retiring in 2002. Shortly thereafter, the NCAA placed the school's basketball program on probation for infractions committed during Tarkanian's tenure. Tarkanian's long feud with the NCAA prompted him to complain that while the NCAA was aggressively seeking rules violations at lesser schools such as Long Beach State and UNLV, it overlooked similar misconduct at powerful programs such as the University of Kentucky. He quipped, "The NCAA is so mad at Kentucky they'll probably slap another three years' probation on Cleveland State."

22. Alexander Wolff and Armen Keteyian, *Raw Recruits: The High Stakes Game Colleges Play to Get Their Basketball Stars and What It Costs to Win* (New York: Pocket Books, 1991), p. 136.

23. Oriard, *Bowled Over*, p. 214; Watterson, *College Football*, p. 376; Jerry Kirschenbaum, "An American Disgrace," *Sports Illustrated*, February 27, 1989.

24. Crowley, *In the Arena*, p. 118.

25. Ibid.;. Smith, *Pay for Play*, pp. 168–69.

26. Crowley, *In the Arena*, p. 119.

27. Crowley, *In the Arena*, pp. 119–20; Smith, *Pay for Play*, p. 169; Watterson, *College Football*, p. 365.

28. Quoted in Crowley, *In the Arena*, p. 120.

29. Peter Applebome, "Is There Life after Football?" *New York Times Sunday Magazine*, October 4, 1987, p. 75; Watterson, *College Football*, pp. 364–72.

30. Applebome, "Is There Life after Football?" p. 73.

31. Ibid.

32. "Colleges Majoring in Scandal," *New York Times*, April 17, 1986, p. A26; John C. Weistart, "Will College Sports Reform Be Business as Usual?" *New York Times*, June 16, 1985, p. A20.

33. Crowley, *In the Arena*, pp. 94–95.

34. Ibid.

35. Crowley, *In the Arena*, pp. 116–17; Smith, *Pay for Play*, pp. 155–56.

36. Crowley, *In the Arena*, p. 117; Smith, *Pay for Play*, pp. 157–58.

37. *Proceedings of the Annual NCAA Convention*, New Orleans, Louisiana, 1986, pp. 65–68. The 1986 convention did, however, pass a modification of Prop 48 that created a sliding scale so that an entering freshman athlete who had a high school GPA above 2.0 could qualify for varsity play if his or her SAT or ACT scores were below 700 or 15, respectively, and an athlete whose test scores were above 700 or 15, respectively, could qualify if his or her GPA was below 2.0.

38. *Proceedings of the Annual NCAA Convention, San Diego, California*, 1987, pp. 120–30.

39. William C. Rhoden, "Thompson's Protest over Freshman Rule Is Drawing Some Criticism," *New York Times*, January 19, 1989, p. D28; Andrew Zimbalist, *Unpaid Professionals: Commercialism and Conflict in Big-Time College Sports* (Princeton, NJ: Princeton University Press), p. 30.

40. Atchley quoted in William C. Rhoden, "Thompson Returns as N.C.A.A. Acts to Delay Rule," *New York Times*, January 21, 1989, p. 51. See also Smith, *Pay for Play*, p. 159; Crowley, *In the Arena*, p. 125.

41. Quoted in Crowley, *In the Arena*, p. 126.

42. Tom McMillen, *Out of Bounds: How the American Sport Establishment Is Being Driven by Greed and Hypocrisy—and What Needs to Be Done about It* (New York: Simon and Schuster, 1992), p. 107.

43. "McMillen Proposes Bill to Reform College Sports; Board of Presidents to Distribute Money," *Baltimore Sun*, July 26, 1991; Smith, *Pay for Play*, pp. 159–60; Crowley, *In the Arena*, p. 169; Zimbalist, p. 195.

44. Oriard, *Bowled Over*, p. 151; Crowley, *In the Arena*, p. 126.

45. Knight Foundation, "About the Foundation," http://www.knightfoundation.org/about/

46. Knight Commission on Intercollegiate Athletics, "Keeping Faith with the Student Athlete: A New Model for Intercollegiate Athletics" (Miami, FL: Knight Foundation, 1991), p. v.

47. Ibid. p. vi.

48. Ibid. p. 3.

49. Ibid. p. 6.

50. Ibid. pp. 7–8, 11.

51. Ibid. pp. 12–22.

52. Ibid., p. 36.

53. Ibid.

54. Ibid., p. 37.

55. Ibid., pp. 37–38.

56. Ibid., p. 38.

57. Ibid.

58. Ibid., p. 39.

59. Smith, *Play by Play*, pp. 161–64, 174–75.

60. Knight Commission on Intercollegiate Athletics, "Academic and Athletic Spending Database for NCAA Division I," http://spendingdatabase.knightcommission.org/; "Knight Commission unveils college sports database," *USA Today Sports*, December 4, 2013, http://www.usatoday.com/story/sports/college/2013/12/04/knight-commission-collegiate -sports-spending-database/3862595/.

61. Joel G. Maxey, "The 1997 Restructuring of the NCAA: A Transactions Cost Explanation," in John Fizel and Rodney Fort, eds., *Economics of College Sports* (Westport, Conn.: Praeger, 2004), p. 17.

62. *NCAA v. Tarkanian*, 488 U.S. 179 (1988).

63. Rick Telander, *The One Hundred Year Lie: The Corruption of College Football and What We Can Do to Stop It* (Urbana: University of Illinois Press, 1990), p. 55.

64. Crowley, *In the Arena*, p. 116.

65. Michael Goodwin, "N.C.A.A. Session Rebuffs Presidents," *New York Times*, July 1, 1987, p. B9.

Chapter 7. The M Connection: Media and Money

1. Information on the University of Louisville has been derived from Steve Eder, Richard Sandomir, and James Andrew Miller, "At Louisville, Athletic Boom Is Rooted in ESPN Partnership," *New York Times*, August 26, 2013; University of Louisville, Biography [of James R. Ramsey], http://louisville.edu/president/biography; "John H. Shumaker," *Wikipedia*, last modified October 19, 2014, http://en.wikipedia.org/wiki/John_W. Shumaker; "Tom Jurich," University of Louisville Athletics website, http://www.gocards.com/genrel/ jurich_tomoo.html.

2. Both quotations from Eder, Sandomir, and Miller, "At Louisville."

3. George Will, "Pigskin Piggy Bank," *Washington Post*, January 7, 2010.

4. Keith Dunnavant, *The Fifty-Year Seduction: How Television Manipulated College Football from the Birth of the Modern NCAA to the Creation of the BCS* (New York: St. Martin's Press, 2004), pp. 92–96; Heather Dinich, "Playoff Plan to Run through 2025," ESPN.com http://espn.go.com/college-football/story/_/id/8099187/ncaa-presidents -approve-four-team-college-football-playoff-beginning-2014. Bowl games provide one of the few sanctioned opportunities for athletes to benefit materially, because many bowl

committees provide gifts, such as Sony PlayStations and video-game disks, to playing participants. The NCAA allows such rewards but puts a value cap of $750 on them.

5. Jerry Hinnen, "ESPN Reaches 12-Year Deal To Air College Football Playoffs," CBSsports.com, November 21, 2012, http://www.cbssports.com/collegefootball/eye-on-college -football/21083689/espn-reaches-12year-deal-to-air-college-football-playoffs.

6. Eric Chemi, "The Amazing Growth in College Football Revenues," *Business Week,* September 26, 2013, http://www.bloomberg.com/bw/articles/2013-09-26/the-amazing-growth -in-college-football-revenues.

7. Allicia Jessup, "The Economics of College Football: A Look at the Top 25's Revenues and Expenses," *Forbes,* August 31, 2013, http://www.forbes.com/sites/aliciajessop/ 2013/08/31/the-economics-of-college-football-a-look-at-the-top-25-teams-revenues-and -expenses/; Dashiell Bennett, "Only 22 of 120 Division I Athletic Programs Made Money Last Year," businessinsider.com, June 15, 2011, http://www.businessinsider.com/ncaa -revenue-expense-report-2011-6.

8. Alexander Wolff and Armen Keteyian, *Raw Recruits: The High Stakes Game Colleges Play to Get Their Basketball Stars—and What It Costs To Win* (New York: Pocket Books, 1991), pp. 31–32.

9. Charles T. Clotfelter, *Big-Time Sports in American Universities* (Cambridge, MA: Cambridge University Press, 2011), Table 3A.2, pp. 233–34.

10. Ronald A. Smith, *Play by Play: Radio, Television, and Big-Time College Sport* (Baltimore, MD: Johns Hopkins University Press, 2001), pp. 186–91; Brad Wolverton, "NCAA Agrees to $10.8-Billion Deal to Broadcast Its Men's Basketball Tournament," *Chronicle of Higher Education,* April 22, 2010, http://chronicle.com/article/NCAA-Signs-108-Billion -De/65219/; Thomas O'Toole, "NCAA Reaches 14-Year Deal With CBS/Turner for Men's Basketball Tournament, Which Expands to 68 Teams For Now," *USA Today,* April 22, 2010, http://content.usatoday.com/communities/campusrivalry/post/2010/04/ncaa-reaches-14 -year-deal-with-cbsturner/1#.VTpN32Yrenc.

11. Smith, *Play by Play,* p. 190; Sara Bibel, "2013 NCAA Final Four Is Highest-Rated and Most-Viewed in Eight Years," *TV by the Numbers,* April 7, 2013, http://tvbythenumbers .zap2it.com/2013/04/07/2013-ncaa-final-four-is-highest-rated-and-most-viewed-in-eight -years/176862/.

12. Kevin Trahan, "The Three Big Things to Know about the SEC Network for Launch Day," *SB Nation,* August 13, 2014, http://www.sbnation.com/college-football/2014/8/ 13/5967845/sec-network-channels-subscribers-launch.

13. "2010–13 NCAA Conference Realignment," *Wikipedia,* last modified on March 24, 2015, http://en.wikipedia.org/wiki/2010%E2%80%9313_NCAA_conference_realignment.

14. Sally Jenkins, "NCAA Lost Its Teeth in Court in 1984, and No One's Been in Charge Since," *Washington Post,* September 23, 2011, http://www.washingtonpost.com/sports/ colleges/ncaa-lost-its-teeth-in-court-in-1984-and-no-ones-been-in-charge-since/2011/ 09/23/gIQAVDyoqK_story.html.

15. Figures taken from *USA Today online,* "NCAA Finances," last updated June 4, 2014, http://www.usatoday.com/sports/college/schools/finances/

16. Steve Berkowitz, Jodi Upton, and Eric Brady, "Most NCAA Division I Athletic Departments Take Subsidies," *USA Today,* July 1, 2013, http://www.usatoday.com/story/ sports/college/2013/05/07/ncaa-finances-subsidies/2142443/.

17. "Colorado Banks on Football, and Coach Cashes In," *USA Today*, November 7, 2013, pp. 1A, 1C.

18. Daniel de Vise, "Athletic Fees Are a Large, and Sometimes Hidden, Cost at Colleges," *Washington Post*, October 24, 2010, http://www.washingtonpost.com/wp-dyn/content/article/2010/10/24/AR2010102403002.html. Longwood supports fourteen varsity sports, the minimum to qualify for Division I, six men's teams and eight women's teams, but no football team.

19. Daniel L. Fulks, "Revenues and Expenses, 2004–2012 (Indianapolis: National Collegiate Athletic Association, 2013), p. 17.

20. Delta Cost Project, "Academic Spending versus Athletic Spending: Who Wins?" (Washington, DC: American Institutes for Research, January 2013), p. 7. Football Subdivision schools support, on average, just over 600 student-athletes; other Division I football schools support around 500 student-athletes, and Division I schools without football teams support 360. Fulks, "Revenues and Expenses."

21. Delta Cost Project, "Academic Spending," pp. 8–9. Some economists have pointed out that scholarship costs distort the expenditure side of athletic budgets, claiming that the full dollar amount—"list price"—of a scholarship is far higher than the actual institutional cost of educating the scholarship recipient, meaning to them that the expense of athletic scholarships is almost negligible. Consequently, they say, the deficits of athletic budgets are exaggerated. Nevertheless, an institution still has to provide a scholarship recipient with real funding to pay for tuition, room and board, and books, and so the costs are real. See, for example, Brian Goff, "Effects of University Athletics on the University: A Review and Extension of Empirical Assessment," in Scott R. Rosner and Kenneth L. Shropshire, eds., *The Business of Sports* (Sudbury, MA: Jones and Bartlett, 2004), pp. 540–43.

22. Steve Berkowitz and Jodi Upton, "Salaries Rising for New Football Coaches," *USA Today*, January 17, 2012, http://usatoday30.usatoday.com/sports/college/football/story/2012-01-16/College-football-coaches-compenstion/52602734/1; Knight Commission reference is unnecessary, so I removed it.

23. *USA Today*, http://sports.usatoday.com/ncaa/salaries.

24. "College Basketball Coaches' Salaries, 2011–2012," *USA Today*, March 28, 2012, http://usatoday30.usatoday.com/sports/college/mensbasketball/story/2012-03-28/ncaa-coaches-salary-database/53827374/1, table; Knight Commission on Intercollegiate Athletics, *Restoring the Balance: Dollars, Value, and the Future of College Sports* (Miami, FL: John S. and James L. Knight Foundation, 2010), chapter 2.

25. Steve Weinberg and Jodi Upton, "Success on the Court Translates into Big Money for Coaches," *USA Today*, March 8, 2007, http://usatoday30.usatoday.com/sports/college/mensbasketball/2007-03-08-coaches-salary-cover_N.htm.

26. See Michael Oriard, *Bowled Over: Big-Time College Football from the Sixties to the BCS Era* (Chapel Hill: University of North Carolina Press, 2009), p. 197.

27. Pete Myerberg and Steve Berkowitz, "What Quirks Can You Find in an FBS Coach's Contract?" *USA Today*, November 6, 2013, http://www.usatoday.com/story/sports/ncaaf/2013/11/06/fbs-ncaa-coaches-contracts-quirks-mike-leach-bill-obrien-tuberville/3456549/. It is important to note that, if a coach decides to skip out on a contract and move to another school, his new employer will take care of the buyout from the vacated school, though the coach is required to pay income tax on the buyout.

28. Jeff Benedict and Armen Keteyian, *The System: The Glory and Scandal of Big-Time College Football* (New York: Doubleday, 2013), p. 99.

29. The category of prime contains several divisions, each more expensive than the other, and the purchase of each is critical in helping a school finance stadium upgrades. When, for example, Washington State University undertook a $80 million makeover of its football stadium in 2011, it set annual season ticket prices as follows:

> Outdoor club seats between the 0- and 20-yard line: $1,700
> Outdoor club seats between the two 20-yard lines: $2,000
> Indoor club seats: $2,500
> Four-person loge boxes: $10,000
> Six-person loge boxes: $15,000
> Twelve-person suites: $30,000
> Eighteen-person suites: $40,000
> Twenty-four person suites: $50,000

Within days after a new football coach, Mike Leach, was announced, all twenty-one luxury suites, including all those costing $50,000, were sold. See Benedict and Keteyian, *The System*, pp. 249, 252.

30. Charles Clotfelter, "Stop the Tax Deduction for Major College Sports Programs," *Washington Post*, December 31, 2010, http://www.washingtonpost.com/wp-dyn/content/article/2010/12/30/AR2010123003252.html; Darren Rovell, "The High Price of Supply and Demand," ESPN.com, January 13, 2006, http://sports.espn.go.com/ncf/news/story?id=2286027. In 1950, in an effort to restrict tax-exempt charities from using their money to make profits, Congress passed legislation to tax unrelated business income but exempted income from college athletic ticket sales. In 1986, the Internal Revenue Service tried to rule that ticket-sale income, which by this time included fees for luxury suites in new and expanded stadiums, should not be exempt, but in 1988, Congress voted to continue the tax break on 80 percent of the fee costs. See Curtis Eichelberger and Charles R. Babcock, "Football-Ticket Tax Break Helps Colleges Get Millions," Bloomberg.com, October 25, 2012, http://www.bloomberg.com/news/2012-10-25/got-college-football-tickets-take-a-tax-break.html.

31. Eichelberger and Babcock, "Football-Ticket Tax Break."

32. Ibid.

33. Steve Weinberg, "Tycoon's $165M Gift to Oklahoma State Raises Both Hopes and Questions," *USA Today*, February 21, 2007, ay.com/sports/college/2006–08–15-pickens-oklahoma-state-donation_x.htm; Oliver Staley, "T. Boone Pickens: OSU's Big, Big Man on Campus," *Bloomberg Business Week Magazine*, April 14, 2011. Unfortunately for all concerned, the donation was invested in a Pickens-controlled hedge fund, and the financial crisis that rocked the country, starting late in 2008, wiped out a big chunk of it.

34. Greg Bishop, "Oregon Embraces 'University of Nike' Image," *New York Times*, August 2, 2013, http://www.nytimes.com/2013/08/03/sports/ncaafootball/oregon-football-complex-is-glittering-monument-to-ducks-ambitions.html?_r=0; Associated Press, "College Football Facilities: Alabama, Oregon among Most Lavish Football Palaces," September 12, 2013, http://www.huffingtonpost.com/2013/09/12/college-football-facilities-alabama-oregon_n_3915431.html.

35. Bishop, "Oregon Embraces."

36. Log Cabin Democrat, "2013–2014 Bowl Payouts," http://thecabin.net/slideshow/2013 -12-19/2013-2014-bowl-payouts#slide-37.

37. Craig Harris, "Trips to BCS Bowl Games Can Cost Some Schools Big Money," *USA Today,* September 28, 2011, http://usatoday30.usatoday.com/sports/college/football/ story/2011-09-28/bcs-bowl-games-cost-some-schools/50582512/1.

38. Chris Smith, "A Single NCAA Tournament Victory Is Worth $1.5 Million," *Forbes Magazine,* March 21, 2013; http://www.ncaa.org/wps/wcm/connect/public/NCAA/ Resources/Basketball+Resources/Basketball+Resource+Distribution+Fund; "NCAA Men's Basketball Tournament: This Year's Unit Payouts," http://winthropintelligence .com/2013/04/01/ncaa-mens-basketball-tournament-this-years-unit-payouts-after/ ac-cessed 1/20/14. Aside from the basketball payouts, the NCAA distributes other moneys to members, both large and small. About 96 percent of NCAA income, now more than $200 million annually, is returned to schools. About 60 percent goes to Division I mem-bers and 36 percent to Divisions II and III. Basketball money is unrestricted, but other distributions are intended for items such as student-athlete assistance for emergency needs, academic enhancement, and a sports-sponsorship fund to encourage funding for nonrevenue sports. These moneys assist budgets of smaller schools but comprise miniscule proportions of large-school budgets. See http://www.ncaa.org/about/resources/finances/ distributions accessed 1/24/14.

39. Sean Silverthorne, "The Flutie Effect: How Athletic Success Boosts College Ap-plications," Forbes.com, April 29, 2013, http://www.forbes.com/sites/hbsworking knowledge/2013/04/29/the-flutie-effect-how-athletic-success-boosts-college-applications/.

40. See William C. Dowling, *Confessions of a Spoilsport: My Life and Hard Times Fighting Sports Corruption at an Old Eastern University* (University Park : Penn State University Press, 2007). Using mostly impressionistic evidence, Dowling, a Rutgers University English professor, claimed that after opting to join the Big East Conference and engage in the arms race of big-time college football and basketball, his institution became a "jockocracy," wildly spending money it did not have on sports while allowing academic programs to wither. A consequence, he said, was that the character and academic aptitude of the stu-dent body declined. Dowling, along with concerned students and other faculty, organized Rutgers 1000, a group that attempted, unsuccessfully, to restore academic priorities over athletics.

41. Douglas J. Chung, "The Dynamic Advertising Effect of Collegiate Athletics," sum-marized in Silverthorne, "Flutie Effect."

42. Study by Arts and Science Group, cited in Welch Suggs, "Study Casts Doubt on Idea that Winning Teams Yield More Applicants," *Chronicle of Higher Education,* March 30, 2001, p. A-51.

43. Eichelberger and Babcock, "Football-Ticket Tax Break."

44. Staley, "T. Boone Pickens"; Benedict and Keteyian, pp. 149–61.

45. These studies have been summarized by Ellen Staurowsky in *The Relationship be-tween Athletics and Higher Education Fund Raising: The Myths Far Outweigh the Facts,* a report prepared for the United States Department of Education Commission on Op-portunities in Athletics, http://priorities.weebly.com/uploads/8/8/6/0/8860813/athletics _and_fundraising.pdf.

46. Andrew Zimbalist, *Unpaid Professionals: Commercialism and Conflict in Big-Time College Sports* (Princeton, N.J.: Princeton University Press, 1999), p. 168.

47. National Center for Education Statistics, "Fast Facts," http://nces.ed.gov/fastfacts/display.asp?id=98; U.S. Census Bureau, "After a Recent Upswing, College Enrollment Declines, Census Bureau Reports," http://www.census.gov/newsroom/releases/archives/education/cb13–153.html.

48. Ben Cohen, "At College Football Games, Student Sections Likely to Have Empty Seats," *Wall Street Journal*, August 27, 2014, http://online.wsj.com/articles/at-college-football-games-student-sections-likely-to-have-empty-seats-1409188244.

49. Jake New, "Empty Seats Now, Fewer Donors Later?" *Inside Higher Ed*, September 11, 2014, https://www.insidehighered.com/news/2014/09/11/colleges-worry-about-future-football-fans-student-attendance-declines.

50. Dan Wolken, "UAB Shuts Down Its Football Program," *USA Today*, December 2, 2014, http://www.usatoday.com/story/sports/ncaaf/cusa/2014/12/02/uab-blazers-football-shutdown-program-dropped/19781387/.

51. Just days after the UAB announcement, Texas A&M University purposely blew up one end of its football stadium as part of a $450 million renovation to the facility. Unlike UAB, a big-time program has no reservations about big-time athletic spending.

52. Wolff and Ketcyian, *Raw Recruits*, p. 294.

53. Brad Wolverton, "Is There a Smarter Way to Divvy Up NCAA Tournament Money?" *Chronicle of Higher Education*, March 31, 2012, http://chronicle.com/blogs/players/are-wealthy-schools-getting-too-much-ncaa-money/29893.

54. A study undertaken by Richard Lapchick, director of the DeVos Sports Management program at the University of Central Florida, found that in 2013, 78.4 percent of the nation's athletic directors and 100 percent of conference commissioners were white males. Associated Press, "Study: Top College Leaders Remain White, Male," http://bigstory.ap.org/article/study-top-college-leaders-remain-white-male.

55. Quoted in Mark Yost, *Varsity Green: A Behind the Scenes Look at Culture and Corruption in College Athletics* (Stanford, CA: Stanford University Press, 2010), p. 13. See also Clotfelter, *Big-Time Sports in American Universities*, p. 243.

Chapter 8. What's to Become of College Sports?

1. Tim Lemke, "O'Bannon Files Suit v. NCAA," *Washington Times*, July 22, 2009, http://www.washingtontimes.com/news/2009/jul/22/obannon-files-suit-vs-ncaa/.

2. A year later, the NCAA restored the number of scholarships to twenty.

3. Remy quoted in Chip Patterson, "Northwestern Players Start Union in College Athletics," CBSSports.com, January 28, 2014, http://www.cbssports.com/collegefootball/eye-on-college-football/24422752/northwestern-players-start-union-movement-in-college-athletics. See also Sara Ganim, "Northwestern Football Players Take Union Hopes to Labor Board Hearing," CNN.com, February 18, 2014, http://www.cnn.com/2014/02/18/us/northwestern-unionization-attempt/.

4. Mark Tracy, "N.C.A.A. Votes to Give Richest Conferences More Autonomy," *New York Times*, August 7, 2014, http://www.nytimes.com/2014/08/08/sports/ncaafootball/ncaa-votes-to-give-greater-autonomy-to-richest-conferences.html?_r=0; Brad Wolverton,

"NCAA Considers Adding Student Representation to Division I Board," *Chronicle of Higher Education*, March 25, 2014; Zac Ellis, "NCAA Considering Direct Student-Athlete Input, Autonomy for Major Conferences," *Sports Illustrated Campus Union*, March 4, 2014, http://college-football.si.com/2014/03/04/ncaa-reform-governance-proposals/; George Schroeder, "NCAA Board Endorses Div. I Changes, Streamlines Process," *USA Today*, April 24, 2014, http://www.usatoday.com/story/sports/college/2014/04/24/ncaa-board -of-directors-meeting-big-conference-autonomy/8108647/.

5. NCAA, "Amateurism" (Indianapolis: NCAA, n.d.), http://www.ncaa.org/remaining -eligible-amateurism.

6. *New York Times Magazine*, December 30, 2011, http://www.nytimes.com/2012/01/01/ magazine/lets-start-paying-college-athletes.html.

7. Taylor Branch, "The Shame of College Sports," *The Atlantic*, October 2011, p. 83.

8. Marlen Garcia, "NCAA President: 'We Can Never' Get to Place Where Athletes Are Paid,'" *USA Today*, December 15, 2010, http://usatoday30.usatoday.com/sports/college/ 2010-12-15-mark-emmert-ncaa-pay_N.htm.

9. An example of this reasoning is "Jay Paterno: Pay Student Athletes? They're Already Getting a Great Deal," http://www.statecollege.com/news/columns/jay-paterno -pay-studentathletes-theyre-already-getting-a-great-deal,766175/. It must be noted that some economists dispute the monetary value of these benefits. For example, some say that though scholarships carry a dollar amount, they really are paper amounts because in the grand scheme of total undergraduate enrollment, they do not cost a school much, if anything. Coaching, according to others, has no dollar value to the vast majority of college athletes who never play professionally after graduation. Still, many advantages that athletes have are real. The dollar cost of medical insurance is relatively small, usually between $700 and $1,200 per year, but the value is large if and when an athlete is injured, providing the injured player with free access to rehabilitation facilities and personnel. Also, varsity athletes receive free equipment and uniforms—basketball players can wear out six pairs of sneakers in a year—often worth thousands, which no intramural or club athlete receives. Free tickets, limited by the NCAA to four per game in basketball, can add up to $2,000 per year, not counting extra amounts if the team makes it to a postseason tournament. Other advantages cannot be calculated. For example, varsity athletes have exposure that can ease their ability to attain postcollege employment, often through a network of alumni. For one breakdown of full benefits in 2011, see Jay Weiner and Steve Berkowitz, "*USA Today* Finds $120K Value in Men's Basketball Scholarship," *USA Today*, March 20, 2011, http://usatoday30.usatoday.com/sports/college/mensbasketball/2011 -03-29-scholarship-worth-final-four_N.htm.

10. "Athletes Rights Group Set Up," *New York Times*, September 28, 1981, http://www .nytimes.com/1981/09/29/sports/athletes-rights-group-set-up.html; Walter Byers, with Charles Hammer, *Unsportsmanlike Conduct: Exploiting College Athletics* (Ann Arbor: University of Michigan Press, 1990), p. 342.

11. Pete Thamel, "Top Grades and No Class Time for Auburn Players," *New York Times*, July 14, 2006, http://www.nytimes.com/2006/07/14/sports/ncaafootball/14auburn.html ?pagewanted=all&_r=0.

12. Ibid.

13. Sara Ganim, "UNC Hires Independent Attorney to Investigate Academic Irregularities," CNN.com, February 21, 2014, http://www.cnn.com/2014/02/21/us/ncaa-athletes-unc/index.html.

14. Sara Ganim and Devon M. Sayers, ""UNC Report Finds 18 Years of Academic Fraud to Keep Athletes Playing," CNN.com, October 23, 2014, http://www.cnn.com/2014/10/22/us/unc-report-academic-fraud/.

15. Amy Julia Harris and Ryan Mac, "Stanford Athletes Had Access to List of 'Easy' Courses," *Stanford Daily*, March 9, 2011, http://www.stanforddaily.com/2011/03/09/1046687/; Jacob D. H. Feldman, "For Accused Jocks, Athletic Regulations Complicate Decisions," *Harvard Crimson*, September 6, 2012, http://www.thecrimson.com/article/2012/9/6/athletes-cheating-regulations-ad-board/.

16. NCAA, "Academic Performance Rate" (Indianapolis: NCAA, n.d.), http://www.ncaa.org/about/resources/research/academic-progress-rate-apr; "UConn loses final appeal," ESPN.com, April 5, 2012, http://espn.go.com/mens-college-basketball/story/_/id/7779554/uconn-loses-final-appeal-play-2013-ncaa-tournament.

17. Dan Kane, "By One Measure, UNC Athletes' Academic Performance Takes a Big Dip," Raleigh (N.C.) *News and Observer*, June 29, 2013, http://www.newsobserver.com/2013/06/29/2999195/by-one-measure-unc-athletes-academic.html; "UConn Basketball Reports Perfect APR, ESPN.com, October 11, 2013, http://espn.go.com/mens-college-basketball/story/_/id/9810748/uconn-huskies-expect-post-perfect-academic-progress-rate-basketball; Gerald S. Gurney and Richard M. Southall, "College Sports' Bait and Switch," ESPN.com, August 9, 2012, http://espn.go.com/college-sports/story/_/id/8248046/college-sports-programs-find-multitude-ways-game-ncaa-apr.

18. Michael Oriard, *Bowled Over: Big-Time College Football from the Sixties to the BCS Era* (Chapel Hill: University of North Carolina Press, 2009), p. 183.

19. Nicole Auerbach, "Oklahoma State Narrowly Avoids Postseason Ban for APR," *USA Today,* May 14, 2014, http://www.usatoday.com/story/sports/college/2014/05/14/ncaa-academic-progress-rate-postseason-bans/9082853/. Penalties for substandard APRs are usually imposed when low rates persist for three consecutive years; a one-year APR can be overlooked if the school shows progress toward developing a program to assist student-athletes whose grades and progress toward completing a major are deficient. The NCAA has instituted a program to help limited-resource schools and historically black colleges and universities to assist student-athletes at academic risk, and at both types of schools the overall APR rose slightly—about 1.5 percent—between 2007–08 and 2011–12. See *NCAA Champion*, 6 (Summer 2013), p. 21.

20. Byers, *Unsportsmanlike Conduct*, p. 315.

21. See, for example, Harry Edwards, "Crisis of Black Athletes on the Eve of the 21st Century," *Society* (March–April, 2000), 9–13; and L. Harrison Jr., C. K. Harrison, and L. N. Moore, "African American Racial Identity and Sport," *Sport, Education and Society* 7 (2000), 21–33.

22. See Michael J. Cusack, "The Academic Progress Rate: Good PR, Bad Policy," *Chronicle of Higher Education* 54, no. 11 (November 2007), B2.

23. Sara Ganim, "CNN Analysis: Some College Athletes Play Like Adults, Read Like 5th Graders," CNN.com, January 8, 2014, http://www.cnn.com/2014/01/07/us/ncaa-athletes-reading-scores/.

24. Merrill Hope, "Expert: Most US College Freshmen Read at Seventh-Grade Level," Breitbart.com, January 3, 2015, http://www.breitbart.com/texas/2015/01/03/expert-most -us-college-freshmen-read-at-7th-grade-level/.

25. James L. Shulman and William G. Bowen, *The Game of Life: College Sports and Educational Values* (Princeton, NJ: Princeton University Press, 2001), p. 44.

26. Ann Killion and Annette Asimov, "Cal's Shockingly Low Admission Standards," SFGate. com, November 15, 2013, http://www.sfgate.com/collegesports/article/Cal-s-shockingly -low-athletic-admission-standards-4984721.php.

27. Jeff Baker, "'Special Admissions' Bring Colleges Top Athletes, Educational Challenges," *Baltimore Sun*, December 22, 2012, http://articles.baltimoresun.com/2012-12-22/sports/ bs-sp-acc-sports-special-admits-20121222_1_athletes-graduation-success-rate-college -courses.

28. Report summarized in Lynn O'Shaughnessy, "Do College Athletes Have Time to Be Students?" CBSNews.com, February 18, 2011, http://www.cbsnews.com/news/do-college -athletes-have-time-to-be-students/. See also Chris Isidore, "Playing College Sports: A Long, Tough Job," CNNmoney.com, March 31, 2014, http://money.cnn.com/2014/03/31/ news/companies/college-athletes-jobs/; and Mark Edelman, "Syracuse's Road to the 2014 NCAA Men's Basketball Championship Would Likely Cost Players 17 Days of Class; 24.2% of Overall Semester," Forbes.com, January 7, 2014, http://www.forbes.com/sites/ marcedelman/2014/01/07/syracuses-road-to-the-mens-basketball-championship-would -cost-players-17-days-of-class-24–2-of-overall-semester/.

29. Shulman and Bowen, *Game of Life*, pp. 260–61, 272–73.

30. NCAA, *2009–10 Division I Manual* (Indianapolis: National Collegiate Athletic Association, 2009), p. 1.

31. Kevin Trahan, "Will the NCAA's 'Big Five' Reform Be Enough to Save Amateur-ism?" SBNation.com, April 24, 2014, http://www.sbnation.com/college-football/2014/ 4/24/5594090/ncaa-changes-power-conferences-unions-lawsuits.

32. Dennis Dodd, "Boise State President Blasts NCAA Reform in Letter to Media," CBSSports.com, May 21, 2014, http://www.cbssports.com/collegefootball/writer/dennis -dodd/24569414/boise-state-presidents-blasts-ncaa-reform-in-letter-to-media.

33. Ibid.

34. Doug Lederman, "Settlement Raises Questions for NCAA," InsideHigherEd. com, February 4, 2008, http://www.insidehighered.com/news/2008/02/04/ncaa#sthash .5HLnCyRT.ID8KxkED.dpbs.

35. Tom Farrey, "Jeffrey Kessler Files against NCAA," ESPN.com, March 18, 2014, http:// espn.go.com/college-sports/story/_/id/10620388/anti-trust-claim-filed-jeffrey-kessler -challenges-ncaa-amateur-model.

36. Steve Eder, "Players Seek Approval of $40 Million Deal in Video Games Case," *New York Times*, June 1, 2014, p. D12; Steve Berkowitz, "Proposed Video Game Settlement Could Help Current NCAA Players," *USA Today*, May 30, 2014, http://www.usatoday .com/story/sports/college/2014/05/30/ed-obannon-ncaa-name-and-likeness-lawsuit -settlement/9789605/; Steve Berkowitz, "As Trial on O'Bannon Lawsuit Begins, Related Case Settled," *USA Today*, June 9, 2014, http://www.usatoday.com/story/sports/college/ 2014/06/09/anti-trust-lawsuit-ed-obannon-against-the-ncaa/10226241/.

37. Steve Berkowitz, "New Lawsuit Targets NCAA and Every Division I School," *USA Today*, October 23, 2014, http://www.usatoday.com/story/sports/college/2014/10/23/ncaa -class-action-lawsuit-obannon-case/17790847/.

38. Deborah Rankin, "Taxes and Accounting: Tackling College Football TV Revenue," *New York Times*, July 5, 1977, p. 45; "Colleges Fear TV Taxation to 'Sink' Them," *Chicago Tribune*, May 12, 1977, p. C3; Ronald A. Smith, *Play by Play: Radio, Television, and Big-Time College Sport* (Baltimore, MD: Johns Hopkins University Press, 2001), p. 140; Allen Sack and Ellen J. Staurowsky, *College Athletes for Hire: The Evolution and Legacy of the NCAA's Amateur Myth* (Westport, CT: Praeger, 1998), pp. 106–9.

39. "It's Time to Tax College Athletics," ProfessorBainbridge.com, http://www.professor bainbridge.com/professorbainbridgecom/2011/04/its-time-to-tax-college-athletics.html.

40. "NCAA Reaches Proposed Settlement in Concussion Lawsuit," NCAA.com, July 30, 2014, http://www.ncaa.com/news/ncaa/article/2014-07-29/ncaa-reaches-proposed- settlement-concussion-lawsuit; John Keilman and Michelle Manchir, "NCAA Reaches $75 Million Settlement in Concussion Lawsuit," *Chicago Tribune*, July 29, 2014, http:// www.chicagotribune.com/news/local/breaking/chi-ncaa-reaches-75-million-settlement -in-concussion-lawsuit-20140729-story.html; Jon Solomon, "Attorneys Push Back to Ap- prove NCAA Concussion Settlement," CBSSports.com, September 6, 2014, http://www .cbssports.com/collegefootball/writer/jon-solomon/24697066/attorneys-push-back-to -approve-ncaa-concussion-settlement.

41. Upton Sinclair, *The Goose-Step: A Study of American Education* (Pasadena, CA: printed by the author, 1922), pp. 370–71.

42. Dennis Dodd, "Sun Is Shining on NCAA Reforms as Power Conferences Push for Change," CBSSports.com, January 17, 2014, http://www.cbssports.com/collegefootball/writer/ dennis-dodd/24412332/sun-is-shining-on-ncaa-reforms-as-power-conferences-push-for -change.

43. There is good reason for the criticism. Many "one-and-done" individuals register for classes in their first semester, pass enough to stay eligible to play, register for classes in second semester, then never attend, because since they are leaving school to (hopefully) play professionally, their eligibility status would not be determined until the semester is over and it would not matter whether they passed those courses.

44. Byers, *Unsportsmanlike Conduct,* pp. 348–50, 372–75.

45. Ibid., pp. 374–87.

Index

HOWARD P. CHUDACOFF is George L. Littlefield Professor of American History and Professor of Urban Studies at Brown University and a faculty representative to the NCAA. His books include *Children at Play: An American History*.

Sport and Society

The University of Illinois Press
is a founding member of the
Association of American University Presses.

Composed in 10.5/13 Adobe Minion Pro
at the University of Illinois Press
Manufactured by Cushing Malloy, Inc.

University of Illinois Press
1325 South Oak Street
Champaign, IL 61820-6903
www.press.uillinois.edu